Negative Interest Rates and Financial Stability

This book sheds new light on a recently introduced monetary tool – negative interest rates policy (NIRP). It provides in-depth insight into this phenomenon, conducted by the central banks in several economies – for example, the Eurozone, Switzerland and Japan – and its possible impact on systemic risk.

Although it has been introduced as a temporary policy instrument, NIRP remained widely used for a longer period and by a greater range of central banks than initially expected. Thus, the book explores its effects and implications on the banking sector and financial markets, with a particular focus on potentially adverse consequences. There is a strong accent on the uniqueness of negative policy rates in the context of financial stability concerns. The authors assess whether NIRP has any – or in principle a stronger – impact on systemic risk than conventional monetary policy. The book is targeted at presenting and evaluating the initial experiences of NIRP policy during normal, i.e., pre-COVID, times. Consequently, the periods in which pre-established macroeconomic relations are rapidly disrupted or, specifically, when the source of the disruption is not purely economic in nature (unlike in systemic crisis) remain rather beyond the scope of the book.

The authors adopt both theoretical and most notably practical approaches to explore the key issues and outline the policy implications for both monetary and macroprudential authorities, with respect to negative interest rate policy. Thus, the book will provide a useful guide for policymakers, academics, advanced students and researchers of financial economics and international finance.

Karol Rogowicz is an Assistant Professor in the Financial System Department at SGH Warsaw School of Economics, Poland and a Senior Economist at the National Bank of Poland.

Małgorzata Iwanicz-Drozdowska is Professor of Finance and Head of the Financial System Department at SGH Warsaw School of Economics, Poland.

Routledge International Studies in Money and Banking

Moral Hazard
A Financial, Legal, and Economic Perspective
Edited by Juan Flores Zendejas, Norbert Gaillard and Rick Michalek

Mergers, Acquisitions, and International Financial Regulation
Analysing Special Purpose Acquisition Companies
Daniele D'Alvia

Pension Fund Capitalism
The Privatization of Pensions in Developed and Developing Countries
Leokadia Oręziak

Central Banks in Organizational Networks
Entangled Market Actors
Christoph F-D. Wu

Responsible Finance and Digitalization
Implications and Developments
Edited by Panu Kalmi, Tommi Auvinen and Marko Järvenpää

Digital Currencies and the New Global Financial System
Edited by Ranjan Aneja and Robert Dygas

Negative Interest Rates and Financial Stability
Lessons in Systemic Risk
Karol Rogowicz and Małgorzata Iwanicz-Drozdowska

For more information about this series, please visit: www.routledge.com/Routledge-International-Studies-in-Money-and-Banking/book-series/SE0403

Negative Interest Rates and Financial Stability

Lessons in Systemic Risk

Karol Rogowicz and
Małgorzata Iwanicz-Drozdowska

Routledge
Taylor & Francis Group
LONDON AND NEW YORK

First published 2023
by Routledge
4 Park Square, Milton Park, Abingdon, Oxon OX14 4RN

and by Routledge
605 Third Avenue, New York, NY 10158

Routledge is an imprint of the Taylor & Francis Group, an informa business

British Library Cataloguing-in-Publication Data
A catalogue record for this book is available from the British Library

Library of Congress Cataloging-in-Publication Data
Names: Rogowicz, Karol, author. | Iwanicz-Drozdowska, Małgorzata, author.
Title: Negative interest rates and financial stability : lessons in systemic risk / Karol Rogowicz and Małgorzata Iwanicz-Drozdowska.
Description: Abingdon, Oxon ; New York, NY : Routledge, 2023. | Series: Routledge international studies in money and banking | Includes bibliographical references and index.
Identifiers: LCCN 2022025550 (print) | LCCN 2022025551 (ebook) | ISBN 9781032319490 (hardback) | ISBN 9781032319506 (paperback) | ISBN 9781003312116 (ebook)
Subjects: LCSH: Interest rates—Case studies. | Risk—Case studies. | Banks and banking—Case studies.
Classification: LCC HG1621 .R64 2023 (print) | LCC HG1621 (ebook) | DDC 332.8—dc23/eng/20220801
LC record available at https://lccn.loc.gov/2022025550
LC ebook record available at https://lccn.loc.gov/2022025551

ISBN: 978-1-032-31949-0 (hbk)
ISBN: 978-1-032-31950-6 (pbk)
ISBN: 978-1-003-31211-6 (ebk)

DOI: 10.4324/9781003312116

Typeset in Times New Roman
by codeMantra

Contents

Figures

Tables

Acknowledgements

The authors would like to express their gratitude to Professor Paweł Smaga, who was the auxiliary supervisor of Karol Rogowicz, for his involvement in various and long discussions and invaluable, in-depth comments during preparation of the PhD thesis. Special thanks should go also to Professor Monika Marcinkowska, from the University of Lodz, and Professor Krzysztof Jackowicz, from Kozminski University, who provided invaluable reviews for the PhD thesis supervised by Małgorzata Iwanicz-Drozdowska. The reviews indicated shortfalls and weaker points that were addressed in this book and much improved the final version of the conducted analysis.

We also thank the participants of Intentional Risk Management Conference 2021, Vietnam Symposium in Banking and Finance 2021 and VII Wrocław Conference in Finance for their helpful comments. All errors remain our own.

Last, but no means least, Karol Rogowicz would like to thank his wife for her patience, support – and broadly understood presence – when they were needed.

***

This book is based on a research project that has been financially supported by the Polish National Science Centre (no. 2017/25/N/HS4/01405).

Authors

Karol Rogowicz

Karol Rogowicz has a PhD in finance and is a CFA charterholder. He is an assistant professor at the Financial System Department at SGH Warsaw School of Economics (Poland). He is also a senior economist at the National Bank of Poland, responsible for analyzing financial market developments, identifying risk and pricing market distortions and assessing monetary policy effects on the financial markets. His research interests concentrate around financial markets and monetary policy issues. He is the author of articles published in JCR journals, such as *Journal of Financial Stability* and *Economic Modelling*.

Małgorzata Iwanicz-Drozdowska

Małgorzata Iwanicz-Drozdowska is a full professor of finance and a head of the Financial System Department at SGH Warsaw School of Economics (Poland). She has been involved for about 30 years in the business practice, including as a Deputy Chair of Polish Financial Supervision Authority. She was granted a scholarship from Georgetown University, Washington, DC and Deutsche Stiftung fuer Internationale Rechtliche Zusammenarbeit EV. She was a visiting researcher at New York University – Stern School of Business, a visiting fellow at Columbia University and a visiting professor within the Erasmus Programme. She is the author of more than 180 publications on banking and the financial services market and has been a participant of many research projects. Her specialization includes financial safety net, financial stability, management of financial institutions and financial education.

1 Introduction

In post-WWII history, there were three structural breaks in the banking system linked to the interest rates and the monetary policy. The first one occurred in the form of the inverted shape of the yield curve in the 1980s, which had changed significantly the way banks (especially in the United States) operated. The lifting of administrative regulations and the change in the shape of the yield curve forced banks to strengthen their interest rate risk management and expanded the use of variable interest rates in their transactions with customers. The second one is related to the application of so-called non-conventional monetary policy tools shortly after the outbreak of the global financial crisis (GFC). The use of such tools, including quantitative easing (QE), led to increased market liquidity and the "swelling" of central banks' balance sheets as well as changed the way monetary policy has been conducted. Moreover, the outbreak of the GFC questioned the idea that price stability is a key – and sufficient – factor for financial stability. The third structural break is linked to ultra-low interest rates which in certain cases became negative and questioned the zero-bound policy (or ZLB – zero lower bound) of central banks. This recent structural break occurred in the period following the GFC. As the phenomenon of negative interest rates is still unexplored, this monograph fills the gap in the literature by showing the role of negative interest rates policy (NIRP). Unique in comparison with other publications, this volume combines theoretical and empirical perspectives to help the reader understand the implication of negative policy rates and place them within other monetary policy tools. In particular, we try to position this monetary policy tool in the context of systemic risk from the perspective of the banking sector and financial markets. Thus, we look at the interest rates from the angle of financial stability.

Certain risks are associated with extremely low and negative interest rates that are important from a systemic risk perspective. The vast majority of these risks are concentrated in the financial sector and most notably include cash withdrawals from the banking sector and the erosion of banks' profitability. In simple theoretical models, the nominal interest rate cannot normally be negative; if it were, economic agents would instead choose to hold cash, which does not give a negative rate of return. Therefore, banks would

DOI: 10.4324/9781003312116-1

be reluctant to pass negative rates through the credit channel. On the one hand, this would deteriorate their profitability and/or, on the other hand, hamper the monetary transmission mechanism. However, since cash does not constitute a friction-free alternative to electronic money, this opens the door to nominal rates in fact being negative.

We find this subject important in the macroeconomic environment until the end of 2021. Although NIRP has been introduced as a temporary tool, it remained widely used for a longer period and by a greater range of central banks than expected. Hence, we find it necessary to study the effects of such a tool with particular attention to its adverse effects. Moreover, since NIRP was introduced relatively recently, there is a need to contribute a complex evaluation of this kind of policy to the literature.

We approach the negative interest rate policy from various perspectives. First, we present the theoretical framework on interest rates (Chapter 2), then both macro- and microeconomic aspects, showing central banks' policies (Chapter 3) and the following reactions of financial markets (Chapter 4) and institutions (Chapter 5). Finally, we address the issue of systemic risk (Chapter 6) and the role of interest rates in this phenomenon (Chapter 7). As the question arises about how the role and impact of the positive and negative rates differ, we frequently point out these differences.

As already mentioned, the main goal of this study is to analyse the role of the negative interest rates for systemic risk. To achieve this goal, we suggest, for further exploration, six research hypotheses:

H1: Channels of negative rates transmission to the real economy are not structurally different from the ways positive rates are transmitted. However, NIRP policy is characterized by some unique factors that may affect the effectiveness of the pass-through process.
H2: There are many ways to implement NIRP policy to mitigate its direct consequences to the banking sector.
H3: Negative rates are fully transmitted only to the money market rates; however, they enhance the influence of other monetary policy instruments on the long-term yields.
H4: Banks are reluctant to transmit negative rates to deposit and credit rates.
H5: The interest rate policy of central banks has a significant impact on systemic risk in the banking sector, regardless of the implemented tool.
H6: NIRP adds more to systemic risk than a monetary policy that uses positive nominal rates as the main tool.

Chapter 2 addresses H1 and is based on an extensive review of the literature. This chapter presents the definitions of various types of interest rates, paying special attention to negative rates. We focus on a theoretical approach to show negative rates alongside well-established economic theorems. We present the theoretical, historical and recent ways to implement negative interest rates, defining the range of lower bounds for interest rates and pointing out which types of them have been broken with an introduction of NIRP. To properly address this topic, we discuss traditional and modern theories of interest rates. Finally, the chapter presents possible channels of NIRP transmission to the financial sector and real economy together with differences between positive and negative rates.

Chapter 3 refers to H2 and focuses on the most recent experiences of negative interest rate policy conducted by five central banks that introduced negative rates, namely the European Central Bank, Swiss National Bank, Sveriges Riksbank, Danmarks Nationalbank and Bank of Japan, which are treated as case studies. We consider the motivation and macroeconomic context for NIRP and analyse this tool against the background of other tools employed by the central banks. Additionally, the chapter discusses also the technical aspects of the implementation of negative policy rates and indicates crucial differences between analysed central banks. Finally, we discuss the future of NIRP. The analysis relies on references to official central banks' documents and communication as well as on the data analysis of the macroeconomic environment from the period of introduction of negative rates.

Chapter 4, which addresses partly H1 and H3, is based on a comprehensive empirical analysis of first experiences with NIRP. We analyse the transmission of negative rates to short-term (money market) and long-term (fixed-income market) rates in NIRP economies, with special attention paid to the Eurozone. To this aim, we decompose long-term yields into the components of the expected path of short-term rates and the term premium. Our analysis tries to evaluate whether the NIRP policy affects these markets comparably to other monetary policy tools, including pricing and volumes. We also discuss the phenomenon of a rising share of negative-yielding debt, its major drivers and motivation for holding such instruments in the investment portfolios. Moreover, we analyse also the stock market and currency market implications of NIRP. All in all, this chapter shows a broader understanding of a negative interest rate environment encompassing more than just negative central bank rates; this is the concept that we use in the following chapters.

Chapter 5 investigates the further transmission of NIRP and the banking sector behaviour, dealing with H4 and partly H1 and H3. Largely, we discuss the interest rate channel of monetary policy to address directly H4 based on the to-date experience of the banking sectors in NIRP economies. With the use of empirical data, we analyse whether interest rates on loans and deposits reflect central banks' negative rates and to what extent this pattern has been disturbed recently and how all this may affect the profitability of the banking sector. Moreover, we analyse credit and risk-taking channels, accounting for a broader definition of the negative interest rate environment. In that vein, we discuss potential sources of the changing distribution of the mentioned rates and assess whether their nature is purely economic or arising from regulations. As the NIRP policy differs structurally from positive rates since banks are burdened with additional costs when relying on deposits in the central bank, the introduction of NIRP is usually complemented with additional monetary policy tools with the aim to relax some undesirable consequences. That might also mean that NIRP policy may add to arising distortion between real-economy entities and the financial sector. Against this background, we compare the transmission pattern across NIRP economies and formulate the overall and country-specific findings.

In the next two chapters, namely Chapters 6 (H5 is partly addressed) and 7 (H5 and H6 are addressed), the systemic risk is analysed for a selected group of countries, which implemented a wide range of monetary policy tools. Thus, in the first place, we consider the United States, United Kingdom, Eurozone and Japan as the economies where central banks faced the ZLB for nominal interest rates and were pushed to implement non-standard monetary policy, in some cases including negative policy rates. This kind of instrument has also been implemented in other economies, such as Switzerland, Denmark, Norway and Sweden, and thus, we include them in our dataset. As a benchmark, we select six countries using a conventional interest rate toolbox, i.e., three advanced economies (Canada, Australia and South Korea) and three emerging economies (Brazil, Russia and China). We estimate our models for the full sample period from the beginning of 2000 to the end of 2019 and for subsamples of NIRP periods.

In Chapter 6, the concept of systemic risk – regarding its definitions, sources and dimensions – is presented, as well as a wide range of systemic risk measures including a comprehensive comparison between them. So far, there has been no consensus in the academic literature on the quantification of systemic risk. Thus, the analysis presented in this chapter should indicate the most suitable measure to implement in the core analysis of NIRP. This approach to quantifying systemic risk is expected to provide a relatively broad and robust picture.

Chapter 7 presents the major empirical outcome of the study that combines findings from analyses presented in previous chapters into a comprehensive quantitative approach. We aim to identify the similarities and differences between negative and positive interest rates environments as well as to assess whether the whole group of NIRP economies is homogenous in terms of interest rates impact on systemic risk. To properly address a wide range of constraints, we rely on a four-stage methodological approach. First, we quantify systemic risk at the microeconomic level. Second, we map the banking sector from an international perspective by constructing a causality network among individual entities. Third, we quantify these relations to measure the potential contagion effect at the global level and – as the main object of interest – monetary policy transmission within the constructed network. Finally, we simulate a range of monetary policy impulses to investigate their propagation – depending on the initial scale – across the network under given circumstances. Notably, we do not restrict the monetary impulses to affecting only domestic banks, but allow them to spill over internationally. As a result, what is very important is that the empirical approach presented in the book takes into account not only the direct monetary policy impact on systemic risk but also the contagion effect arising between banks.

According to the presented structure, it should be noted that the study is conducted in several steps and uses various research approaches. The review of the existing literature on the issues relevant for each of the discussed topics – namely the negative interest rates as well as systemic risk – is a starting point for the analysis. We also rely on the case study analysis of different central banks' approaches toward negative rates. However, the main findings that will be presented in empirical part of the book rely on a broad-based quantitative approach. By implementing such a broad-based approach, we believe that this book will analyse the negative interest rate topic in a comprehensive manner.

As mentioned above, our research does not cover the recent COVID-19 pandemic outbreak, which, among others, may have impacted systemic risk. Our approach is motivated by two considerations. First, the aim of this analysis is to investigate the NIRP relationship with systemic risk during 'normal' times rather than in periods in which pre-established macroeconomic relations are rapidly disrupted or, specifically, when the source of the disruption is not purely economic in nature (unlike in systemic crisis). Second, our sample spans the entire period of the non-tiered ECB NIRP, which we compare with preceding monetary policy experiences. The scheme of tiered negative rates, in our opinion, is in fact a mixed policy rate from the perspective of the banking sector, particularly when direct costs are considered. Therefore, our time sample additionally allows us to focus on a 'pure' NIRP environment (conducted by the ECB only) with the aim not only of distinguishing between positive and negative rates but also of investigating heterogeneity within the NIRP countries.

In the final chapter, we summarize conclusions derived from previous ones and present policy implications for both monetary and macroprudential authorities with respect to negative interest rate policy. As mentioned above, we do not cover the period of the COVID-19 pandemic (from March 2020) and the outbreak of the war in Ukraine (from February 2022); however, in the final chapter, we show their role and challenges for the future.

2 Negative Interest Rate Policy – A Theoretical Outline

2.1 The Concept of Interest Rate in Economics and Finance

In market economy, interest rate is among the key parameters underlying economic decision-making process. The economic literature provides several interest rate definitions, including the structure of its functions and its typology. Typically, interest rate in the economy is construed as a particular type of price/money cost (i.e., intertemporal price), much as definition approaches vary depending on the school of economic thought. Notwithstanding the tentative interest rate definition, the literature points out to its four major functions (e.g., Masiukiewicz, 1994): (i) allocation, which involves affecting aggregate investment and production structure in the economy; (ii) regulation, which comes down to maintaining balance on the capital and money markets whereby the interest rate is a tool for balancing supply and demand of loan capital; (iii) calculation, which enables examining the profitability of business entities' investment decisions; and (iv) yield, which involves calculating income on capital investment. Analysis of the above functions is crucial as introducing a negative interest rate policy may induce a disruption of this fundamental mechanism.

2.1.1 Interest Rate Theories

According to the classical school of economics, the interest rate – although the classical economics alone did not relatively elaborate much on its very concept – may be viewed as a part of profit (e.g., according to A. Smith) or as premium paid for holding goods now versus the possibility to use them in the future (e.g., according to I. Fisher, 1930). It should also be emphasized that the classical theory assumes neutrality of money in the long term and it ignores the effect it has on setting the interest rate. It means that the existence of money is not a prerequisite for the interest rate to exist. From this perspective, classicists and neo-classicists (including I. Fisher) viewed the interest rate as a non-monetary category. At the same time, in their considerations, they denied it could be used as an active monetary policy instrument (Bilski, 2012). It is because, following Fisher's theory, interest rate was

DOI: 10.4324/9781003312116-2

market-developed by equating savings (supply of liquid capital, positively dependent on interest rate level) with investments (demand for liquid capital, reversely dependent on interest rate level). It is only K. Wicksell's elaboration on this approach that showed the interest rate is determined by both real and monetary factors (Brózda-Wilamek, 2018). It was the first time in the history of economic thought that the role of monetary policy could be deemed as giving rise to interest rate fluctuations around the rate's natural level. Moreover, K. Wicksell expanded the classical interest rate theory to include two additional interest rate types – a monetary rate (as a money cost charged by commercial banks on loans originated, set by supply and demand on the money market; Wicksell, 1934) and the natural rate of interest (defined further in the chapter). As for economic fluctuations, he related them to the relationship between these two.

It was the Austrian school of economic thought that referred to the Wicksellian theory. The school's representatives positioned the interest rate as a monetary phenomenon and they defined it as the cost paid for borrowing capital. Thus, the interest rate determines the yield floor for deposited capital while deciding whether the investment was profitable or not. Still, Austrians opposed any state intervention in the economy, that is, also the role of monetary policy. F.A. Hayek, one of the neo-Austrian school representatives, showed that the interest rate may be defined as difference in preference between the price level of consumption goods (providing present income) and capital goods (providing future income; Brózda-Wilamek, 2018). In this approach, interest rate decline arises from an increase of capital goods' price versus that of consumption goods, that is, from a shrinking of so-called time preference (Hayek, 2009). In the context of relationship between these two categories of goods, the Austrian school also mentioned the role of money amount in the economy, thus declining the money's neutrality. It is because fluctuations of amount of money in circulation affect the real allocation processes which give rise to shifting production factors from the upcoming production stages (consumption goods) to those more distant (investment goods).

J.M. Keynes presented a different point of view, including the interest rate theory. He argued that a direct relationship between savings and investments is non-existent since savings depend on income which, in turn, depends on investments (Grabowski, 1966). His theory held that money supply on the market does not only depend on the level of savings in the economy but also on their form. When business entities keep their savings in cash, they do not affect the interest rate and, consequently, they do not obtain any compensation for deferring consumption. It follows that the savings owner must give up disposing of their own funds to obtain compensation, the so-called liquidity premium. So, the interest rate equals the ratio of what you can obtain if you give up disposing of a given amount for a predetermined period versus the debt value (Keynes, 1936). Unlike in the classical theory, the interest rate equates money supply (considered to be an exogenous factor, stemming from the central bank's operations) with demand for it (as a result of three major motives – transaction, prudential and speculative ones). Keynes attributed to the interest rate a special role in determining the volume of capital expenditure. He maintained that businesses undertake investments whereby capital efficiency is higher than the present market interest rate at which they can obtain financing in the form of a bank loan.

The risk factor may also be of importance in shaping the interest rate curve. It was noted by J. Tobin (1961) who, as a neo-Keynesian, defined the interest rate as a premium for giving up liquidity, that is, for taking a risk of investing in securities. In that view, the interest rate was interpreted as a monetary phenomenon with some real sphere elements. In his theory, the interest rate, on the one hand, defines the interest level for bank loans and financial instruments and it was also considered a possible rate of return on real capital goods (Szydło, 2002).

In this context, the varying importance of interest rates from theoretical perspectives may also be addressed. Much as the classical theory perceived the real long-term interest rate being of key relevance in determining economic processes, J.M. Keynes considered the real short-term nominal interest rate to prevail (Duménil and Lévy, 1999). Important relations among various categories of interest rates produce a simplified approach in economic models which is restricted to just one general interest rate theory being applied. It is often assumed that changing the level of one interest rate type usually implies the same focus for change in the other categories. Still, in the context of negative interest rates, it is crucial to differentiate between the nominal and real, as well as short- and long-term categories, to be elaborated on in subsequent sub-chapters.

2.1.2 Nominal and Real Interest Rate

The differentiation between real and nominal interest rates, originally made by I. Fisher, became vital for economic considerations. The nominal interest rate defines an alternative cost incurred in keeping funds as cash, i.e., so-called cost of lost interest (Begg et al., 1994). In turn, the real interest rate specifies the increase of the purchasing power of money to be attained if invested at a given nominal rate. In line with an original Fisher effect, a difference between those two was the level of inflation. Such a varied approach to interest rates translated into them being considered as economic surplus tools, which is, capital-generated income. The surplus could be claimed by the lender when the capital rate of return equals the interest rate, or by the borrower in case the inflation rate equals the interest rate (Domański, 2016). It follows that the relation between interest rate and inflation (so, the real interest rate) is made equivalent to the structure of economic surplus partition between the lender and the borrower.

At this point, it should also be noted that the novelty and unprecedented character of a negative interest rate is connected with its nominal category. Concomitantly, negative real interest rates used to be a commonly known

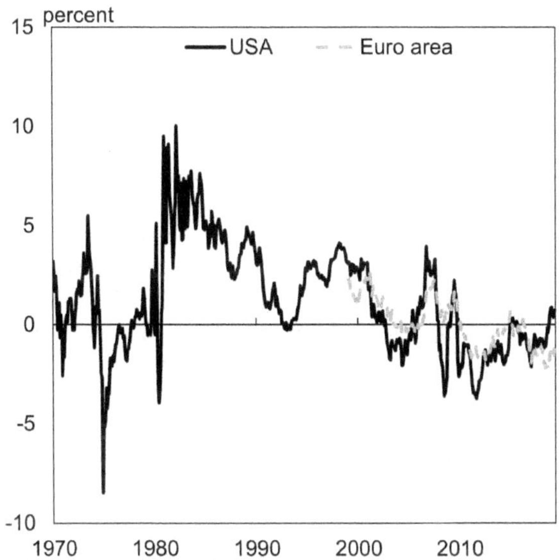

Figure 2.1 Real interest rates in the USA and Euro area
Note: Real interest rate calculates on ex-post basis with reference to consumer price index.
Source: Bank for International Settlements, own calculations.

and quite a popular phenomenon in the past, usually during high inflation (Figure 2.1). For deflation times, however, such a phenomenon was considered impossible to occur (Błaszczyk, 2010). At the same time, the literature points out that the materialised negative short-term real interest rates normally relate to *ex-post* treatment, i.e., estimates based on the actual change in prices. In turn, estimates based on inflationary expectations of businesses (*ex-ante* treatment) point out to a negative real interest rate occurring much less frequently. Importantly, negative real interest rates were recorded during various monetary policy regimes, which makes it difficult to bring them into direct comparison on account of varying structural conditions (Borio et al., 2017).

2.1.3 Short- and Long-Term Interest Rates

J.R. Hicks (1975) was one with the greatest impact on how the entire theoretical interest rate framework works (including the rates' term structure). He distinguished between two interest rates with varying terms they pertain to – short- and long-term. His assertion was that the long-term interest rate is a compound of the short-term rate and its future levels which carry certain risk premium component estimated by the lender. In turn, future interest rate levels were to derive directly from what businesses expected them to look like in the future. In this approach, under stable business conditions, the long-term interest rate should exceed short-term rates by the above-mentioned premium component. The premium compensates for uncertainty brought on by adverse changes of future economic environment (the higher the uncertainty, the higher the interest rate term).[1]

Next to the Keynesian liquidity preference, the factors which affect the varying character of the mentioned interest rates include: uncertainty deriving from the loss of all or a part of funds (i.e., insolvency risk, credit risk), the above-mentioned uncertainty regarding future interest rate levels and the advantages of funds being used by alternative methods (maintained as short-term instruments, mainly cash). With respect to the last factor, interest rate level also measures the "nuisance" of funds being converted into securities. J.R. Hicks claimed that money and other assets create a chain of substitutes which accounts for the positive value of interest rate (Brózda-Wilamek, 2018).

The discrimination between interest rates depending on their term to maturity enabled their so-called term structure. In practice, a yield curve is developed as an approximation of the term structure. It is made for instruments of varying maturities, yet with similar credit risk and liquidity (Sławiński, 1996).[2] In turn, later theories accounting for the shape of yield curves allowed to identify economic factors, at the same time expanding earlier considerations which solely focused on interest rate level analysis. As (in accordance with the pure expectations theory) long-term interest rates arise from the present and expected short-term rates (Sławiński, 2006), central banks employ the term structure today to monitor the expectations on future monetary policy and to relate them to such ideas through, e.g., inflation level or economic growth prospects. Other theories hold that certain investor groups have preferences for the length of investment horizon (habitat preference theory) or that they are confined to a particular market segment, e.g., as a result of their regulatory environment or the character of business operations (market segmentation theory). On the other hand, such an approach implies that the institutional structure of the domestic financial market may affect the yield curve. For instance, a high share of long-term investors, such as pension funds or insurance companies, will be fostering a decline in long-term interest rates (Sławiński, 1996).

2.1.4 Natural Rate of Interest

K. Wicksell (1934) is considered to have originated the natural rate of interest theory.[3] He defined it as such a level of the real interest rate that equates investments with savings in the context of a simultaneous price level stabilization. In addition, K. Wicksell brings up thus defined interest rate on a par with marginal productivity of capital. From this perspective, if the real interest rate exceeds marginal productivity, a company acting reasonably should reduce investment. However, the literature shows that such a definition provides room for several variants of natural rate of interest (e.g., Brzoza-Brzezina, 2003): one attributable to savings being equated with investment, a second one relating to a general price level and a third one equating the natural rate of interest with marginal capital productivity. While in K. Wicksell's opinion all of the three definitions described the same object, they should be considered separate definitions according to today's economists (Laidler, 1991).[4]

The contemporary definitions deviate from the above original approach. The most widely applied is the one which identifies the natural rate of interest with such a real rate for which inflation is stable. In such an approach, the growth of real rates above their natural level will trigger economic processes reducing inflation, whereas their decline below the natural rate – inflation acceleration. Given the monetary policy role in determining interest rates, the above definition allows to define the stance of the very monetary policy. That stance may be defined as natural in case the central bank's effect favours maintaining real interest rates on the level of a natural rate of interest, restrictive for the first of the variants named above and expansionary for the second one.

The natural rate of interest level typically does not arise from the central bank's actions, but it depends on the prevailing economic conditions, i.e., labour and capital resources and their efficiency, as well as the societies' preferences for consumption and savings (Michałek, 2012). Nevertheless, some economists (e.g., Rzońca, 2012) note that – based on the New-Keynesian analytical scheme – the central bank may theoretically affect the natural rate of interest as long as capital expenditure underlies the reasoning. Having an effect on capital expenditure, changes of the central bank's interest rate may affect the capital resources, and ultimately, the capital's marginal productivity.

Unlike the interest rate categories described above, the natural rate of interest is not directly observable; hence, attempts are made to estimate it. The literature points to several estimation methods starting with the assumption of stability over time, that is, relatively stable economic conditions – through the application of a long-term weighed average for real interest rates (Williams, 2003) – to the application of econometric methods which take account of the dynamics of economic changes. With respect to the last one, the most prevalent is the method put forward by Laubach and Williams (2001, 2016). It is based on a total estimate of the economy's growth trend, the natural real interest rate and the potential product. Still, notwithstanding the measurement method, the metric carries uncertainty, which may reduce the advantages of incorporating this theory into the decision-making process of central banks (Orphanides and Williams, 2007).

The literature is not clear on whether the natural rate of interest should be related to the long- or the short-term rate (Kotłowski, 2016). K. Wicksell's understanding is that the rate was identified with the long- (Amato, 2005) or at least medium-term rate, with the latter's maturity corresponding to the duration of economic shocks (Bomfim, 2001). However, the majority of authors who address this issue from the perspective of optimum monetary policy (see, e.g., Garnier and Wilhelmsen, 2005; Brzoza-Brzezina, 2006; Andrés et al, 2009) identify it with the short-term rate corresponding to monetary policy's operational target.

This approach changed following the GFC and with the central banks resorting to unconventional monetary policy tools which also affect the long-term rates. Under such circumstances, the real picture of the monetary policy may not be captured if the conclusions on monetary conditions in the economy are based only on the short-term rate. Thus, the economic literature put forward a concept which partly resolves the problem and takes into account the whole term structure – the natural yield curve theory (see, e.g., Brzoza-Brzezina and Kotłowski, 2014). Simultaneously, it was pointed out that these two metrics (natural rate of interest and natural income curve) have clearly desynchronised in the post-GFC environment.

The theory of natural rate of interest was covered in this sub-chapter more extensively than the other interest rate categories. It is because the central banks pushing interest rates below zero are, *inter alia*, attributable to a systematic and large-scale decline of the natural rate of interest. This tendency has only strengthened following the GFC (Figure 2.2). In the major economies, the decline (even below zero for the eurozone) prevented central banks from stimulating the economy which would have otherwise called for lowering the real short-term interest rate below the natural rate. Summers (2014) claimed that the natural rate of interest going below zero was possible

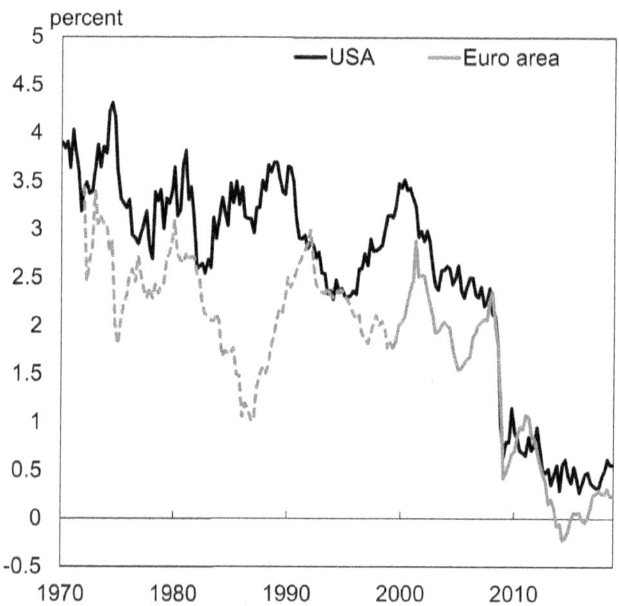

Figure 2.2 Natural interest rates in the USA and Euro area
Note: Dashed line denotes estimates for Germany.
Source: Laubach and Williams (2016).

due to a chronic (and fostered by the latest crisis) rise in saving tendency (deferring consumption) in the developed countries and a decline in a tendency to invest. In highly developed countries, the phenomenon contributes to rising excess of savings in business. Consequently, the natural rate of interest going well below zero made it difficult for the central banks to bolster the economy, which – amid low inflationary expectations – meant that it was actually necessary to bring the nominal interest rates below zero.

In spite of numerous comments and critical voices, as well as empirical evidence (see, e.g., Rogoff, 2015; Bernanke, 2016), the mainstream economics has so far failed to develop a consensus whether the natural rate of interests are now indeed below zero. Economic models taking into account the very capacity for the natural rate of interest to fall below zero also remain sort of a challenge. For instance, introducing a natural negative interest rate in classical growth models is feasible, yet it requires a hardly realistic assumption that the economy is affected by technological regression and the high capital saturation in production. The latter particularly indicates that the marginal contribution of capital into a product is lower than the capital depreciation.

2.1.5 Shadow Interest Rate

In response to the effects of the GFC, central banks in numerous developed economies first lowered interest rates to their zero lower bound (see Figures 2.3–2.5) and then used other unconventional monetary policy tools

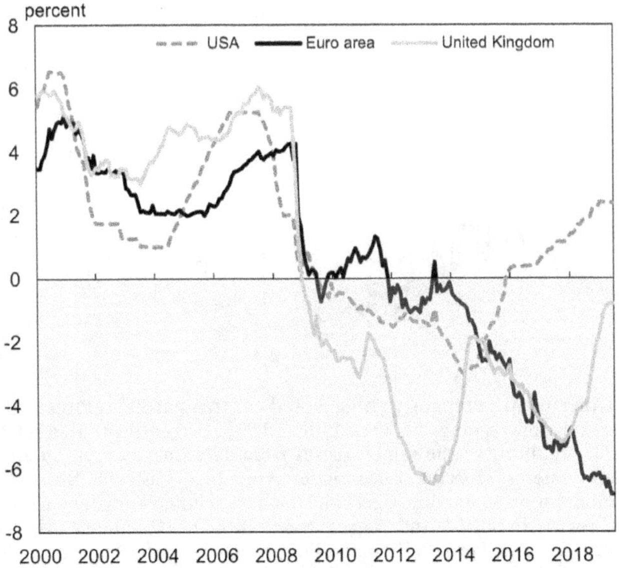

Figure 2.3 Shadow interest rate in selected economies
Source: Bloomberg data, Wu and Xia (2016) estimates.

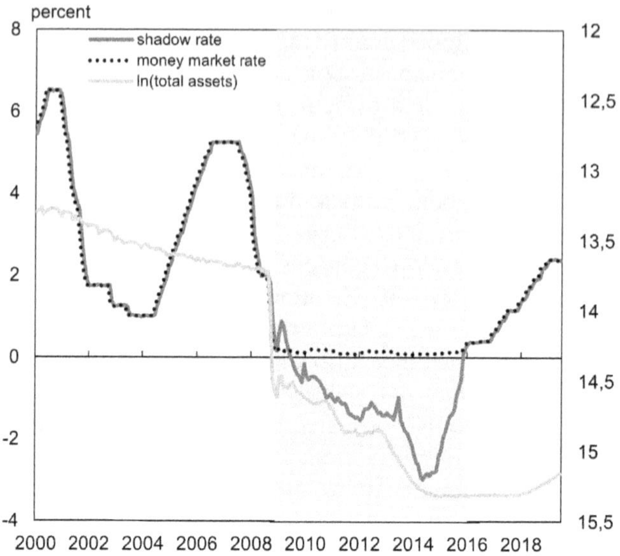

Figure 2.4 Relationship between shadow interest rate and central bank's balance sheet – case of USA

Note: Grey area denotes the period when zero lower bound was binding in the USA.

Source: Bloomberg data, Wu and Xia (2016) estimates.

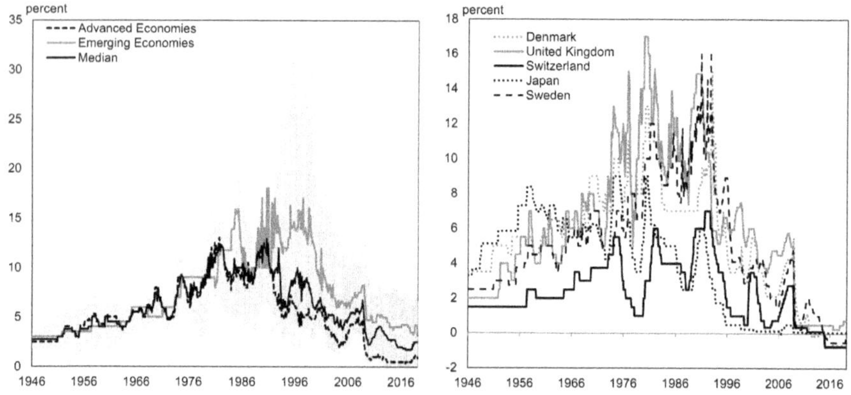

Figure 2.5 Long-term perspective of selected central banks' interest rates

Note: Grey area denotes a range between 10th and 90th percentile; thus, a relatively narrow range at the beginning of the sample arises from data unavailability. Left chart counts central banks' interest rates for 38 economies: Argentina, Australia, Brazil, Canada, Switzerland, Chile, China, Columbia, Czechia, Denmark, United Kingdom, Croatia, Hungary, Indonesia, Israel, India, Iceland, Japan, South Korea, Macedonia, Mexico, Malaysia, Norway, New Zealand, Peru, Philippines, Poland, Romania, Serbia, Russia, Saudi Arabia, Sweden, Thailand, Turkey, USA, South Africa, Eurozone.

Source: Bank for International Settlements, central banks.

for further monetary stimulation. However, in analyses of the effect of monetary policy on economic variables, the majority of economic models is based on the central bank's main tool, i.e., the interest rate. Consequently, it was necessary to put forward a synthetic indicator for monetary policy to cover both the central bank's interest rate policy and the unconventional measures. The shadow interest rate was such a theoretical and not readily observable indicator. It addresses the question of what the level of the central bank's nominal interest rate should be to provide for similar monetary conditions assessed through the spectrum of market interest rates (Krippner, 2013; Wu and Xia, 2016, 2017).

The main advantage of such an economic figure is ensuring comparability among the monetary policy tools applied. The foregoing is confirmed by the degree of correlation of the shadow interest rate with macroeconomic variables being similar to that of money market rate in the period before the lower bound was reached, i.e., before the expansion of central banks' instrumentation to include unconventional measures. In addition, the rate is not limited by the bound, so it is free to take on negative values. The rate's characteristics mentioned above are corroborated by its estimates for economies which employ financial assets purchase programmes. In particular, the rate overlaps with the central bank's key interest rate in the periods when monetary policy unconventional tools are not in use. And it goes below zero whenever central banks intensify asset purchase. In this way, it is possible to compare several central bank tools, including their role for the economy's natural rate interest level. Concomitantly, the shadow interest rate is recommended only in the environment of expansionary monetary policy pursued with the use of several monetary policy channels.[5]

2.2 The Role of Monetary Policy in Determining Interest Rates

One of the ways to directly control interest rates on the interbank market is to subordinate them to the central bank's interest rates level, which translates into alignment in other financial market segments. As a result, in the modern central banking paradigm, it is the interest rate that has become the primary monetary policy tool affecting monetary and real variables and historically replacing money supply regulation. On the other hand, an approach proposed by Goodfriend and King (1998) and referred to as the New Keynesian school of thought currently prevails with respect to the tool's effect on the economy. This approach is based on the real variables being the main reason for the volatility of business activity, and the impact of monetary policy on the volatility being relatively modest in the medium term, albeit significant in redressing the economy's balance after a real shock (e.g., Przybylska-Kapuścińska et al., 2008).

Once considered a monetary policy tool, nominal interest level may, however, be sort of a simplification in terms of operational aspects, and it requires more extensive clarification. The fact is that there can be named three categories of monetary policy goals in central banking operations which can, as a whole, function as the monetary policy strategy:[6]

- the primary or the ultimate goal that the central bank was established to achieve. The primary goal of the monetary policy is typically price stability, often expanded to include promotion of economic growth, full employment or securing financial stability.
- intermediate goals to achieve the primary goal. Typically, the goal is the nominal interest rate level. Advocates of Keynesian money theory opted for the nominal interest rates being the intermediate goal of monetary policy (Kaźmierczak, 2019). They assumed that demand for money is highly elastic with respect to the rate. Practically speaking, the choice of interest rate as the intermediate goal is due to this variable being observed on a day-to-day basis (in real time for the money market), which also means it is easily controlled and communicable for broader audience.[7]
- operational goals, that is, short-term variables strictly and directly controlled by the central bank. Monetary policy's operational goal is usually the level of nominal short-term interest rates of the money market while central bank instruments which provide the control include open market operations, FX operations, reserve requirements, as well as the central bank's communication with their audiences (Przybylska-Kapuścińska et al., 2008).

As shown previously, monetary policy affects short-term rates, while business entities' investments in fixed assets are decisions for a longer time-span, also with respect to the expected cost of financing. Therefore, it is the long-term interest rate that represents a category which, to a higher extent (at least recently), has affected such decisions. It follows that the central bank, in order to influence the real economy more effectively, should affect the long-term interest rate level. This dependence was already brought up by J.M. Keynes whose idea was for the central banks to fix prices of the safest securities of numerous maturities (Keynes, 1936).

Progress of the global financial crisis of 2007–2008 changed the way central banks perceived the role of short-term interest rates being the primary instrument of monetary policy. It is because, for effective business stimulation and monetary policy goals to be achieved, it was also necessary to bring down long-term interest rates. With risk premium in crisis remaining at levels higher than usual, the central banks would have had to set a negative short-term interest rate in order to lower the long end of the yield curve (Kotłowski, 2016). Importantly, such an approach would have had been hardly thinkable a few years back. Central banks take this problem into account in running their monetary policy – originally, by overtly communicating the future interest rates (among others publishing their projections; e.g.,

Przybylska-Kapuścińska and Szyszko, 2011), and recently, through unconventional monetary policy tools, including in particular financial assets purchase programmes (e.g., Fawley and Neely, 2013).[8]

What characterises unconventional monetary policy is affecting financial markets while bypassing the short-term interest rate channel (*decoupling principle*; Borio and Disyatat, 2009). There are three channels of influence most commonly referred to in the literature (typically on asset purchase programmes): expectations (influencing the path of central banks' expected interest rates and the term premium), liquidity (influencing liquidity in the banking sector) and portfolio (working through demand on securities, including their, often imperfect, substitutes, purchased by the central bank). The literature points to the portfolio (m.in. Gagnon et al., 2011) and expectation channels (Christensen and Rudebusch, 2012) as affecting the reduction of long-term interest rates the most. Still, a detailed assessment of the magnitude of a given channel's effect may vary depending on the research method and the very definition of respective influence channels (Kotłowski, 2016).

2.3 Lower Bound for Nominal Interest Rates

The nominal interest rate is assumed to be of relatively modest relevance in economic models and the business entities make investment and consumption decisions based on the levels of and mutual relations among real interest rates. Consequently, also the role of lower bound for nominal interest rate is of little importance so long as the central bank may affect the level of expected rates and inflationary expectations, hence the expected real interest rates. Much as perfectly applicable for cash-free economy, this assumption changes along with the change of the relative importance of cash. It is because the alternative cost of holding money in cash is closely related to the real rate of return on any chosen investment and the real rate of return on cash. With zero cost of holding cash, the difference between those two equals the nominal interest rate level (Kimball, 2015).

The topic is all the more important that the economy reaching the lower bound for interest rates considerably increases the risk of deflationary trap (i.e., a situation whereby the expected macroeconomic situation requires further easing of monetary policy, yet the nominal interest rates must not be employed by the central bank for this purpose; Brzoza-Brzezina et al., 2016). Depending on its determinants, the very level of the lower bound for interest rates may, however, be defined in several ways: on the one hand as zero lower bound and as technical or economic bound on the other.

2.3.1 Zero Lower Bound

The theory of zero lower bound is common in the literature. The zero lower bound (ZLB) is considered to be a major – next to downward nominal wage rigidity – phenomenon determining the efficiency of monetary policy with low inflation and deflation, and it is also an important argument in favour of non-zero inflation (IMF, 1999). ZLB risk materialization poses a threat whenever – with adequately strong deflationary shock causing a fall in the general price level and persistent deflationary expectations emerging – the economy may fall into a liquidity trap (Svensson, 2000). Under such circumstances, money becomes a substitute for bonds, expansionary open market operations do not affect nominal and real prices and volumes, the private sector maintains a monetary base instead of bonds and the monetary policy is ineffective (Błaszczyk, 2010).

The consensus in the theory of economics holds that the zero lower bound is triggered by a liquid asset of a nominal fixed rate of return equal zero, i.e., cash (McCallum, 2000). It was already Fisher (1930) who claimed that assuming a zero-storage cost, an interest rate for any good must not be lower than zero. Keynes (1936) was of similar opinion. He emphasized that the costs of storing money are negligible and certainly lower than the liquidity premium. While sufficient capital accumulation could reduce interest rates to zero by limiting the said premium, the rates must not be negative anyway.[9]

From this perspective, in case the central bank introduced a negative interest rate, its transmission to bank loans and deposits would make no sense as business entities – in pursuit of maximizing rate of return – would hold their cash. Similarly, a borrower's optimum strategy would be taking out the highest loan possible as the principal to be repaid (with interest) would be lower anyway. The legal aspect aside, the whole loan amount could be held in an asset free from negative cost (i.e., cash) and then repaid with profit guarantee. In effect, neither bank deposits nor loans would make any sense and the interest they bear would have no macroeconomic role (Brzoza-Brzezina et al., 2016).

Also, in the financial literature on the modelling of interest rates, the prevailing view has been one of interest rates' non-negative character, and for a significant portion of financial models, the assumption of a positive interest rate is considered one of the most important (Pan and Wu, 2006). For an example, such an assumption plays a crucial role in the valuation of derivative instruments, whereby even low likelihood of a negative interest rate translates into high sensitivity of instrument re-valuation (Rogers, 1995) and, as some authors maintain, irrational results.[10]

Given the problems that the zero lower bound caused, the literature considered numerous solutions to mitigate the risk of a deflationary trap. In the original approach, McCallum (2000) proposed that the central bank use exchange rate as a monetary policy tool, thus giving a depreciation stimulus so as to bolster price growth at the same time.[11] It was one of the solutions for monetary policy to continue to affect economic conditions. Other solutions pertained to modifying the strategy of direct inflation target which has in recent years been prevailing among monetary policy strategies in developed economies. Namely, the central bank may set the inflation target higher (Blanchard et al., 2010), which in long-term perspective will translate into higher inflationary expectations implying – with a given natural rate of interest – higher nominal interest rates.[12] The central bank may also modify the monetary policy strategy from the direct inflationary target into price level targeting (Nakov, 2008; Billi, 2013). In this approach, the monetary policy is so pursued as to make the real price level keep close to the pre-defined path (see, e.g., Grostal et al., 2016). It means that as inflation falls, the inflationary expectations rise (conversely to the direct inflation target strategy) since for inflation to revert to the path mentioned above, a period of higher inflation is necessary, which consequently drives the real long-term interest rates down. Finally, the solution used in practice by central banks following their GFC's experience was to directly affect long-term interest rates (Clouse et al., 1999). In this approach, central bank communication is used to credibly ensure that short-term rates remain at their levels over an extended period. The foregoing is to be conducive to lowering the path of the expected interest rates and the related uncertainty, as well as to translate into a decline in long-term interest rates.

The said zero lower bound mechanism, in spite of providing only theoretical solutions, did prove historically effective in maintaining interest rates on positive levels. However, it was challenged as the central banks introduced the negative interest rate policy and the economists became more interested in defining the actual and not the zero bound for interest rates.

2.3.2 Physical Bound for Interest Rates

One of the fundamental assumptions underlying the above-mentioned zero lower bound is negligible or zero cash-holding costs. Still, a physical and less than zero bound for interest rates shows that cash investment is in fact costly. It is because businesses tend to bear only modest costs associated with the safety or convenience of keeping their cash with a bank (Neumark, 1948). What is interesting, much as the scholars agree on the physical bound for interest rates being located below zero, some economists show it is possible for the bound to reach positive values. This would be the case if holding cash provided its holders with significant profits which would defy downward trend along with the growth of cash resources (Yates, 2002). This, however, seems to be no more than a theory.

The cost of cash naturally changes with respect to the resources at hand in absolute terms and – what is important for lower bound considerations – relative terms. Academics commonly assume that the cost is notably lower for households (than corporates) since they usually hold relatively little cash *per capita*. In addition, dematerialized money gives businesses extra benefits, including more efficient working capital management. Hence, businesses are more willing to accept negative interest viewed as compensation for access to services offered by banks which are not directly related to the cost of holding cash. From macroeconomic perspective, it means that for developed economies with a fair share of domestic firms, the lower bound for interest rates will take on more negative values than, for instance, that for the economies with a fair share of foreign capital. Consequently, as the relative importance of households, services or the export of goods grows, so will the physical lower bound for interest rates approximate the zero level to a greater extent.

Unlike the zero bound, the physical bound for interest rate may change over time. It is because, whenever it is expected, the central bank's interest rates will be maintained or will continue to fall, businesses (in particular in negative interest rate environment) may adapt to the new environment by lowering their cash storage costs (McAndrews, 2015).[13] In other words, the longer the low or negative interest rate period businesses expect (based on the central bank's communication), the more difficult it will be to pursue expansionary policy based on interest rate only.

It should also be mentioned that by the time the cash is renumerated with interest other than zero, the physical bound for interest rates is the valid bound for the monetary policy. Some scholars emphasise, however, that the central banks introducing NIRP does not mean the zero bound for interest rates has been crossed as it only approximates the physical lower bound (McAndrews, 2015).[14]

2.3.3 Economic Bound for Nominal Interest Rates

Another theory seeking to determine the lower bound for interest rates is based on defining the minimum point at which monetary policy loses it expansionary character. From economic perspective, such a point may be reached whenever the central bank's interest rate equals the natural rate of interest. In theory then, as the former falls, the latter may go down as well, which will be attributable to long-term economic conditions and which will be conducive to the expiry of the said expansionary character of monetary policy. Notwithstanding, the situation is not identical with the economic lower bound for interest rates, also known as effective lower bound. It needs to be noted that once the economic bound is reached, further pushing interest down by the central bank gives rise to tightening monetary policy conditions which is due to limiting the effect of monetary policy's credit channel. Reversal interest rate – proposed by Brunnermeier and Koby (2017) – is the most commonly known form of effective bound.

The idea of reversal interest rate assigns a special role to the banking sector and it is based on a direct relation between monetary and macroprudential policy. In this approach, excessively low interest rates in the conditions of regulatory constraints, including capital requirements, will prevent commercial banks from increasing lending and, consequently, they will limit the effect of monetary policy on business operations. In this way, the more restrictive the said requirements, the higher the effective bound for interest rates. In particular, next to economic factors (e.g., a more elastic demand for money), what raises the effective bound is also bank balance sheet structure, such as a considerable share of household deposits, lower bank equity or tightening macroprudential regulations which bear both on the banks' capital as well as on the banks' risk appetite (Brunnermeier and Koby, 2017). It follows that restrictive macroprudential regulations applied during economic downturn may withhold the impact of expansionary monetary policy by raising the effective bound for interest rates. Such a situation may partly arise directly from temporal diversification of both the policies' reaction functions. The idea also takes account of the coordination failure of both the policies which becomes of particular relevance in terms of NIRP analysis. For instance, if negative nominal interest rates are introduced when the banking sector is in good shape (in particular with respect to a high capital base being due to internal policies or regulatory recommendations), the expansionary character of negative interest rates is reflected in the sector's credit policy. On the other hand, when NIRP is introduced with the banks' weaker capital position and/or when macroeconomic policy takes up measures aiming to mitigate possible systemic risks, the lower effective bound for interest rates will move upwards, which may diminish the scale of monetary policy's effect on banks' lending (Kimball, 2016).

Further, much as the relation between zero and the physical bound being lower at all times was clear-cut, it grows more complex for the economic bound. Theoretically speaking, the economic bound may be both positive (so, higher than the other two) and negative. The latter is the most probable estimate in the light of NIRP, albeit not necessarily so from historical perspective (e.g., Poloz, 2015). In addition, this lower bound category is the most variable category of all those in question. For instance, if the effect of maintaining interest rates low has a negative pressure on the revenue of the banking sector, and the lending capacity based on the capital accumulated earlier is shrinking, the effective lower bound understood as reversed interest rate curve may rise gradually (McAndrews, 2015). In other words, the central bank's activity is not necessary for the interest rate effective bound to be crossed. Still, empirical research shows that the central banks' unconventional measures in the form of the purchases of financial asset historically had a rising effect on the bound by reducing the share of "safe assets" in the form of treasury bonds on commercial banks' balance sheets (Eisenschmidt and Smets, 2018). In addition, quantitative easing programmes give rise to a substantial rise of the scale of liquidity surplus in banking, which directly makes the sector more vulnerable to interest rate changes. It should be pointed out that next to a volatile nature of the economic bound for interest rates, the bound is also the most empirically difficult among all of its counterparts in question.

Yet another approach to defining interest rate level triggering the expiry of monetary policy expansionary potential, referred to as expansionary lower bound, was developed by Cavallino and Sandi (2019). The idea expands the approach discussed earlier to include the marginal interest rate being placed in international context, based on the importance of international capital flows (the so-called monetary policy trilemma).[15] This idea holds that expansionary monetary policy contributes to the outflow of foreign portfolio capital, which has an effect of driving up the yield on domestic treasury bonds which also make up the balance sheets of national banks. So long as the balance sheet structure of commercial banks meets regulatory requirements with respect to balance between capital and the scale of risk exposure, the expansionary monetary policy will have a conventional effect on the activity of banks, thus, on subsequent stages of the transmission mechanism. Notwithstanding, in case of a sufficiently strong impulse of the monetary policy and balance sheet structure constraints, and with the intention to absorb the treasury bond market surplus yielding positive rate of return, the banking sector will seek to curb credit supply by raising interest (Cavallino and Sandi, 2019). Interest rate level at which the above mechanism will be observable is identified by the academics precisely as effective bound for interest rates which bears characteristics similar to those described earlier on.

Unlike its predecessors, the next concept in question points to the importance of business entities' perception of the expected future business risk. Namely, the entities are willing to bear the cost of investing in "safe assets" (e.g., a bank deposit or treasury bonds) to safeguard against future risk. Some sources of this approach may be traced back with as early as with Marshall (1962). He claimed that in an economy in which eager consumers outnumber the capital providers, some entities may accept negative interest rate just to keep capital. The above scenario is supposedly due to the accumulated wealth being incapable of fetching profit and concerns about future consumption. It follows that, according to this concept, the higher the uncertainty of the economic environment, the lower the economic bound for interest rates.

2.4 Negative Interest Rate Phenomenon

Based on the earlier demonstrated theoretical foundations for the overall idea of an interest rate, its particular variety (i.e., the negative value) lends itself to being defined in several ways. First, the negative interest rate interpreted as a price for any good (assuming it is not equilibrium price) may denote a clear decline in demand for money versus its supply. Second, it can be identified with negative premium for using given goods in the future, that is, a disadvantage expected in the future. Such an approach is consistent with the financial definition typically quoted in terms of the current NIRP which implies that future revenue is of higher value than the present revenue. Third, according to the Austrian school of thought, a negative interest rate may mean negative time preference, i.e., a higher preference for capital rather than consumption goods. Fourth, in terms of uncertainty, it may mean on the one hand higher uncertainty or risk attributed to the current rather than future events, or on the other hand, lesser investment risk due to keeping securities rather than cash. Fifth, a negative interest rate may be indicative of a high substitutability between cash and other forms of holding capital. In the Keynesian view, this may be due to a negative liquidity premium and it may show that cash has lost on its mobility versus securities. Such an approach identifies the negative interest rate with a preference for lesser nuisance associated with converting cash into securities rather than holding cash alone. This concept may be substantiated by the contemporary meaning of cash and the development of new technologies which result in a broad access to a wide range of (highly dematerialised) financial instruments in real time at historically low transaction costs. It follows that the negative interest rate may demonstrate that the spectrum of money substitutes has clearly expanded from historical perspective.

Next to defining the very phenomenon of negative interest rates, it should be considered to what extent the theory of economics allows its very existence. In the classical view, such a phenomenon is allowed if it is a necessary solution for the economic system to redress its balance. Notwithstanding, the foregoing implies two characteristics of negative interest rates that are required for consistency with the classical theory. First is a market character of such rates, albeit not attributable to the monetary policy pursued. Second, given money neutrality, the newly introduced interest rate character is a narrower term than under the classical theory as it only covers monetary aspects. The Keynesian approach to the negative nominal interest rate is not clear-cut either. On the one hand, this theory was visibly sceptical with regard to the importance of active monetary policy, which implies the same for NIRP – especially if it was supposed to be just a temporary tool (Palley, 2016), which the central banks basically emphasized. Moreover, both J.M. Keynes and J.R. Hicks firmly believed that the interest rate must not be negative, as it could translate into economic system instability (Brózda-Wilamek, 2018). On the other hand though, the Keynesian approach itself does not question short-term negative interest rates whenever necessary to attain a zero long-term interest rate (Maclachlan, 2019).[16] In turn, the Austrian school's representatives claim that the present negative interest rates must not be identified with free market rates either (Hoppe, 1992). It is due to the negative rates being rather a product of central banks than of a changed time preference among businesses. As a result, a risk-free market interest rate is still most likely in the positive territory.

As previously indicated, this sub-chapter will also pertain to negative interest rate types, including in particular paper currency and non-paper currency interest rate, and the discount rate, in order to provide a correct theoretical framework for negative interest rates (Table 2.1).

2.4.1 Negative Non-Paper Currency Interest Rate

The issue of negative non-paper currency interest rate refers to the category of nominal interest on money excluding its materialised form, i.e., cash. Thus, such an approach suggests that it is the right category to provide the

Table 2.1 Theoretical classification of negative interest rates definition

School of economic thought	*Selected representative*	*Definition of interest rate*	*Category of interest rate*	*Possible meaning of negative interest rate*
Classical, Neoclassical	A. Smith; I. Fisher	Premium paid/ received as a reward for possessing goods at the present moment rather than in the future	Non-monetary (real)	Disadvantage expected in the future, i.e., negative premium for possessing goods at present moment
Austrian	L. von Mises; F.A. Hayek	Price paid for lending of capital; Difference between preference of consumer and capital goods	Monetary (nominal)	Negative time preference, i.e., capital goods are preferred over consumer goods
Keynesian, Neo-Keynesian	J. M. Keynes; J. Tobin	Price that equates demand and supply in the money market; Reward for resignation from liquidity (or cash balances)	Monetary (with elements of non-monetary perspective)	Significant oversupply in the money market; Negative premium for investment risk, i.e., preference to hold financial securities instead of cash; Decline of cash mobility/ liquidity below the mobility of securities

Source: based on literature review.

context for the analysis of NIRP now being pursued by the central banks. The said distinction into paper currency and non-paper currency interest rates is, however, a particular feature conditioned by the very policy as in the environment of positive interest rates the concepts are normally equated. The distinction produces a risk of shifting cash between the said money forms, which in turn may result in macroeconomic imbalances. In other words, if implemented in non-cash financial instruments, central bank's negative interest rates pose a risk that the investors who want to minimize the nominal loss will shift their funds to cash, an asset not affected by negative interest, which limits the rates' efficiency (Buiter, 2009; Mankiw, 2009;

McAndrews, 2015). Consequently, given limited likelihood of such a risk materializing, the extent to which non-paper currency interest rate introduced under NIRP can go down is relatively low. A mechanism which could enable its downward movement to continue (down to several percent below zero) is a theory of negative paper currency interest rate (PCIR).

Simultaneously, it should be pointed out that the non-paper currency interest rate should not be confused with the concept of non-monetary interest rate. It is because the latter category is a broader term and is relatively more common in economic dealings. Its existence is due to the costs of storing non-cash assets and certain assets depreciating over time. If these factors' magnitude is significant and they outweigh the benefits of holding the non-monetary asset, then, in the absence of other factors that may affect price changes over time, a negative interest rate will emerge. Today, the so-called convenience yield is a form of non-monetary interest rate. It is an observable variable, most of the time on the commodity futures market. As a rule, the negative non-monetary interest rate should not be identified with the negative discount rate either as the latter has different structural foundations.

2.4.2 Negative Paper Currency Interest Rate

What underlies the concept of paper currency interest rate is a separation between money as a medium of exchange and as a store of value proposed originally by S. Gesell (1916), who is considered to be the father of negative interest rate theory.[17] Still, the theory in which cash is charged with a cost identical with the negative interest for non-cash products, is itself much more complex, both method- and implementation-wise. Consequently, what the academics put forward can be analysed from several perspectives (see Table 1.2).

The first perspective defines the categories of entities through which negative interest for cash is implemented – directly, through business agents (households, firms) or the banking sector. It is worth mentioning that for a non-paper currency interest rate, such a distinction was not necessary as the interest rate was implemented by the financial sector, mainly banking. The banking sector is perceived as the expected transmission channel for the paper currency interest rate, too, as it enables cutting down on operational or political costs associated with implementing NIRP, *inter alia*, in relations with retail clients (Agarwal and Kimball, 2019).[18] The second, scope-related perspective defines whether negative interest will be implemented in prices or as a quantitative constraint. The third perspective will, in turn, be based on cash being perceived as a financial asset which offers its holder a nominal rate of return made up of two components: income (in this case as negative cash-flow) and price (here: money depreciation; Agarwal and Kimball, 2019). Consequently, the method of introducing a negative interest rate varies with respect to transmission mechanism type which will actually apply.

As already mentioned, the first economic author to propose a theoretical approach of charging the cost to cash was S. Gesell (1916). This approach identified the negative interest rate with a form of taxing cash by introducing extra cash-holding costs, and the consequence was to discourage paper currency. In the original version of the theory, cash-holding costs were to take on a form of banknote stamp fee which depended on the nominal value of cash.[19] This theory has come back also in a somewhat more modern form of placing magnetic readers on banknotes which record the time a given banknote spent outside the banking system and charging a cost proportionate to the period (Goodfriend, 2000). Such a theory is relatively simpler to classify in terms of the said perspectives, as it charges directly cash holders with an extra fee based on the price mechanism. Other proposals being part of this trend, albeit enjoying much less interest among the economists, are those associated with introducing the cost of cash through random withdrawals of banknotes, e.g., of a given series or with a specific digit in the series number (Li, 1995; Mankiw, 2009).

An alternative treatment (also based on the price mechanism, but in terms of cash depreciation) was originated by Eisler (1932) and further elaborated on by Buiter (2009). This approach assumed a nominal depreciation of electronic money versus cash, which was to discourage holding the latter and finally to enable the introduction of negative interest in whatever form. Buiter (2009) slightly highlighted the division of money categories by advocating the introduction of two parallel ones – means of payment and medium of exchange. The former was to pay liabilities, including taxes, and take on an electronic form, which is, to be easily charged with non-paper currency interest rates. The latter was to provide for cash exchange in trade and to undergo gradual depreciation to the former category.

Historically speaking, price mechanisms directly charging cash are the oldest concepts we know, that were developed long before it was actually necessary to implement the mechanisms. Much more recent are those which emerged as interest rates approached the zero bound. They took account of implementation burden related to previous proposals, based on quantitative mechanism and/or reliant on the banking sector for transmission. A total withdrawal of cash from circulation is the best-known approach of all quantitative mechanisms (Buiter, 2009; Rogoff, 2015). Although there are economies with quite a large share of non-cash transactions (e.g., Sweden), abolishing cash completely does entail negative consequences. They are said to include changes in how transactions are carried out (Rogoff, 2017), a rising risk of economic exclusion or a considerable increase of costs associated with avoiding the exclusion (Agarwal and Kimball, 2019) or a risk of domestic currency being converted into foreign currencies. The aforementioned factors spurred the popularity of the more moderate form which involved abolishing only high-denomination banknotes or retaining only coins, whereby the cost of holding cash would go up (Rogoff, 2017).

A common characteristic for all of the above proposals is direct charging cash holders with a cost. The most recent literature mentions it is possible to employ the entire banking sector as an intermediary in the process, thus shifting a vital part of operations from the central bank. There are four ideas which come into play here: (a) clean approach (Agarwal and Kimball, 2015), (b) rental fee (Agarwal and Kimball, 2019), (c) withdrawal limit (Goodfriend, 2016) and (d) deposit limit.

The first one was proposed by Buiter (2009) and draws on relations between the central bank and commercial banks and is based on the latter's need for cash. In this approach, the central bank sets the rate of exchanging non-cash to cash for the commercial bank. It has the form of a "crawling peg" known from FX theories and it corresponds to adjustment by the scale

Table 2.2 Theoretical possibilities of negative rates introduction

		Direct negative rates for economic agents	*Negative rates transmitted through banks*
Negative rate based on price system	Cash depreciation	(1) Eisler (1932); Butier (2009) (2) Tax approach (Feldstein, 2002; Correia et al., 2013)	Clean Approach (Agarwal and Kimball, 2015)
	Negative dividend on cash	(1) Gesell (1916); Goodfriend (2000) (2) Li (1995); Mankiw (2009)	Rental Fee Approach (Agarwal and Kimball, 2019)
Negative rate based on quantity restrictions	Cash depreciation	Withdrawal of cash from circulation (Buiter, 2009; Rogoff, 2015)	(1) Limits on withdrawal (Goodfriend, 2016) (2) Limits on deposits (Agarwal and Kimball, 2019)
	Negative dividend on cash	(1) Cash limits (Agarwal and Kimball, 2019) (2) Withdrawal of high-denomination banknotes (Rogoff, 2017)	Prohibition ban on cash electrification (Agarwal and Kimball, 2019)

Source: Agarwal and Kimball (2019).

of negative interest (Agarwal and Kimball, 2015). Consequently, the value of cash will differ from the nominal value, which may be conducive to psychological barriers and difficulties (e.g., clearly calculation-related) arising from the use of cash. It should additionally discourage cash; however, legal constraints may emerge due to the above-mentioned value variations versus the nominal value.

What addresses such a risk is the second approach which entails similar economic consequences and charges commercial banks with a direct cost proportionate to the cash "rented" from the central bank (Agarwal and Kimball, 2019). It should be pointed out that this approach approximates the most the current central banks' policy of negative interest rates whereby the commercial banks incur a direct cost of the deposit surplus held with the central bank above the reserve requirement.

The last mechanism reliant on the banking sector is quantitative mechanisms. The mechanisms come down both to limiting the amount of cash alone and to limiting deposits (versus cash) that can be hoarded by a respective commercial bank. Still, there is a belief prevalent in the literature that the most effective approach to the introduction of negative interest for cash is the price (and the not quantitative) mechanism which employs the entire banking sector as an intermediary (Agarwal and Kimball, 2019).

2.4.3 Negative Discount Rate

The discount rate reflects intertemporal consumption preferences. It seems a natural assumption for a discount rate to be positive as its zero or negative values paired with a positive rate of return on savings would defer consumption indefinitely (e.g., Koopmans, 1960; Hirshleifer, 1970; Frederick et al., 2002).

It also seems natural to analyse the relationship between discount and interest rate in the first place as discounted utility theory is strictly related to the interest rate theory (Fisher, 1930). As the interest rate is a component of the discount rate, the link between these two is directly proportional. Still, one should also take note of the inverse relationship. Whenever the discount rate falls across the society, it means that the present consumption is compromised for future consumption, which – in the classical theory of economics – raises the level of savings in the economy and puts a concomitant pressure on the market interest rate to go down. In addition, as mentioned before, the natural rate of interest may be split into technological progress function and the time preference rate of households. It means that the change of discount rate on the macroeconomic scale may affect the change of natural rate of interest and thus, indirectly, the central bank's interest rate, providing that it is sought to maintain the monetary policy stance unchanged.

It is also of vital importance that despite the interplay between interest rates and discount rates, they are also influenced by independent idiosyncratic factors. In spite of being reliant on macroeconomic factors just like the interest rate, the discount rate has some subjective elements. The literature brings up identified asymmetries for profits and losses (so-called sign effect), non-linear effect of advantage being deferred versus accelerated (Loewenstein, 1988), or the dependence of the magnitude of discount rate on the very relative magnitude of the discounted object (so-called absolute magnitude effect; Thaler, 1981).[20]

Accordingly, a negative discount rate means a greater preference for future rather than current events, in spite of their perfect substitutability. Apart from the situations whereby the negative discount rate arises from interest rate decline, yet again the subjectivity may be brought up as mattering much more for the discount rate for non-monetary values. The literature shows that certain events provoke such strong expectations that consumption becomes deferred or negative events accelerated (i.e., discounted at a negative rate; Loewenstein, 1987). Yet another subjective factor (albeit on aggregate scale) is a change of preferences due to the structural determinants of the environment. Historical experience has demonstrated that economic entities normally show a positive time preference (which is provided as rationale for the positive discount rate). Nevertheless, average life expectancy rising in the recent decades (along with the expectations around it) resulting in a future growth in expected consumption may have contributed to the emergence of a negative time preference in that the preference has shifted away from the current consumption (Fels, 2019).

The third factor that provides rationale for a negative discount rate is uncertainty, that is, uncertain events are less discounted than their opposite (por. m.in. Chew and Ho, 1994; Lovallo and Kahneman, 2000). From this perspective, it is worth mentioning a reverse relation between this factor and the interest rate, whereby higher uncertainty comes with higher interest rate. With respect to discount rate for monetary values, the literature provides for two theories for this phenomenon – the theory of preference for rising sequence of reward (Loewenstein and Sicherman, 1991) and low loss preference (Mitchell and Wilson, 2010). In line with the first one, business entities are reluctant to receive cash-flow of a falling sequence and they will opt for that with a rising sequence, even though the latter may be slightly lower. In turn, the preference for rising income may be justified with a preference for rising consumption (Loewenstein and Sicherman, 1991). It follows that the negative discount rate in the economy may be identified with expecting a decline in revenues or consumption.[21]

Summing up, it should be noted that the negative level of interest rates does not have to be identified with negative discounting in intertemporal choices (and *vice versa*), although it will be one of the major determinants underpinning such processes. Still, it is behavioural determinants that are the major factor necessary for a negative discount rate to emerge.

2.5 Mechanism of Negative Nominal Interest Rate Transmission

The phenomenon of negative interest rates and its impact on economic variables requires that the mechanism of monetary transmission be assessed first, with a special focus on its respective stages. What is more, as this phenomenon is a novelty, it is also necessary to indicate potential disruptions to this mechanism, as well as to assess its potential structural changes.

As pointed out before, the purposes of unconventional monetary policy tools[22] included flattening the term structure of interest rates by directly affecting the long end and by managing interest rates expectations. In addition, the term premium component was narrowed while reducing the uncertainty as for the future interest rate levels. Thus, in spite of the short-term interest rate remaining intact, the effect of unconventional tools gave rise to a lower cost of financing investment projects (with fixed risk premium) for medium- and long-term horizon (Figure 2.6). The measures increased the scope of acceptable investment projects, which is, those which offer a positive rate of return above the cost of financing. Notwithstanding, as the potential impact spectrum of the programmes was wearing out (including, due to supply restrictions, market liquidity disruption risk), so was further potential for stimulating the process shrinking. This time, the use of yet another tool – i.e., the negative interest rate policy – provides for shifting the short end of the interest rate curve, which reduces the cost of investment project financing to a larger extent, and for shifting the acceptability point to the left again. However, as the level of financing costs draws closer to zero, so they become more rigid, which pushes up the required risk premium on such a project as the risk-free rate reduction continues (Barth et al., 2016).

Starting with the above simplified scheme in the context of an investment project, it is necessary to address the question to what extent the entire monetary policy transmission mechanism for NIRP differs from that in the positive rate environment. With such an analysis, one should also remember that the mechanism alone – construed in this study as a body of patterns and

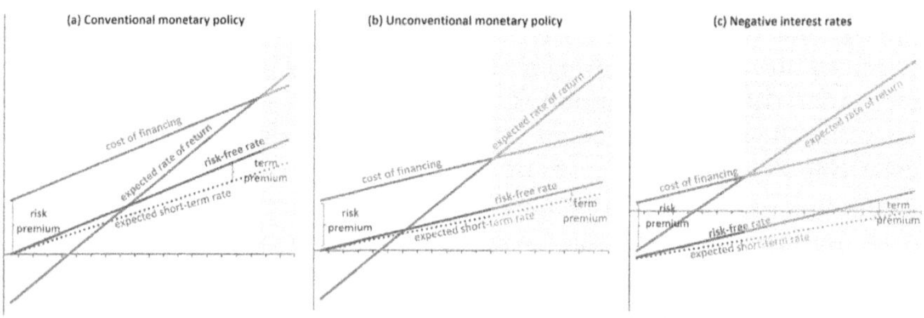

Figure 2.6 Simplified analysis of return on investment for different monetary policy regimes

Note: For simplification purposes, the scheme assumes zero inflation; thus, the real interest rate is equated to nominal rate; grey area denotes the range of acceptable investment projects.

Source: Own elaboration.

relationships through which the monetary policy affects real prices and the real economic growth (Ireland, 2005) – is different across respective economies and it may vary over time. In turn, as in the econometric analysis of the effect of the monetary policy, so in the mechanism's structure, so-called monetary impulses (shocks, disturbances) play a vital role and they determine the emergence of causal links among economic variables (Duwendag et al., 1995). The theoretical literature distinguishes between two fundamental types of monetary impulses: primary (directly created by the central bank by changing the parameters of the monetary policy pursued) and secondary (generated outside the central bank, by the behaviour of business entities).

There are five the most prevalent channels of monetary transmission in the literature – (i) interest rate channel, (ii) expectations channel, (iii) exchange rate channel, (iv) assets prices channel and (v) lending channel (Demchuk et al., 2011). In turn, Boivin et al. (2010) provide for a more detailed division in that they break down the transmission channels into neoclassical (based on theoretical models for investment, consumption, international trade and assuming the financial market is perfect) and non-neoclassical which rely on financial markets being imperfect (such as bank-related channels and the balance sheet channel). This extended division, however, can be incorporated into the traditional four-channel approach (Chmielewski et al., 2018) and such will be the basis for considerations in this sub-chapter. At the same time, it needs to be emphasized that it is often difficult to precisely tell the transmission channels apart given their interconnectedness (Brózda-Wilamek, 2018).

Two effects can be considered as falling under the interest rate channel: the interest rate directly affecting investment through the changes in cost of capital (to which Figure 2.7 referred) and the intertemporal substitution channel (the change of preferences in intertemporal choice). How the interest channel works is due to nominal price rigidity,[23] which is reflected in a proportional change of real rates once the central bank changes the nominal rate (Beyer et al., 2017). The expectations channel, on the other hand, is a certain enhancement of the interest rate channel as it shows that the central bank may affect the real economy by shaping the expectations of business entities. The expectations chiefly concern two categories: the average level of short-term interest rates in the future and the future inflation rate (e.g., Łyziak, 2011), whereas the effect the central banks has on them depends on the credibility of the monetary policy pursued.

The third channel regards monetary policy effect on the exchange rate. In accordance with uncovered interest rate parity, and in spite of the initial appreciation of the domestic currency after monetary policy tightening, if the domestic interest rate is higher than its foreign counterpart, depreciation will ensue in medium term so as to align the rates of return (Chmielewski et al., 2018). Moreover, two effects can be distinguished within the exchange rate channel (Mishkin, 2001): the relative price effect bearing on net exports and its opposite, balance sheet effect which bears on the balance sheet structure of business entities (scale of this influence is determined by the balance sheet net currency position; Demchuk et al., 2011).

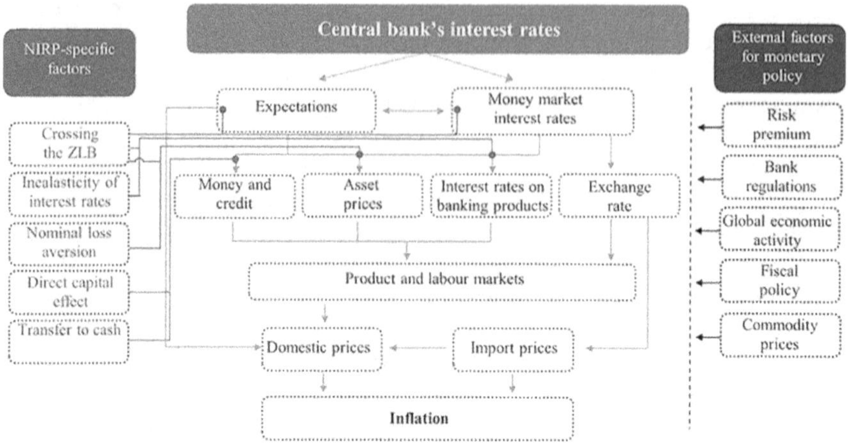

Figure 2.7 Simplified scheme of monetary policy mechanism in negative interest rates environment

Source: Own elaboration.

The asset price channel also follows two mechanisms – the effect of a company's market valuation on investing activity[24] and the wealth effect. In the former case, falling interest rates translate into higher company market valuation (which is due to a lower discount rate) and higher company profits arising from promoted economic upturn. In addition, thanks to lower capital cost, investments become relatively more profitable. What is more, even the investments which were earlier unprofitable finally start fetching profit (see Figure 2.7). The idea of the second mechanism (the wealth effect) is that higher stock prices drive the wealth of households which increase consumption as they feel relatively better off.

The most extensive contemporary monetary policy transmission channel, which is also potentially important in the context of NIRP, is the lending channel. Four smaller channels can be distinguished within it: (i) balance sheet channel, (ii) bank lending channel, (iii) bank capital channel and (iv) risk-taking channel. Within the first one, falling interest rates translate into higher net asset value of business entities, thus improving their creditworthiness and reducing the external finance premium. In line with the second channel, tighter monetary policy causes lending restriction, albeit not by demand (i.e., interest), rather by supply mechanism, in the form of a more restrictive lending policy of commercial banks. As for the third channel, loosening monetary policy translates into an improved bank balance sheet structure by a higher market valuation of capital. This, in turn, will increase the lending potential targeting the non-financial sector. For this channel, it is vital that an opposite scenario is brought up in the case of which higher interest rates translate into lower market valuation of bank capital, the risk of bank capital approximating regulatory limitations rises and the likelihood of curbing credit supply grows stronger (Beyer et al., 2017). The fourth and the youngest mechanisms assume that the interest rate changes affect the perception of risk and its acceptable portfolio level. As a result, entities increase their risk exposure so as to maintain their search for yield (Borio and Zhu, 2008).[25]

The above-described monetary policy transmission mechanism for a particular case of negative interest rate policy (starting from a proposal for the European Central Bank; Strasser, 2018) is depicted in Figure 2.7. Thus, the first conclusion from the said proposal is that the monetary policy mechanism for NIRP works both through traditional and the "modern" monetary policy channels (e.g., Pyka and Nocoń, 2019). It means that, in structural terms, it does not differ significantly from the conclusion for positive (including low) rates. In particular, it is not expected that some new important transmission channels will emerge which would be defined individually for NIRP. The foregoing may be part of the case to show it is a conventional tool used in unconventional way.[26] Notwithstanding, negative interest rate policy has its particular characteristics which sets it apart from both conventional and unconventional monetary policies. Much as they do not translate into new transmission channels being formed, the factors may affect the quality of monetary policy impulses being transmitted into the real economy within the already existing framework. In particular, this disruption would far more likely concern secondary impulses while probably sparing the quality of primary impulses (Borio et al., 2017).

First and foremost, the very fact of breaking through the zero bound for interest rates, next to the obvious effect on the development on monetary market rates, works through the expectations channel. Especially for the interest rates approximating the zero bound, it is natural for expectations to be largely asymmetric, in favour of the rates rising in the future. The truth is that the effect of the expectations channel may be in this case strengthened by forward guidance (e.g., Hubert and Labondance, 2018), policy or QE programmes (e.g., Apergis, 2018); however, this impact is reflected by no more than expecting a longer expansionary period (i.e., flattening the curve of expected rates) rather than eliminating the said asymmetry.

Another particular factor associated with NIRP, the direct capital effect, pertains to the negative rates being directly charged with a cost, which has a character similar to that of tax burden effect. It implies that both the banking sector and, more broadly, the financial sector, as well as non-financial sector entities will be charged (through the wealth effect) with a cost arising from the reverse cash-flow structure. In other words, holder of a given asset offering a negative interest rate will be required to bear an extra cost, unlike in the positive interest rate environment. In banking, this effect seems to be the most robust as in many cases it is a burden on substantial portion of the bank's balance sheets as deposits placed directly with the central bank. Yet another particular NIRP factor which directly affects the banking sector is the so-called interest rigidity. It stands for unwillingness or inability to reduce deposit and credit interest below zero. The two aforementioned particular factors (i.e., direct capital effect and deposit interest rigidity), in affecting net profit, may constrain the benevolent impact of NIRP via bank capital channel (Borio et al., 2017). In this way, they may thus translate into weakening the traditional monetary policy transmission mechanism.

Third, the said monetary transmission may be additionally weakened by economic entities being nominal loss-averse. This factor works both for the nominal money illusion, as well as in the real context given the scale of inflationary expectations in the NIRP economies analysed. This phenomenon contributes to shifting a portion of funds to more profitable (including more risky) investments, or holding them in a form warranting protection against nominal loss (transfer into cash). It follows that the measures undertaken in this context give rise to structural change of money supply in the economy, including its transfer outside the banking sector.

It is worth emphasizing here that the importance of particular factors affecting the transmission mechanism is largely influenced by the negative interest rate level, how their implementation is structured in central banks and for how long such policy has been pursued. Central banks emphasize that NIRP-related risk will not materialize if inflationary or other targets are achieved relatively soon and the negative interest rate period will be but a transitory stage (SNB, 2016; EBC, 2017). Notwithstanding, the factors beyond the control of central banks may, in medium term, necessitate the said period's extension and, albeit not directly, contribute to multiplication of risks and a rising likelihood of them materializing.

Summary

The policy of negative interest rates introduced by selected central banks first and foremost needs to be placed in a theoretical context of the interest rate phenomenon. To this aim, this chapter deals with the issue of negative interest rate in defining it and specifying its several categories which may be (and often were) negative, i.e., the real, natural or the so-called "shadow" interest rate. Recently, however, the said list has been expanded to include the category of a negative nominal interest rate, which stirred up a debate on the paradigm of a non-negative character of this category prevalent in the literature. Consequently, the analysis made in the chapter identifies a number of major aspects. First, the chapter opens up a debate on the lower bound for nominal interest rates in that it presents several types of the rate, first and foremost the so-called reversal interest rate. Second, the idea of an interest rate being negative is not clearly defined in the literature and, judging by the main economic schools of thought, it may take on several variants. Third, NIRP pursued by the central banks is neither direct nor the only reason for the negative nominal interest rates we see now in several economies, mainly in the eurozone. Fourth, given the recent economic conditions, the chapter brought out it is necessary to distinguish between two types of negative nominal interest rate – paper currency and non-paper currency interest rate. It was pointed out that NIRP refers to the latter, while the former remains a theoretical concept. Fifth, in this light, several theoretical possibilities (judged from the perspective of economic entities and the banking sector) to expand the current NIRP to embark on paper currency interest rate territory were presented. Sixth, it was emphasized that in structural terms, the mechanism of transmitting central bank negative nominal interest rates does not significantly differ from that for positive, including low, rates. Notwithstanding, the particular factors of NIRP as defined in this chapter may, particularly through the banking sector, affect the quality of the transmitted monetary policy impulse and spawn new or strengthen the existing risks, including those to financial system stability.

Notes

1 Short-term interest rate can in fact be higher than long-term interest rates. Such circumstances may be evidenced when there is a high-risk premium demanded for the investment in the nearest future or when economic agents present a strong belief that, e.g., central bank's interest rates to be lowered in the future.
2 The yields that are presented in the following chapter can be used for illustrative purposes as an empirical example of the yield curve concept presented in this theoretical chapter.
3 Whereas Wicksell (1934) is commonly referred to while indicating the origins of the concept of a natural interest rate, some economists (Smithin, 2013) also cite Thornton (1802).
4 Keynes (1936) was the person who manifested his scepticism with respect to the concept of natural interest rate. In particular, he claimed that theory the natural rate of interest is an invention that does not exist in the real world (or rather, the monetary world). The system is simply founded on the monetary rate of interest that is permitted to prevail by the financial and/or political authorities (Tily, 2012).
5 However, the measure might not be appropriate to evaluate monetary policy stance when central bank uses unconventional monetary policy tools to reinforce restrictive monetary policy (e.g., through quantitative tightening).
6 Admittedly, academic literature proposes a range of various definitions of monetary policy strategy. Nevertheless, all of them confirm that the main objective of the strategy is central bank's commitment to apply so-called nominal anchor (Mishkin, 2007), i.e., a numerical objective that the monetary policy should achieve. There are many possible nominal anchors (e.g., exchange rate, monetary aggregates, inflation) with possibility for an implicit nominal anchor. The latter involves targeting a particular nominal variable adopted only internally within the central bank without it being announced explicitly.
7 The academic literature and central banking practice point at some alternative intermediate monetary policy objectives, such as monetary aggregates, exchange rate (e.g., Grostal et al., 2016) or even inflation forecast (Svensson, 1997).
8 When zero lower bound is binding, additional accommodative monetary policy impulse can be introduced through three ways: (i) by affecting expectations on interest rates in medium to long term (forward guidance); (ii) by changing the term structure of the central bank's balance sheet (qualitative easing) and (iii) by expanding the central bank's balance sheet (quantitative easing; Smaghi, 2010).

9 Interest rate can be negative only when holding cash is associated with extraordinary costs or mental discomfort (Goodfriend, 2000).

10 Existence of nominal negative interest rate was also rejected in yield curve modelling theories and practices. Majority of the models that were implemented to the interest rate modelling assumed non-negativity (models of Brennan and Schwartz (1979) or Cox et al. (1985) and the ones that allowed rates to be negative (e.g., Vasicek, 1977) were broadly criticized. Literature was dominated by the belief that only rates than can be negative are real interest rates (Constantinides, 1992). Against this background, introduction of NIRP created new uncharted environment in that aspect and put pressure on risk management practices. As a result, financial institutions replaced 'traditional' models with some alternatives (Recchioni et al., 2017; Morgan Stanley, 2018).

11 This framework was applied, e.g., by the central bank of the Czech Republic in November 2013, when the CNB decided to transparently declare a one-sided exchange rate commitment with potentially unlimited foreign exchange interventions (CNB, 2013).

12 It should be pointed that none of the central banks decided to introduce such a strategy in response to outbreak of global financial crises.

13 As a medium-term consequence of negative rates may be the fact that some individuals may find it profitable to set up businesses that "hoover up" paper currency from households and small businesses to centralize paper currency storage. As a result, cost of storing cash would be mitigated, which should allow to lower interest rates deeper into negative territory. Given that, it might be desirable to introduce regulatory framework for mentioned type of business (Agarwal and Kimball, 2019).

14 Literature estimates the cost of storing cash to be around 0.2– 1%, although this could depend in part on the size of bills. Since the purchasing power of large denomination banknotes varies over countries, the cost of storage would also differ internationally. The cost of convenience can be roughly proxied by fees associated with credit and debit card interchange fees, which were around 1–3% annually, on average (Keohane, 2015). This could suggest that negative policy interest rates marginally below 2% are possible without prompting depositor flight, although country-specific factors and the expected duration of negative policy rates will be important factors in determining the effective lower bound for interest rates (Jackson, 2015).

15 The paradigm of trilemma is a constraint on monetary policy making in any country, evaluated from international perspective (e.g., defined for an open economy). It states that a country cannot simultaneously have an open capital account, a stable exchange rate and autonomous monetary policy. Thus, monetary authorities have to decide which one of these characteristics would not be directly controlled by the policy.

16 To encourage investors to hold long-term and less liquid sovereign bonds, their yield should be greater than that offered by short-term debt securities. Thus, if the objective for long-term yield is set to be around zero – given unchanged characteristics (e.g., for monetary policy expectations) – short-term instruments have to offer negative rates.

17 According to Gesell (1916), all goods are depreciating over time and gradually lose their initial value. The only exception to that rule is money. Thus, he claims that owners of money are postponing the moment of purchasing goods until their start to depreciate. Then, owners of goods have to incur a loan from owners of money in order to sustain their productive ability unchanged. Gesell considered such a process to be unfair, and, in order to restore social balance, he proposed a concept of money tax.

18 The most clear example of this approach is a decomposition of return on investment in the stock market, in which investor's profit is generated by dividends (cash flow component) and by changes in prices (price component).

19 Although this concept has been never implemented at the country level, it was widely used in some states in the United States during the Great Depression of 1929–1939 (Gatch, 2006). In majority of cases, banknotes were stamped on every transaction and thus not in regular intervals of time as Gesell originally proposed. However, this practice has raised concerns regarding its impact on economic processes, e.g., in a form of discouraging consumption.

20 As an example, the mentioned factors usually result in discount rates to be greater than the interest rates, assuming that the former are estimated on the basis of real decision-making processes (Frederick et al., 2002).

21 According to the latter theory, economic motivation gives way to psychological motivation in a situation when economic agents prefer to suffer a loss earlier, assuming that it is relatively small. Literature points out that the negative discount rate is a relatively popular phenomenon for the case of negative cash flows (Mitchell and Wilson, 2010).

22 Unconventional monetary policy framework of this book is to include: outright purchases of financial assets (so-called quantitative easing), programmes to support lending activity (e.g., funding for lending schemes) and forward guidance communication policy.

23 Price stickiness is the resistance of nominal prices to change quickly, which is reflected by the process of price changes to be relatively delayed as compared to processes in real economy. Sticky prices are one of market imperfections, caused by illusion of money (thus inability to distinguish between nominal and real terms).

24 The latter is known in the literature as Tobin's q, which is the ratio between a physical asset's market value and its replacement value.

25 It should be noted that balance sheet channel and risk-taking channel are not novel in the literature undertaking monetary transmission mechanism. There were identified earlier; however, due to the rising role financial market regulations and risk management techniques, their role has increased significantly.

26 In that context, an example of unconventional monetary policy tool used in an unconventional way may be the negative interest rate policy but extended to cash level (i.e., negative paper currency interest rates).

Bibliography

Agarwal, R., Kimball, M.S., (2015). *Breaking Through the Zero Lower Bound*, IMF Working Paper, no. 15/224.

Agarwal, R., Kimball, M.S., (2019). *Enabling Deep Negative Rates to Fight Recessions: A Guide*, IMF Working Paper, no. 19/84.

Amato, J.D., (2005). *The Role of the Natural Rate of Interest in Monetary Policy*, BIS Working Papers, no. 171.

Apergis, N., (2018). Expectations and the Quantitative Easing in Eurozone, *Economics and Business Letters*, Oviedo University Press, vol. 7, no. 1, pp. 18–23.

Barth, M., Davies, Z., Pascual, A., G., Keller, C., Maraffino., G., (2016). Negative ascent: Life amid negative nominal interest rates. Equity Gilts study, Barclays investment note, as of 3 March 2016.

Begg, D., Fischer, S., Dornbusch, R., (1994). *Ekonomia*, tom 2, Państwowe Wydawnictwo Ekonomiczne, Warszawa.

Bernanke, B., (2016). *What Tools Does the Fed Have Left? Part 1: Negative Interest Rates*. Brookings Institution (blog), 18 March.

Beyer, A., Nicoletti, G., Papadopoulou, N., Papsdorf, P., & Rünstler, G., Schwarz, C., Sousa, J., Vergote, O., (2017). *The Transmission Channels of Monetary, Macro- and Microprudential Policies and their Interrelations*, Occasional Paper Series 191, European Central Bank.

Billi, R.M., (2013). *Nominal GDP Targeting and the Zero Lower Bound: Should We Abandon Inflation Targeting?* Working Paper Series 270, Sveriges Riksbank.

Bilski, J., (2012). Polityka stopy procentowej w świetle teorii ekonomicznych. Wnioski dla strefy euro, [in:] J. Bilski, A. Kłysik-Uryszek (eds.), *Globalne aspekty kryzysu strefy euro*, Acta Universitatis Lodziensis, Folio Oeconomica, no. 273.

Blanchard, O., Dell'Ariccia, G., Mauro, P., (2010). Rethinking Macroeconomic Policy, *Journal of Money, Credit and Banking*, vol. 42, no. s1, pp. 199–215.

Błaszczyk, P., (2010). *Stabilność cen – sposoby definicji oraz wyzwania dla polityki pieniężnej,* Materiały i Studia, Narodowy Bank Polski, no. 249.

Boivin, J., Kiley, M.T., Mishkin, F.S., (2010). *How Has the Monetary Transmission Mechanism Evolved Over Time?* NBER Working Paper No. 15879, National Bureau of Economic Research.

Bomfim, A.N., (2001). *Measuring Equilibrium Real Interest Rates: What Can We Learn from Yield on Indexed Bond?* Finance and Economics Discussion Series no. 53, Board of Governors of the Federal Reserve System.

Borio, C., Disyatat, P., (2009). *Unconventional Monetary Policy: An Appraisal*, BIS Working Papers No 292, November 2009.

Borio, C., Disyatat, P., Juselius, M., Rungcharoenkitkul, P., (2017). *Why So Low For so Long? A Long-term View of Real Interest Rates*, BIS Working Papers no. 685, Bank for International Settlements.

Borio, C., Gambacorta, L., Hofmann, B., (2017). The Influence of Monetary Policy on Bank Profitability, *International Finance*, vol. 20, pp. 48–63.

Borio, C., Zhu, H., (2008). *Capital Regulation, Risk-taking and Monetary Policy: A Missing Link in the Transmission Mechanism?* BIS Working Paper No. 268, Bank for International Settlements.

Brennan, M.J., Schwartz, E.S., (1979). A Continuous Time Approach to the Pricing of Bonds, *Journal of Banking and Finance*, vol. 3, pp. 133–155.

Brózda-Wilamek, D., (2018). *Stopa procentowa jako kanał transmisji polityki pieniężnej Systemu Rezerwy Federalnej,* Wydawnictwo Uniwersytetu Łódzkiego, Łódz.

Brunnermeier, M.K., Koby, Y., (2017). *The "Reversal Interest Rate": An Effective Lower Bound on Monetary Policy*, Stanford University Working Paper.

Brzoza-Brzezina, M., (2003). Rola naturalnej stopy w polskiej polityce pieniężnej, *Ekonomista*, vol. 5, pp. 593–612.

Brzoza-Brzezina, M., (2006). The Information Content of the Neutral Rate of Interest, *The Economics of Transition*, vol. 14, no. 2, pp. 391–412.

Brzoza-Brzezina, M., Kolasa, M., Szetela, M., (2016). Is Poland at Risk of the Zero Lower Bound? *Bank i Kredyt*, vol. 47, no. 3, pp. 195–226.

Brzoza-Brzezina, M., Kotłowski, J., (2014). Measuring the Natural Yield Curve, *Applied Economics*, vol. 46, no. 17, pp. 2052–2065.

Buiter, W.H., (2009). Negative Nominal Interest Rates: Three Ways to Overcome the Zero Lower Bound. *The North American Journal of Economics and Finance*, vol. 20, no. 3, pp. 213–238.

Cavallino, P., Sandi, D., (2019). *The Expansionary Lower Bound: Contractionary Monetary Easing and the Trilemma*, BIS Working Papers no. 770, Bank for International Settlements.

Chew, S.H., Ho, J.L., (1994). Hope: An Empirical Study of Attitude toward the Timing of Uncertainty Resolution, *Journal of Risk and Uncertainty*, vol. 8, pp. 267–288.

Chmielewski, T., Kapuściński, M., Kocięcki, A., Łyziak, T., Przystupa, J., Stanisławska, E., Wróbel, E., (2018). *Mechanizm transmisji polityki pieniężnej w Polsce. Stan wiedzy w 2017 roku.* Materiały i Studia nr 330, Narodowy Bank Polski.

Christensen, J.H.E., Rudebusch, G.D., (2012). The Response of Interest Rates to US and UK Quantitative Easing, *Economic Journal*, vol. 122, no. 564.

Clouse, J., Henderson, D., Orphanides, A., Small, D., Tinsley, P., (1999). *Monetary Policy When the Nominal Short-Term Interest Rate is Zero*, Manuscript. Board of Governors of the Federal Reserve System.

CNB (2013). *CNB Keeps Interest Rates Unchanged, Decides on Interventions*, Monetary Policy Press Release of Czech National Bank, 7 November 2013.

Constantinides, G.M., (1992). A Theory of the Nominal Term Structure of Interest Rates, *Review of Financial Studies*, vol. 5, pp. 531–552.

Correia, I., Farhi E., Nicolini J.P., Teles, P., (2013). Unconventional Fiscal Policy at the Zero Bound, *American Economic Review*, vol. 103, no. 4, pp. 1172–1211.

Cox, J.C., Ingersoll, J.E., Ross, S.A., (1985). A Theory of the Term Structure of Interest Rates, *Econometrica*, vol. 53, pp. 385–407.

Demchuk, O., Łyziak, T., Przystupa, J., Sznajderska, A., Wróbel, E., (2011). *Monetary Policy Transmission Mechanism in Poland – What Do We Know in 2011?*, National Bank of Poland Working Paper no. 116.

Domański, S.R., (2016). Strategia rozwoju jako efekt polityki pieniężnej, *Kwartalnik Nauk o Przedsiębiorstwie, Szkoła Główna Handlowa*, vol. 3, pp. 29–41.

Duménil, G., Lévy, D. (1999), Being Keynesian in the Short Term and Classical in the Long Term: The Traverse to Classical Long-Term Equilibrium, *The Manchester School*, vol. 67, pp. 684–716.

Duwendag, D., Ketterer, K-H., Kösters, W., Pohl, R., Simmert, D.B., (1995). *Teoria pieniądza i polityka pieniężna*, Wyd. Poltext, Warszawa 1995.

EBC, (2017). *Financial Stability Review*, European Central Bank, November 2017.

Eisenschmidt, J., Smets, F., (2018). Negative Interest Rates: Lessons from the Euro Area. Presented at *XXI Annual Conference of the Central Bank of Chile*, forthcoming.

Eisler, R., (1932). *Stable Money, the Remedy for the Economic World Crisis: A Programme of Financial Reconstruction for the International Conference*, 1933. The Search Pub. Co.

Fawley, B., Neely, C.J., (2013). Four Stories of Quantitative Easing, *Federal Reserve Bank of St. Louis*, vol. 95, pp. 51–88.

Feldstein, M., (2002). T*he Role for Discretionary Fiscal Policy in a Low Interest Rate Environment*, NBER Working Paper no. 9203, National Bureau of Economic Research.

Fels, J., (2019). *Interest Rates: Naturally Negative?* Economic and Market Commentary, PIMCO.

Fisher, I., (1930). *The Theory of Interest as Determined by Impatience to Spend Income and Opportunity to Invest It*, Mamillan.

Frederick, S., Loewenstein, G., O'Donoghue, T., (2002). Time Discounting and Time Preference: A Critical Review, *Journal of Economic Literature*, vol. XL, pp. 351–401.

Gagnon, J., Raskin, M., Remache, J., Sack, B., (2011). Large-scale Asset Purchases by the Federal Reserve: Did They Work? *Economic Policy Review*, vol. 17, pp. 41–59.

Garnier, J., Wilhelmsen, B.R., (2005). *The Natural Real Interest Rate and the Output Gap in the Euro Area - A Joint Estimation*, ECB Working Paper Series, no. 546.

Gesell, S., (1916). *Die Natuerliche Wirtschaftsordnung*, Rudolf Zitzman Verlag [available in English as: *The Natural Economic Order*, Peter Owen Ltd, London, 1958].

Gatch, L., (2006), *Local Scrip in the USA during the 1930s: Lessons for Today?* Presented at the *Conference on Monetary Regionalisation: Local Currencies as Catalysts for Endogenous Regional Development, Bauhaus-University Weimar*, Germany, September 28–29, 2006. http://base.socioeco.org/docs/local_scrip_in_the_usa-gatch.pdf [accessed: 23 June 2019].

Goodfriend, M., King, R.G., (1998). *The New Neoclassical Synthesis and the Role of Monetary Policy*, Federal Reserve Bank of Richmond Working Paper no. 5/1998.

Goodfriend, M., (2000). Overcoming the Zero Bound on Interest Rate Policy, *Journal of Money, Credit, and Banking*, vol. 32, no. 4, pp. 1007–1035.

Goodfriend, M., (2016). *The Case for Unencumbering Interest Rate Policy at the Zero Lower Bound*, Jakson Hole Speech, https://www.cmu.edu/tepper/faculty-and-research/assets/docs/unencumbeInter-rate-policy-zero-bound-2016.pdf

Grabowski, C., (1966). *Współczesne teorie procentu*, PWE, Warszawa.

Grostal, W., Jabłecki, J., Beniak P., Ciżkowicz-Pękała, M., Skrzeszewska-Paczek, E., Wesołowski, G., Żuk, P., (2016). *Alternatywne strategie polityki pieniężnej*, Narodowy Bank Polski.

Hayek, F.A., (2009). *The Pure Theory of Capital*, The Ludwig von Mises Institute, London.

Hicks, J.R., (1975). *Wartość i kapitał*, PWN, Warszawa.

Hirshleifer, J., (1970). *Investment, Interest, and Capital*, Prentice-Hall, Englewood Cliffs, NJ.

Hoppe, H., (1992). The Misesian Case against Keynes, [in:] Skousen, M. (ed.), *In Dissent on Keynes: A Critical Appraisal of Keynesian Economics*, Praeger, New York, pp. 199–223.

Hubert, P., Labondance, F., (2018). The Effect of ECB Forward Guidance on the Term Structure of Interest Rates, *International Journal of Central Banking*, vol. 14, no. 5, pp. 193–222.

IMF, (1999). *Safeguarding Macroeconomic Stability at Low Inflation*, World Economic Outlook.

Ireland, P.N., (2005). *The Monetary Transmission Mechanism*, Federal Reserve Bank of Boston Workin Paper, no. 06/05.

Jackson, H., (2015). *The International Experience with Negative Policy Rates*, Bank of Canada Staff Discussion Paper 2015-13.

Kaźmierczak, A., (2019). *Polityka pieniężna w gospodarce otwartej*, Wydawnictwo Naukowe PWN, Warszawa.

Keohane, D., (2015). *Negative Rates and Gesell Taxes: How Low Are We Talking Here?* FT Alphaville, 2 February.

Keynes, J.M., (1936 [2012]). *Ogólna teoria zatrudnienia, procentu i pieniądza*, Wydawnictwo Naukowe PWN, Warszawa.

Kimball, M.S., (2015). Negative Interest Rate Policy as Conventional Monetary Policy, *National Institute Economic Review, National Institute of Economic and Social Research*, vol. 234, no. 1, pp. 5–14.

Kimball, M.S., (2016). *What is the Effective Lower Bound on Interest Rates Made Of?* Confessions of a supply-side liberal. [accessed: 28 June 2019: https://blog.supplysideliberal.com/post/145194765303/what-is-the-effective-lower-bound-on-interest].

Koopmans, T.C., (1960). Stationary Ordinal Utility and Impatience, *Econometrica*, vol. 28, pp. 287–309.

Kotłowski, J., (2016). *Polityka pieniężna zorientowana na przyszłość. Wybrane aspekty analityczne*, Oficyna Wydawnicza SGH, Warszawa.

Krippner, L., (2013). Measuring the Stance of Monetary Policy in Zero Lower Bound Environments, *Economic Letters*, vol. 118, pp. 135–138.

Laidler, D., (1991). *The Golden Age of the Quantity Theory*, Harvester Wheatsheaf, New York.

Laubach, T., Williams, J.C., (2001). *Measuring the Natural Rate of Interest*, FED Working Paper, 2001-56.

Laubach, T., Williams, J.C., (2016). *Measuring the Natural Rate of Interest Redux*, Finance and Economics Discussion Series 2016–11, Board of Governors of the Federal Reserve System.

Li, V.E., (1995). The Optimal Taxation of Fiat Money in Search Equilibrium, *International Economic Review*, vol. 36, no. 4, pp. 927–942.

Loewenstein, G., (1987). Anticipation and the Value of Delayed Consumption, *Economic Journal*, vol. 97, pp. 666–684.

Loewenstein, G., (1988). Frames of Mind in Intertemporal Choice, *Management Science*, vol. 34, pp. 200–214.

Loewenstein, G., Sicherman, N. (1991), Do Workers Prefer Increasing Wage Profiles, *Journal of Labor Economics*, vol. 9, pp. 67–84.

Lovallo, D., Kahneman, D., (2000). Living with Uncertainty: Attractiveness and Resolution Timing, *Journal of Behavioral Decision Making*, vol. 13, pp. 179–190.

Łyziak, T., (2011). Oczekiwania inflacyjne, [in:] A. Sławiński (ed.), *Polityka pieniężna*, C.H. Beck, Warszawa.

Maclachlan, F., (2019). Negative Interest Rates: A Keynesian Perspective, *Review of Keynesian Economics*, vol. 7, no. 2, pp. 171–184.

Mankiw, N.G., (2009). *It May Be Time for the Fed to Go Negative*, New York Times, 18 April 2009.

Marshall, A., (1962). *Principles of Economics (Eighth Edition)*, Macmillan & Co Ltd, London.

Masiukiewicz, P., (1994). *Stopy procentowe w bankach*, Wydawnictwo Alteria, Warszawa.

McAndrews, J., (2015). *Negative Nominal Central Bank Policy Rates – Where is the Lower Bound?* Federal Reserve Bank of New York, wystąpienie na Uniwersytecie Wisconsin, 8 May 2015.

McCallum, B., (2000). Theoretical Analysis Regarding a Zero Lower Bound on Nominal Interest Rates, *Journal of Money, Credit, and Banking*, vol. 32, pp. 870–904.

Michałek, A., (2012). Szacowanie naturalnej stopy procentowej dla Polski, *Acta Universitatis Nicolai Copernici, Ekonomia*, vol. XLIII, no. 2, pp. 161–181.

Mishkin, F.S., (2001). *The Transmission Mechanism and the Role of Asset Prices in Monetary Policy*, NBER Working Paper, no. 5464.

Mishkin, F.S., (2007), *Monetary Policy Strategy*, The MIT Press, Cambridge.

Mitchell, S.H., Wilson, V.B., (2010). The Subjective Value of Delayed and Probabilistic Outcomes: Outcome Size Matters for Gains But Not for Losses, *Behavioural Processes*, vol. 83, pp. 36–40.

Morgan Stanley, (2018). *Interest Rate Strategy 2-Year Auction Recap: Avoiding the Yield Trap*, investment note, as of 23 July 2018.

Nakov, A., (2008). Optimal and Simple Monetary Policy Rules with Zero Floor on the Nominal Interest Rate, *International Journal of Central Banking*, vol. 4, no. 2, pp. 73–127.

Neumark, F., (1948). *Genel Ekonomi Teorisi (Gözden Geçirilmiş Yeni Baskı)*, İsmail Akgün Matbaası, İstanbul.

Orphanides, A., Williams, J.C., (2007). Robust Monetary Policy with Imperfect Knowledge, *Journal of Monetary Economics*, vol. 54, no. 5.

Palley, T.I., (2016). Why Negative Interest Rate Policy (NIRP) is Ineffective and Dangerous, *Real-World Economics Review*, vol. 76, pp. 5–15.

Pan, E., Wu, L., (2006). Taking Positive Interest Rates Seriously, *Advances in Quantitative Analysis of Finance and Accounting*, vol. 4, pp. 327–356.

Poloz, S.S., (2015). *Prudent Preparation: The Evolution of Unconventional Monetary Policies*, Presentation for Empire Club of Canada, Toronto, ON, 8 December 2015.

Przybylska-Kapuścińska, W., Musielak-Linkowska, M., Cendal, M., Kowalak, M., (2008). *Współczesna polityka pieniężna*, Difin, Warszawa.

Przybylska-Kapuścińska, W., Szyszko, M., (2011). Strategia wyjścia z niestandardowych działań banków centralnych, [in:] Gospodarowicz, A. (ed.), *Finanse – nowe wyzwania teorii i praktyki: bankowość*, Wydawnictwo Uniwersytetu Ekonomicznego, Wrocław, pp. 35–44.

Pyka, I., Nocoń, A., (2019). Negative Interest Rate Risk. Atavism or Normalization of Central Banks' Monetary Policy, *Acta Universitatis Lodziensis. Folia Oeconomica*, vol. 3, no. 342.

Recchioni, M.C., Sun, Y., Tedeschi, G., (2017) Can Negative Interest Rates Really Affect Option Pricing? Empirical Evidence from an Explicitly Solvable Stochastic Volatility Model, *Quantitative Finance*, vol. 17, no. 8, pp. 1257–1275.

Rogers, L.C.G., (1995). Which Models for Term-Structures of Interest Rates Should One Use? *Mathematical Finance*, vol. 65, pp. 93–116.

Rogoff, K., (2015). Costs and Benefits to Phasing Out Paper Currency, *NBER Macroeconomics Annual*, vol. 29, no. 1, pp. 445–456.

Rogoff, K., (2017). Dealing with Monetary Paralysis at the Zero Bound, *Journal of Economic Perspectives*, vol. 31, no. 3, pp. 47–66.

Rzońca, A., (2012). *Kryzys banków centralnych. Skutki stopy procentowej bliskiej zera*, Wydawnictwo C.H.Beck, Warszawa.

Sławiński, A., (1996). Krzywa dochodowości, *Bank i Kredyt*, vol. 11, pp. 25–35.

Sławiński, A., (2006). *Rynki finansowe*, Polskie Wydawnictwo Ekonomiczne, Warszawa.

Smaghi, L.B., (2010). *What Has the Financial Crises Taught Us? The Global Dimension and International Policy Cooperation*, BIS Review 114/2010.

Smithin, J. (2013). *Essays in the Fundamental Theory of Monetary Economics and Macroeconomics*, World Scientific Publishing.

SNB, (2016). *Quarterly Bulletin*, Swiss National Bank, no. 2/2016.

Strasser, G., (2018). *The Monetary Policy Transmission Mechanism in the Euro Area*, ECB Central Banking Seminar, Frankfurt am Main, 11 July 2018.

Summers, L.H., (2014). U.S. Economic Prospects: Secular Stagnation, Hysteresis and the Zero Lower Bound, *Business Economics, National Association for Business Economics*, vol. 49, no. 2.

Svensson, L.E.O., (1997). *Inflation Targeting in an Open Economy: Strict or Flexible Inflation Targeting?* Discussion Paper Series, G97/8, Reserve Bank of New Zealand.

Svensson L.E.O., (2000). *How Should Monetary Policy Be Conducted in an Area of Price Stability?* NBER Working Paper, no. 7516, Cambridge.

Szydło, S., (2002). *Stopy procentowe w gospodarce polskiej*, Oficyna Wydawnicza TEXT, Kraków.

Thaler, R.H., (1981). Some Empirical Evidence of Dynamic Inconsistency, *Economic Letters*, vol. 81, pp. 201–207.

Thornton, H. (1802), *An Enquiry into the Nature and Effects of the Paper Credit of Great Britain*.

Tily, G. (2012). Keynes's Monetary Theory of Interest. [in:] *Threat of Fiscal Dominance?* vol. 65, pp. 51–81, Bank for International Settlements.

Tobin, J., (1961). Money, Capital and Other Stores of Value, *American Economic Review*, vol. 51(2), pp. 26–37.

Vasicek, O., (1977). An Equilibrium Characterization of the Term Structure, *Journal of Financial Economics*, vol. 5, pp.177–188.

Wicksell, K., (1934). *Lectures on Political Economy*, vol. 2: Money, Augustus Kelley, New York.

Williams, J.C., (2003). *The Natural Rate of Interest*, FRBSF Economic Letter 2003-32.

Wu, J.C., Xia, F.D., (2016). Measuring the Macroeconomic Impact of Monetary Policy at the Zero Lower Bound, *Journal of Money, Credit, and Banking*, vol. 48, no. 2–3, pp. 253–291.

Wu, J.C., Xia, F.D., (2017). *Time Varying Lower Bound of Interest Rates in Europe*, Chicago Booth Research Paper, no. 17-06.

Yates, T., (2002). *Monetary Policy and the Zero Bound to Interest Rates. A Review*, ECB Working Paper, no. 190.

3 Negative Interest Rate Policy Experience of Selected Central Banks

3.1 The Decisions and Motivation behind the Introduction of Negative Interest Rates by Central Banks

In recent years, some central banks in developed economies have lowered their nominal interest rates below zero in order to achieve the goals they have been assigned. In this way, a new approach emerged in how to pursue monetary policy, namely, the negative interest rate policy (NIRP). Such measures were interpreted as undermining the prevalent opinion of nominal interest rates being of non-negative character which previously kept the rates to a very low, close to zero, level. The main reason behind pushing interest rates below zero in these economies was a strive to continue to loosen monetary policy in order to mitigate deflation threat amid a rising risk of global economic downturn or, in some of the economies, lessening appreciation pressure on the exchange rate. As a consequence, the negative character of the nominal interest rate no longer is a purely theoretical concept, albeit still being confined to the non-paper currency interest level. This sub-chapter aims to present the reasons for implementation and its details, as well as to give out the differences in how negative nominal interest rates are used as a central bank tool. Consequently, the first part of the analysis is a presentation, and then it becomes a platform for comparison.

This chapter's analysis encompasses five central banks which employ NIRP in the analysed period: the European Central Bank as well as the central banks of Sweden, Switzerland, Denmark and Japan. Although other central banks introduced NIRP as well (including, e.g., the Bank of Hungary[1]), the relevance of these banks in the analysis of broad implications for the negative interest rates is rather low due to NIRP itself being a monetary policy tool of relatively minor importance. In other words, the choice of central banks to be covered in this monograph as well as the hierarchy of analyses and considerations made in this book is substantiated by the relative importance of NIRP among monetary policy tools (assessed through, *inter alia*, the number of interest rate types below zero, the scale of their downward potential or the scale of their direct cost burden on the banking sector) in selected countries and the size of economic territory relevant for this tool.

DOI: 10.4324/9781003312116-3

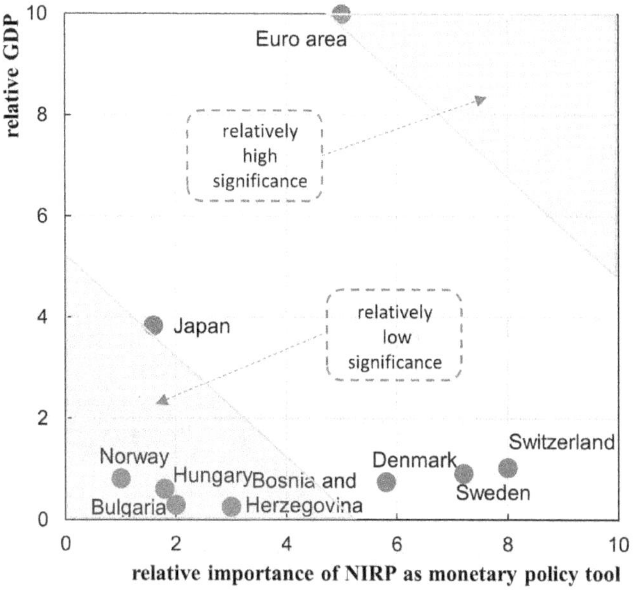

Figure 3.1 Relative significance of NIRP in selected economies

Note: GDP in current USD of selected economy in relations to the euro area (value indexed to range 0–10); relative significance of NIRP in monetary policy toolbox determined with three criteria: (a) level of negative rate; (b) number of central bank's rate set below zero; and (c) introduction of mitigating mechanism (e.g., tiering).

Source: Own work based on central banks and IMF data.

Accordingly, eurozone analyses will predominate given the importance of economic area NIRP is relevant for (the second of the said assessment criteria). In contrast, as NIRP plays a relatively minor role among the monetary policy tools (the first assessment criterion) used by the central Bank of Japan, this country will receive the least extensive coverage (see Figure 3.1).

It should be noted here that the respective central banks introduced their NIRP in roughly similar periods (Figure 3.2), which brings us to two conclusions. First, such a "synchronization" – albeit unintentional – of central banks' measures demonstrates the importance of international factors in economic processes. A rising importance of this factor in recent years (i.e., following the outbreak of the GFC; see, e.g., Kurowski and Rogowicz, 2018) translates into domestic monetary policies becoming less diversified. Second, this phenomenon makes it difficult to identify the effects of the domestic monetary policy alone. Owing to an international transmission, particularly in the context of a large economy (like the eurozone) affecting small open economies, the international factor may be of major importance, which is also substantiated by the said criterion of selecting the economies for analysis.

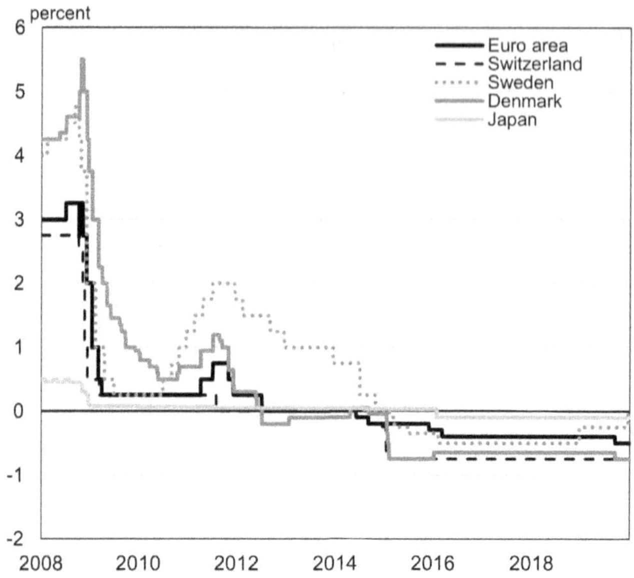

Figure 3.2 Selected central banks' interest rates in NIRP economies

Note: Japan – overnight deposit rate (since January 2016), Switzerland – mid-range for 3M LIBOR CHF or SNB policy rate (since June 2019), Sweden – 7-day repo rate, Denmark – certificates of deposit rate, euro area – O/N deposit rate.

Source: Bloomberg data.

In spite of the aforementioned temporal coincidence as for its introduction, the purposes and ways of introducing NIRP varied with respect to the central bank's mandate and the interest rate system prevailing in a given economy (Brózda-Wilamek, 2017).

3.1.1 The Swiss National Bank

Historically, the Swiss National Bank (SNB) was the first one to use negative nominal interest rates. Although in a different form than today, the system was introduced as early as in the 1970s. In order to counter excessive appreciation of the Swiss franc,[2] in June 1972, SNB introduced negative interest for non-resident deposits denominated in the Swiss currency. Initially, the interest was −2% per quarter; in 1978, it went down to −10% accordingly. Ultimately, this tool turned out to be inadequate and the investors, instead of depositing the Swiss francs bought earlier, invested them in stocks and real estate (Kowalewski, 2015). Finally, the period drew to its end on SNB's decision to introduce an exchange rate target. In spite of NIRP being used only to a narrow extent in the period, it did provide two major conclusions for the contemporary negative interest rate policy. The first and the most important one is that technically it is possible to introduce negative nominal interest rates, and the second one saying that even quite an unconventional measure like lowering interest rates below zero may be an inadequate tool of affecting the exchange rate (Meggyesi, 2010).

Nowadays, SNB has employed a wider scope of NIRP, much as the rationale behind was similar. Namely, the bank yet again sought to reduce the scale of capital flowing due to EBC's introduction of the asset purchase programme. In December 2014, a decision was made to push the operational target of monetary policy below zero with a corresponding yield alignment of the monetary policy tools used. In pursuing the monetary policy operational target, it was decided to reduce the floor for acceptable fluctuations of LIBOR CHF 3M down to −0.75%. As a result, a respective corridor determined by the central bank for this rate was set from −0.75% to 0.25%. It means that the ceiling of this corridor remained positive, so interbank interest rates could still take on positive values. Another decision in this regard was taken in January 2015 whereby the central bank shifted the said corridor of interbank rates' fluctuations to more negative levels, i.e., −1.25% to −0.25%, so this time both its ceiling and the floor went down below zero. At the same time, SNB introduced negative interest for deposits held with the central bank above a pre-determined threshold of −0.75%, i.e., at the mid-point of the corridor of acceptable interbank rate fluctuations.

It is also important that, as the interest rates went below zero, in January 2015, SNB decided to abandon the asymmetric exchange rate target in their monetary policy, that is, to cease to defend the minimum EUR/CHF at 1.20 (SNB, 2015). The decision was made in spite of the central bank's assurance it was determined to maintain the lower bound for the exchange rate. It was probably down to a pronounced rise in FX reserves stemming from central bank's currency intervention and the prospects of the domestic currency's appreciation pressure amid quantitative easing announced by ECB.

3.1.2 The Central Bank of Sweden

The first central banks to have used NIRP nowadays are the central banks of Sweden and Denmark.

The world's oldest central bank, the central bank of Sweden (Riksbank) was the first one to have lowered the deposit rate below zero in August 2009 in response to the consequences of the GFC. Since absorbing liquidity from the banking sector is rather a marginal function of overnight deposits, hence at that time the downward movement was not that relevant either for Riksbank's operational implementation of the monetary policy or for the valuation of financial instruments and the banking system.

Therefore, it is the moment of pushing below zero the repo rate, i.e., the central bank's main interest rate (one which sets out monetary policy operational target), that is considered to be the actual period in which Sweden's central bank introduced NIRP. In attempt to prevent the strengthening of the domestic currency, Riksbank drove O/N deposit rate below zero in July 2014 and the seven-day repo rate in February 2015. Swedish krona's appreciation would only have added to the inauspicious prospects of inflation growth which had approximated zero in the months preceding the decision.[3]

Swedish central bank is the only one which put an end (marked by raising the main interest rate up to 0% in December 2019[4]) to NIRP after an almost five-year period. Much as the central bank justified the interest rate change with favourable macroeconomic environment, with respect to the rates' very level, yet again only a temporary character of NIRP was emphasized. It was also brought up that such a policy being pursued for a long period may cause "unfavourable adaptations of economic entities" (JP Morgan, 2019). That NIRP's side effects were among the reasons behind Riksbank's having put an end to the policy was also shown in the bank's official communication. It claimed that the decision did not commence a cycle of tightening the monetary policy by the central bank (Riksbank, 2019), all the more that at the same time a treasury bond purchase programme was maintained, which identified an expansionary character of the monetary policy.

3.1.3 The National Bank of Denmark

The National Bank of Denmark (DNB) pushed one of its interest rates, i.e., the rate of certificate of deposit, down below zero, and O/N deposit rate down to zero after ECB's asset purchase programme was initiated in September 2014. At this point, it is worth turning to the particular character of DNB's interest rates' operational system which defines four rates' categories, i.e., discount rate, rate of certificates of deposit, credit rate and current account rate. Like in other central banks, it is the discount rate that shows the monetary policy direction, however, currently the rate is of no practical use. It is because it has not defined the yield of any monetary policy instrument since 2009. Consequently, what matters more, given the perspective of monetary policy implementation, is the rate of certificates of deposit and the credit rate, both of which demonstrate the yields of open market operations – certificates of deposits are issued as part of open market operations and secured loans originated by the central bank, accordingly.

What underlay the decision to introduce negative interest rate was the idea to curb the scale of capital inflow into Denmark and thus, to limit the appreciation pressure on domestic currency. It should be pointed out that as Denmark is one of ERM II participants, the indirect goal of monetary policy is to maintain a stable relation of Danish krona to euro. Thus, the monetary policy's operational system is strictly subordinated to DNB's achievement of the exchange rate target. In turn, the decisions concerning the level of the Danish central bank's interest rates first and foremost correspond to the changes (or the expected changes) of European Central Bank's monetary policy. As a result, ECB's decision which broadened the scale of expansionary character of the eurozone's monetary policy, somewhat "forced" a similar measure on Denmark's central bank (DNB, 2015). Also, subsequent decisions to continue interest rates reduction made in January and February 2015 were an aftermath of DNB's currency interventions which did not prove sufficient enough to stabilize the exchange rate (DNB, 2015).[5]

Just as the central bank of Sweden, so did DNB first introduced NIRP earlier, in July 2012, in the form of the aforementioned negative interest on certificates of deposit. As the central bank itself emphasized, the then adjustment was also connected with ECB's monetary policy, and more specifically, ECB's lowering interest rates to a similar extent (DNB, 2012). Consequently, the rate of certificates of deposit was driven then below zero, down to −0.2%, and it remained on the negative level until May 2014.

3.1.4 The European Central Bank

The European Central Bank (ECB) was the first among the central banks to use NIRP in the current cycle of monetary policy.[6] However, unlike the Swiss National Bank, the policy is restricted to a narrower scope of interest rates categories, only the deposit facility which went down below zero in June 2014 (initially, to −0.1%, then to −0.5%) with the reference rate being driven down to zero.

The introduction of NIRP was among the elements of a broader scope of measures regarding three areas: loosening monetary policy, improving transmission mechanism and ensuring unconventional mechanisms can be introduced (EBC, 2015b). The measures included: (i) a decision (vital for our study) to apply negative interest also to funds held with ECB in excess of the reserve requirement, (ii) a series of *Targeted Longer-Term Refinancing Operations* (TLTROs) which supports lending for households and non-financial entities, (iii) intensifying preparations for the introduction of direct purchase on asset-backed securities (ABS) market to foster monetary policy transmission mechanism, (iv) actions aiming to strengthen forward guidance and mitigate money market volatility.[7] The main motive behind those measures was to additionally loosen the monetary policy and to counter de-anchoring inflationary expectations in the eurozone. Namely, in the months preceding the decision, eurozone inflation went down below what ECB considered as consistent with price stability definition, and the then pending significant euro appreciation added to the risk of lower inflation extending over a longer period.

Five years passing from NIRP introduction in September 2019, ECB decided to apply important changes in its implementation. In particular, ECB introduced *tiering*, a mechanism of varying the interest rate on funds deposited by commercial banks with ECB so as to, as the bank itself put it, limit the adverse effect of more negative interest rates on the banks' situation (EBC, 2019). Concomitantly, as for the very decision implementing NIRP, also in this case, a number of other tools came into play, in particular, relaunch of the financial asset purchase programme (called QE II).

3.1.5 The Bank of Japan

Among the central banks in question, the last one to resort to negative interest rate policy was the Bank of Japan (BoJ). The bank introduced negative interest for a minor part of O/N deposit operations in January 2016[8] (at −0.1%). Importantly, the decision was unexpected and the Bank of Japan had not communicated such an option earlier, unlike the other central banks introducing NIRP (Morgan Stanley, 2016). This measure aimed to counter deflationary pressure and to strengthen the commitment to meet the inflationary target (BoJ, 2016), at the same time ensuring a further reduction in interest rates in the negative territory, if necessary. Thus, NIRP became one of the elements of expansionary monetary policy, be it the case of ECB. Prior to NIRP introduction, in Japan, monetary policy was loosened still with the use of two earlier implemented types of measures – qualitative and quantitative. The quantitative measures are identified with growing the central bank's balance sheet, while the qualitative dimension with the structural change of the portfolio of assets held by the bank, with the intention to include higher-risk or lower liquidity instruments (Kuroda, 2017). Consequently, monetary policy of the Bank of Japan following the introduction of negative interest rates was defined as quantitative and qualitative monetary easing with a negative interest rate.[9] Moreover, the Bank of Japan had already been through a 20-year history of zero interest rate policy that the bank was the first to use.

3.2 NIRP Implementation Details

Negative nominal interest rates were implemented across all the central banks largely through the existing monetary policy operational systems, much as they required adaptation to the new environment.[10] Notwithstanding, each of the central banks in question employed a different NIRP implementation model for commercial banks' deposits with the central bank. The implementation model is important since it generates varying consequences of NIRP and its transmission mechanism, and, what is crucial, the effects on the banking sector.

The prevailing implementation model of NIRP regarding charging commercial banks with a negative cost of depositing funds with the central bank is the model of multi-layered interest applied for the funds, called *tiering*. This model assumes that the negative interest rate is not a burden on the entire excess liquidity of the banking sector as there is a system of cut-offs or buffers in place which reduces a potential direct cost for the commercial bank. Such an attitude to negative interest rate implementation was originated by the central banks of Denmark and Sweden, and then it was expanded by the Bank of Japan. Still, the approach to the said model clearly varies across the respective central banks using NIRP – the central banks of Denmark, Sweden and Switzerland introduced a two-tier, and the Bank of Japan – a three-tier model of interest on funds with the central bank.

The central bank of Denmark introduced two current account limits (an individual and a global one) defining the scale of funds at the central bank for which negative interest rate applies. Thanks to NIRP's particular character, it was possible to use the said limits as an additional monetary policy instrument. As a result, a change of interest rate level is not (to certain extent) required for the scale of expansionary character of monetary policy pursued by DNB to change.

The balance of funds on commercial banks' current accounts must not exceed the global limit pre-determined by DNB. The limit falls into individual limits for funds held by each of the entities having a current account and it is set by the central bank based on the activity of respective interbank participants. In case funds deposited on the current accounts exceed the global limit, the excess above individual deposits' limits is automatically converted by the central bank into certificates of deposit bearing negative interest. Only in such an event does NIRP effectively charge the direct cost to the banking sector.

Also, in the case of Switzerland, negative interest is charged only on the value of funds held with the central bank (i.e., *sight deposits*) above a predefined level (*exemption threshold*). The thresholds are set individually for each of the credit institutions and they are determined on the basis of one out of two methods (the threshold must be at least CHF 10m).

- The threshold based on the reserve requirement (domestic banks) amounted to 20-fold the reserve required over a month before negative interest rates were introduced, plus/less relevant increase/decrease of funds held by a given entity.
- Fixed threshold – for the other institutions on which the reserve requirement is not binding (foreign banks, securities' dealers, clearance houses, insurance companies, international organizations, central banks), SNB sets a fixed threshold (no principles for its forming have been specified, though).

What the above models have in common is that there is a general level for all the banks that allows to avoid negative interest. The Bank of Sweden, on the other hand, has a different approach in that the scale of proportion of excess liquidity with respect to a given bank is subject to a uniform criterion. In this approach, for each commercial bank's funds held with the central bank, the negative interest does not apply based on the threshold proportional to the funds' volume[11].

In turn, the Bank of Japan introduced relatively the most sophisticated system of charging the direct cost of negative interest rates. It is made up of three elements (BoJ, 2016):

- Basic balance – a fixed level equal to the average value of deposit with the central bank in the period immediately preceding NIRP introduction for which positive interest rate applies. This approach aimed to prevent against a hike of the direct cost for banks with respect to the pre-NIRP level.
- Macro add-on balance – balance which incorporates the level of reserve requirement and the funds provided to commercial banks under the lending support programme, for which the zero interest rate applies. The balance was gradually adjusted along with the rise in excess liquidity of the banking sector.
- Policy-rate balance – the remaining portion of funds deposited with the central bank for which a negative interest rate applies.

In spite of varying methods used for all the models, the common and most important advantage is constraining the scale of direct cost burden on the banking sector, the cost arising from negative interest on the deposit with the central bank. This constraint allows the central bank to cut interest rates to more negative levels without reaching the effective lower bound for interest rates. The experience of central banks which use the said differentiation mechanism indeed shows that even a non-significant direct NIRP cost burden on the banking sector, as in Japan, is enough for negative interest rates to enter the money or bond market. In practice, given their universal character and ease of implementation, mainly two approaches to the multi-tier model became popular – individualized (Swedish approach) or aggregate cut-off system (Danish approach).

In contrast, what distinguished the system of interest rates on commercial bank deposits with the ECB from those of other central banks for most of the NIRP policy period to date, was the lack of introduction of tiering scheme.[12] In such an event, in the environment of negative interest rates, all the excess liquidity funds in the banking sector deposited with the central bank were charged with identical cost equal to deposit rate. The absence of such a model was ECB's intention suggesting the bank

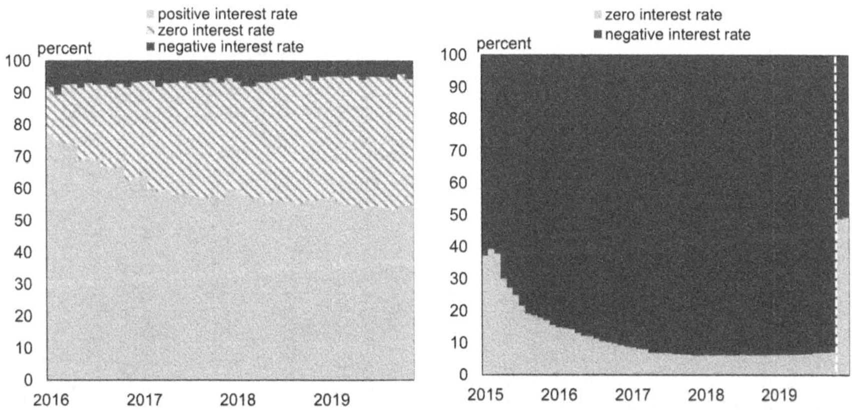

Figure 3.3 Structure of direct cost burden on the banking sector – cases of Japan (left panel) and the euro area (right panel)

Note: Dashed line on the right figure denotes the introduction of two-level tiering scheme by the European Central Bank.

Source: Own work based on central banks data.

was not willing to bring the interest rates any lower and thus, in the form of soft forward guidance, constraining the valuation of such a measure by financial market participants (EBC, 2016). Ultimately, however, ECB introduced a system of varying deposits with the central bank. In line with the mechanism adopted, commercial banks were exempt from negative interest for funds representing sixfold of the reserve requirement made by a given bank (EBC, 2019).

Summing up the analysis of NIRP implementation solutions, it should be identified to what extent the methods varying among respective central banks impact the effective structure of interest on the banking sector's excess liquidity. Figure 3.3 presents the structure of a direct cost burden on the banking sector with the use of two extreme scenarios – the most sophisticated differentiation mechanism (the Bank of Japan) and the differentiation-free mechanism (used by ECB for most of the analysed period). For the first model, only some of the funds of commercial banks deposited with the central banks are effectively charged with a negative interest rate, whereas in the other case, it is the vast majority of them. In other words, in the context of generating direct costs for the Japanese banking sector, the importance of NIRP is relatively low, whereas for the eurozone, the said policy is economically relevant (more in Chapter 4).

A summary of the above considerations on NIRP in the analysed central banks is depicted in Table 3.1.

Table 3.1 Comparison of major characteristics of central banks' NIRP

	European Central Bank	*Riksbank*	*Denmark's National Bank*	*Swiss National Bank*	*Bank of Japan*
Introduction date **Type of negative rate**	January 2014 Deposit rate	February 2015[c, d] Repo rate, deposit rate	September 2014[e] Current account rate, certificates of deposit rate, lending rate	December 2014 Policy rate [range of 3-month LIBOR CHF][f]; deposit rate	January 2016 Deposit facility rate
Lowest level of negative rate	−0.50%	−0.50% −1.25%	−0.75%	−1.25% to −0.25%; −0.75%	−0.10%
Other non-standard monetary policy activities	Financial assets purchases,[a] lending activity support programme (TLTRO)	Financial assets purchases, possibility of discretionary FX interventions	Ceasing of sovereign bonds issuance (X 2014–V 2015)	NIRP introduction coinciding with abandon of exchange rate floor policy	Financial assets purchases
Interest rate scheme for deposits with central bank	(1) June 2014–November 2019: negative rate on deposits with central bank with amount exceeding reserve requirement[b]; (2) Since December 2019: deposits with central bank with amount below six-times the reserve requirement (0.0%), other deposits charged with negative rate	Majority of deposits with central bank is remunerated close to repo rate	Negative rate is applied to certificates on deposits	(1) Deposits with central banks with amount below 20× reserve requirement or CHF 10 bn (0.0%); (2) Other deposits (−0.75%)	(1) Deposits established during BoJ purchases of financial assets (0.1%); (2) Reserve requirement and measures granted to support lending (0.0%); (3) Other deposits (−0.1%)
Cause of introduction	Price stability and anchoring of inflation expectations	Price stability and anchoring of inflation expectations	Preventing the capital inflow, mitigation of the currency appreciation pressure	Mitigating the currency appreciation pressure and easing deflationary pressure	Deflationary pressure counteraction, strengthening of central bank inflation commitment

Note: [a]financial asset purchases under APP programme were terminated with the end of 2018; [b]interest rate on deposits with central bank below the reserve requirement amounts to rate on main refinancing operations (currently 0.0%); [c]Riksbank introduced the negative rates (in a form of deposit rate) for the first time in August 2009; [d]Riksbank ended its NIRP on January 2020; [e]DNB introduced negative rate on certificates of deposits also earlier (July 2012–April 2014); [f]SNB replaced the target range for the three-month Libor as its main monetary policy tool in June 2019, when SNB policy rate was introduced.
Source: Own work based on central banks' information.

3.3 Expectations for the Persistence of Negative Interest Rates

An essential part of analysing the impact of a new phenomenon (NIRP in this case) should be the question of its persistence. The persistence of a given phenomenon is implied by no less than a medium term of its duration and, unlike for temporary phenomena, it allows business entities to adapt to the new environment.

At the moment of introducing NIRP, the central banks highlighted the phenomenon's temporary character (see, e.g., EBC, 2015a; SNB, 2016). It was viewed as a tool for a faster achievement of monetary policy goals. Such a rhetoric of the central banks may be verified by the expectations of financial market participants (expressed in the quotations of financial instruments) which are, on the other hand, dependent on the very rhetoric. Such metrics allow for a twofold analysis – based on the expected level of interest rates only or the expectations for how long they will potentially remain on a given level. The conventional monetary policy was primarily the area for which the first approach was relevant. However, as unconventional tools came to be used, the time factor also became of importance (directly addressed also under, *inter alia*, forward guidance) for a given interest rate level. In order to incorporate the time factor, a synthetic indicator may be estimated which would allow for both the level and the time horizon of the expected negative interest rate levels. Moreover, such an indicator may be interpreted in the context of business entities' motivation to migrate to cash, that is, the expectations for nominal interest rates to reach the lower bound.

The above metrics being analysed for the eurozone shows that, in line with the said ECB rhetoric, originally, financial market participants deemed it was highly likely the interest rates would revert to their positive territory relatively soon after they took on the negative values (Figures 3.4 and 3.5). Consequently, at its initial stages, the negative interest rate phenomenon was, in objective terms, of temporary character.

However, the above circumstances changed considerably over time and they became settled for several years with respect to the expectations for a somewhat lower level of interest[13] rates and a longer time-span for the negative values to remain. It was also at that time that, given the expectations were medium term, the said phenomenon should have been considered as displaying characteristics of persistence. The said factor was additionally strengthened in mid-2019 whereby, as the degree of monetary policy expansionary character was expected to rise worldwide, so did the horizon for NIRP in the eurozone (Figure 3.4) and other analysed economies greatly extend.

The aforesaid issue is one of the grounds for the research topic addressed in this monograph. Namely, the persistence of negative interest rates may be one of the reasons to analyse their major effect on systemic risk which is a medium-term issue and which also requires structural adaptations in the financial system to be taken account of. This aspect is presented in the following chapters.[14]

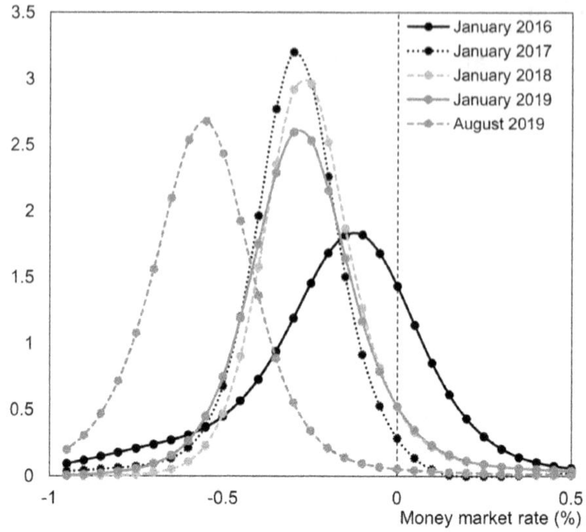

Figure 3.4 Market-implied expectations on short-term market rate in the euro area
Note: The distributions of expected market rates implied from interest rates options.
Source: Own work based on Bloomberg data.

Figure 3.5 Synthetic indicator of market-implied expectations on negative rates in the euro area
Note: Synthetic indicator of market-implied expectations on negative rates measured by the area over the curve of implied forward interest rates for the period up to moment of interest rate return to zero. The measure thus includes two factors – the level of the negative rate and the length of period during which the negative rates are expected to remain in place. The lower the expected interest rate or the longer the period of NIRP, the higher the level of proposed synthetic index.
Source: Own work based on Bloomberg data.

Summary

In recent years, some central banks in developed economies pushed their nominal interest rates below zero, thus challenging the prevailing view of interest rates never reaching negative values, and initiating a new approach to how a monetary policy may be pursued. The reasons for the introduction of NIRP, however, varied across the said economies. On the one hand, they indicated a tendency to continue to loosen the monetary policy and the new tool was employed as an addition to other unconventional central bank's measures. On the other hand, though, they were an element of containing appreciation pressure on exchange rate. Negative nominal interest rates across all the central banks are implemented via the existing monetary policy operational systems. At the same time, however, the models of charging commercial bank's funds deposited with central banks clearly varied.

The latter aspect seems to differentiate group of NIRP economies to the greatest extent and in fact leads to an important consequences for further analysis. Specifically, the ECB did not launch a tier scheme for remuneration of excess reserve holdings when it introduced its NIRP. All other NIRP central banks took steps to partly mitigate the direct impact of negative rates on banking sector profitability and introduced such a scheme. Therefore, these banks *de facto* introduced a blended interest rate policy. Against this setting, the ECB should be considered the only central bank that introduced a pure NIRP, which was in effect during much of the time the eurozone experienced negative rates. As a result, our further findings with respect to NIRP in the eurozone should be considered general findings for negative rates.

Notes

1 The National Bank of Hungary cut its overnight deposit rate to −0.05% in March 2016. However, since it is implemented only to a small share of deposits with central bank, its impact on the banking sector is negligible. The bank suggested, however, that one of the reasons for lowering the rate into the negative territory is to put a downward pressure on long-term market yields.

2 The strong appreciation pressure on Swiss franc, both in 1970s and recently, is associated with these currency-specific features. Namely, alongside, e.g., the Japanese yen, Swiss franc is globally perceived as a safe haven currency. It means that, regardless of the local economic factors, the currency is sensitive to the market perception of global risk aversion.

3 In order to make monetary policy more expansionary, the decision to introduce negative repo rate in February 2015 was accompanied by the decision on purchases of government bonds as well.

4 At the same time, the deposit facility rate in Sweden remained in the negative territory. However, due to the mentioned minor importance of that rate, the end of 2019 can be nevertheless considered as an end of NIRP conducted by Riksbank.

5 DNB activity (FX market interventions, interest rates cuts) was supported by the fiscal policy in a form of increased issuance of sovereign debt. The objective of this action was to discourage foreign investors to flow into the country and to ease appreciation pressure on Danish krone.

6 In fact, Danish central bank lowered its rates into negative territory before the ECB did; however, due to policy normalization, they came back into positive levels in 2014.

7 These actions included: (i) to continue conducting its main refinancing operations (MROs) as fixed rate tender procedures with full allotment for as long as necessary; (ii) to conduct the longer-term refinancing operations (LTROs) to be allotted before the end of the Eurosystem's reserve maintenance period ending in December 2016 as fixed rate tender procedures with full allotment; (iii) to suspend the weekly fine-tuning operation sterilising the liquidity injected under the Securities Markets Programme.

8 It should be noted that the phenomenon of negative interest rate was evidenced in Japan a long before the NIRP was introduced and did not arise from monetary policy decisions. Crisis of confidence in deflationary environment with almost-zero interest rates caused that Japanese banks in 1998 preferred to set up deposits with foreign commercial banks. This was exploited by foreign subsidiaries of banks operating in Japan that agreed to deposit money with local banks but with a charge of negative rate (see, e.g., Wakatabe 2012; Yoshino and Taghizadeh-Hesary 2015).

9 This framework evolved further (in September 2016) into a concept of Quantitative and Qualitative Monetary Easing with Yield Curve Control.

10 Adaptation of operational framework, which is mentioned in this chapter, mostly comes down to economic characteristics (like tiering scheme). It should be noted, however, that introduction of NIRP pushed pressure to adaptation of computerized systems as well, both in central bank and in other financial institutions, in a way that allows for negative interest to be introduced in the system (Bech and Makhozov, 2016).

11 It should be pointed that Riksbank, unlikely other central banks, does not actively use a reserve requirement as a tool in monetary policy implementation framework.

12 Some economists claim that implementation framework of ECB's NIRP can be, in fact, described as a tiering scheme since one of the 'tiering level' was defined by reserve requirement remunerated at zero rate. Nevertheless, the approach presented is this book is based on a banking sector cost burden perspective. Consequently, ECB's early experience with NIRP is not described as a tiering scheme.

13 It might have partly arisen from ECB decision to cut deposit rate in March 2016. Still, market expectations to such an action built up much earlier and they should be – at least to some extent – included in to presented distributions of future interest rates from early 2016.

14 With respect to expectations on central bank's interest rate, the minimum for such rate still remains an unresolved question. To date experience suggests that neither technical nor economical bounds have been reached yet. Survey measures points that the lower bound for central banks to be around minus 1.5% (Jeffery, 2019). This translates into uncertainty associated with this monetary policy tool, which may increase further as the period of negative rates extends.

Bibliography

Bech, M., Makhozov, A., (2016). *How Have Central Banks Implemented Negative Policy Rates?* BIS Quarterly Review.

BoJ, (2016). *Introduction of "Quantitative and Qualitative Monetary Easing with a Negative Interest Rate"*, Bank of Japan, 29 January.

Brózda-Wilamek, D., (2017). *Polityka ujemnych stóp procentowych – doświadczenia Europejskiego Banku Centralnego*, Prace naukowe Uniwersytety Ekonomicznego we Wrocławiu, nr 499/2017.

DNB, (2012). *Interest Rate Reduction, Monetary Policy Decision*, Monetary Policy Press Release, 5 July.

DNB, (2015). *The Interest Rate Reduction follows Danmarks Nationalbank's Purchase of Foreign Exchange in the Market*, Monetary Policy Press Releases, 19, 23, 29 January and 5 February 2015.

EBC, (2015a). *Economic Bulletin*, European Central Bank, no. 2/2015.

EBC, (2015b). *Introductory Statement to the Press Conference (with Q&A), Monetary Policy Decision*, 3 June 2015.

EBC, (2016). *Introductory Statement to the Press Conference (with Q&A), Monetary Policy Decision*, 10 March 2016.

EBC, (2019). *ECB Introduces Two-tier System for Remunerating Excess Liquidity Holdings*, Press Release, European Central Bank, 12 September 2019.

Jeffery, Ch., (2019). *Central banks face loss of independence – Central Banking survey*, [available online: https://www.centralbanking.com/central-banks/4376401/central-banks-face-loss-of-independence-central-banking-survey].

JP Morgan, (2019). *Riksbank Hikes as Expected; Policy Rate Now on Hold for Foreseeable Future*, Europe Economic Research, investment note, 19 December 2019.

Kowalewski, P., (2015). *Flirt z ujemnymi stopami procentowymi*, Obserwator finansowy, 5 January 2015 [available only in Polish].

Kuroda, H., (2017). *Quantitative and Qualitative Monetary Easing and Economic Theory*, Speech at the University of Zurich in Switzerland, 13 November.

Kurowski, Ł.K., Rogowicz, K., (2018). Are Business and Credit Cycles Synchronised Internally or Externally? *Economic Modelling*, vol. 74, pp. 124–141.

Meggyesi, P., (2010). *Reflections on Negative Interest Rates in Switzerland*, Global FX Strategy, JP Morgan, 14 May.

Morgan Stanley, (2016). BoJ Surprise: Implications for Macro, Equities, Fixed Income and Foreign Exchange, *Japan Economics and Strategy*, investment note, 29 January.

Riksbank, (2019). *Repo Rate Raised to Zero Per Cent*, Press Release, Sveriges Riksbank, December 2019.

SNB, (2015). *Swiss National Bank Discontinues Minimum Exchange Rate and Lowers Interest Rate to –0.75%*, Monetary Policy Press Release, Swiss National Bank, 12 January 2015.

SNB, (2016). *Quarterly Bulletin*, Swiss National Bank, no. 2/2016.

Wakatabe, M., (2012). *Turning Japanese? Lessons from Japan's Lost Decade to the Current Crisis*, Center on Japanese Economy and Business, Working Paper Series no. 309.

Yoshino, N., Taghizadeh-Hesary, F., (2015). *Japan's Lost Decade: Lessons for Other Economies*, Asian Development Bank Institute, Working Paper Series no. 521.

4 Initial Experience of Negative Rates Transmission

4.1 The Impact of Negative Interest Rates on Financial Asset Prices and the Exchange Rates

4.1.1 Money Market

Through its influence on the interbank market, or rather on the development of interest rates on the market, monetary policy indirectly affects the level of deposit and credit interest offered by the banking sector and then also the prices and profitability of other deposit and credit instruments (Szpunar, 2000). It means that the first step to take in assessing the quality of monetary transmission – also for negative interest rates – should be the assessment of how the transmission affects the interbank market.

The experience to-date with regard to negative nominal interest rates being transmitted to the interbank rates provides grounds to believe that it follows the positive rates' transmission pattern (Bech and Makhozov, 2016). Across all of the NIRP economies under scrutiny, interbank interest rates followed the central bank rate to the same degree as they did for positive rates in the environment of the central bank's unconventional tools (Figure 4.1).[1] Denmark seems to be the only exception here as this is where the dependence is somewhat less conspicuous. During some periods, the interbank rate approximated O/N deposit rate of the central bank, whereas at other times – the certificate of deposit rate, while it is the latter one that comes as the central bank's main rate. This dependence is chiefly due to a peculiar character of market liquidity, which NIRP affected only indirectly. In the environment of low market liquidity, the interest rate is primarily developed by interbank operations which do not bear negative cost, whereas in the other case, by another bank group, i.e., those with a higher scale of excess funds (Andersen et al., 2018). It follows that, admittedly, in the case of international market's limited liquidity,[2] NIRP drives up the volatility of interest rates on this market, which – with very little volatility in the preceding period (e.g., owing to a belief that zero lower bound holds for interest rates) – may be a source of risk to commercial banks' short-term financing management.

DOI: 10.4324/9781003312116-4

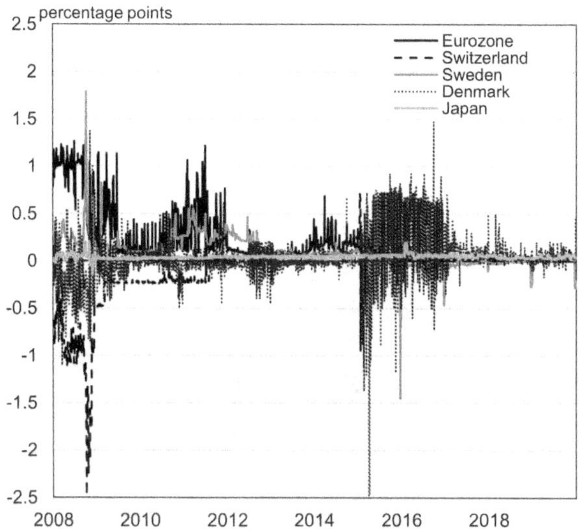

Figure 4.1 Daily spread between money market rate and central bank interest rate in NIRP economies

Source: Bloomberg data.

The scale of turnover should be the second element of interbank assessment. In this case, experience of the economies in question shows a more diversified character. Immediately following NIRP introduction, the transaction volume on the eurozone interbank market did not significantly change (Figure 4.2), still, it clearly dropped along with the increase in excess liquidity of the banking sector after asset purchase was launched by ECB beginning in 2015. Thus, it can be concluded that the sharp decline of turnover in the eurozone is attributable to the respective monetary policy rather than NIRP alone directly. At the same time, however, a drop in turnover on the interbank market in Denmark may be attributed to NIRP, as it is immediately following its introduction that the market turnover went down. It reflects to a large extent NIRP implementation details whereby the limit of funds deposited by commercial banks in the central bank was increased, which thus influenced shifting some operations from interbank to the central bank directly (Tan, 2019). Conversely, a different NIRP implementation structure (i.e., in particular, the system of negative interest cut-offs) gave rise to higher turnover on the interbank market in Switzerland (BIS, 2016). In this case, banks' inclination to take out loans on the interbank market clearly increased in the case of entities for which excess liquidity is below the negative interest threshold. The inclination was simultaneously confronted with higher supply on the part of the banks which exceed the mentioned threshold (Bech and Makhozov, 2016).[3]

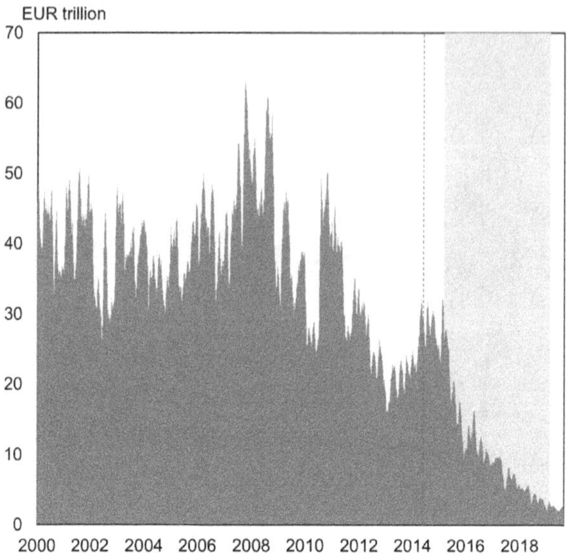

Figure 4.2 Daily turnover in O/N unsecured deposit market in the euro area
Note: Dashed line denotes the introduction of NIRP by the ECB, while the grey area refers to the ECB's Asset Purchase Programme.
Source: European Central Bank.

4.1.2 Bond Market

As central banks were introducing NIRP, other unconventional monetary policy instruments were in use. Such a co-occurrence is of particular importance for bond market analysis. It is down to the fact that the tools were largely to affect the bond yield curve, both its medium-term end (e.g., forward guidance) and long-term interest rates (financial assets purchase). Due to these factors, it is difficult to isolate empirically the effect of NIRP alone on the bond market. What the literature provides in this respect is mainly qualitative analyses.

Given the above determinants, this sub-chapter puts forward several perspectives for the analysis of bond markets in the environment of negative interest rates, providing relatively more in-depth insights than for the other financial instrument categories. It is due to the relatively highest effect of NIRP on this market the chance to draw similar conclusions regarding other categories of financial instruments. Thus, bond market considerations will have a tripartite structure. First, the immediate reaction of bond valuation to NIRP introduction is analysed, then the market structure in the environment of negative interest rates, and finally we attempt to evaluate whether the central banks' NIRP is a prerequisite to observe negative interest rates on the bond markets.

4.1.2.1 Direct Impact of NIRP on the Bond Market

In the context of the impact of negative interest rates on financial markets, it should first and foremost be pointed out that their introduction by central banks was surrounded by uncertainty – in economic, operational and institutional terms (Bech and Makhozov, 2016; IMF, 2017). With respect to the first category, it was down to uncertainty as for to what extent it is only a temporary tool, as well as to expectations for business activity underpinned by interpretations that the central bank is forced to use its instrument in an unprecedented way (Barr et al., 2016; Barth et al., 2016). Operational uncertainty was due to NIRP being incorporated in financial instruments valuation and their settlement (e.g., the method of paying interest on variable rate bonds bearing negative interest) and to the IT infrastructure capacity to cope with the new situation. Operational uncertainty manifested by technical difficulties was nevertheless a short-lived phenomenon. Moreover, the scale of this uncertainty was partly contained by profitability remaining in the positive territory for a majority of financial instruments in the environment of slightly negative interest rates. The foregoing restricted the scope of required operational adjustments and enabled their gradual implementation along with a preparation for possible further interest rates cuts. In turn, institutional uncertainty was down to potential determinants which prevented financial institutions from holding portfolios containing negative yield securities. In addition, for a large portion of, *inter alia*, pre-originated mortgage loans, there were domestic regulations in place which precluded the use of negative interest payments.

Notwithstanding the above-mentioned uncertainty, the introduction of negative interest rates provided expansionary impulse for the valuation of financial assets. The scale of this influence, however, clearly varied among the economies on both short- and medium-term basis. Such conclusions can be drawn on the basis of event studies for the decisions to introduce and then to reduce negative interest rates (Figure 4.3). In line with such an analysis, in the eurozone, the prices of selected financial assets were identified as adjusted relatively to the lowest, whereas in Switzerland, Denmark and, in some cases, for Japan, to the highest extent. Such a differentiation may be attributable to a broader scale of interest changes for the second group of central banks. Still, it would not be the case for Japan, whereby a slight interest rate alteration resulted in proportionally stronger assets' reaction, particularly long-term yield. What may have contributed to the differentiation was also the scale of expectations regarding the decision made (much as the very introduction decisions were unexpected, the later cuts were not any more), as well as the accompanying decisions.

The above analysis is short term only, and it shows the immediate reaction of instrument valuation to monetary policy decision. An advantage of this approach is ignoring other factors which have a medium-term impact and may distort the identification of this type of immediate influence of a

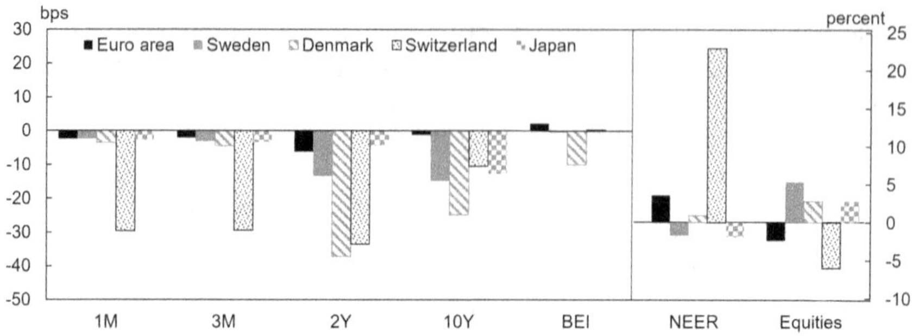

Figure 4.3 Direct short-term reaction of selected financial assets to the interest rate decisions in the NIRP environment

Note: Calculations in a 1-day window for selected assets on the basis of IMF (2017); cumulative change for all interest rate decisions in NIRP environment; 1M. 3M, 2Y, 10Y – the maturity of government bonds, BEI – break-even inflation, NEER – nominal effective exchange rate (increase denotes appreciation of the local currency). Changes of NEER and stock prices presented in percent, while for other assets, they are in basic points.

Source: Own calculations based on Bloomberg data.

given event, speaking of NIRP introduction in this case. However, at the same time, adjustments of economic (and financial in particular) variables may not immediately follow such a decision. In certain cases, they may even take place before the event, based on how the expectations of market participants develop.

4.1.2.2 Structural Changes of the Bond Market in the Environment of Negative Interest Rates

The policy of negative interest rates strengthened the impact of the monetary policy's signalling channel which is attributable to the central bank's desire to affect the medium- and long-term interest rates as well. This is very important as there is a consensus in the literature of aggregate demand in the economy being dependent more on long-term interest rates rather than short-term rates (see, e.g., Woodford, 1999). The analysis of this channel – for both eurozone and other economies using unconventional monetary policy tools – may be two-dimensional: from the "zero-cost" perspective and NIRP. The former pertains to *forward guidance*[4] and is referred to in the literature (very broadly speaking) as "zero-cost" since it largely comes down to the central bank's communication (de Groot and Haas, 2018). Much as forward guidance came to be identified in empirical research as an effective tool for affecting future interest rates expectations, its impact is substantially lessened as it draws closer to the relevant zero lower bound (Figure 4.4). In turn, along with the reduction of nominal interest rates below zero and thus crossing the bound, so was the signalling mechanism for

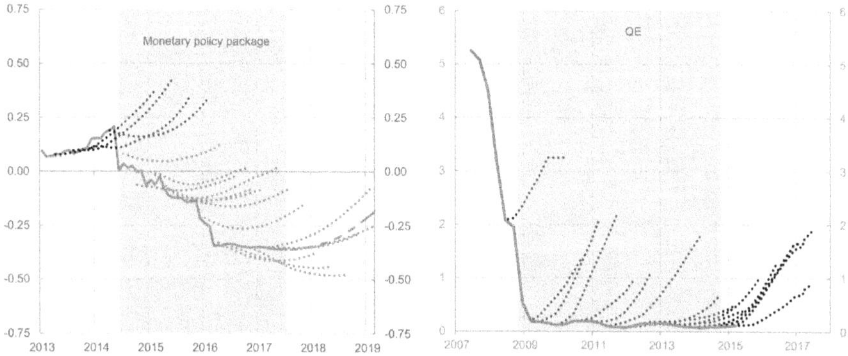

Figure 4.4 Market-implied expectations on future interest rates in negative rates environment (euro area, left panel) and in regime of positive rates (United States, right panel)

Note: Market expectations on interest rates (denotes by dotted line) implied from forward rate agreement (FRA) contracts.

Source: Eisenschmidt and Smets (2018).

future interest rates permanently shifted into the negative nominal territory (Draghi, 2017). Such a strategy of affecting future interest rates, however, is not referred to as zero-cost on account of its direct cost to the banking sector (see Chapter 5.2. *Direct Effect of Negative Interest Rates on the Banking Sector*). A comparison of how market metrics for central banks' expectations for interest rates in the eurozone and the United States develop (as examples of the economies in which central banks employ the policies of, respectively, positive and negative interest rates) is what well captures this dependence (Figure 4.4).

The above observation is important as it differentiates the monetary policy transmission on the bond market in the positive versus negative interest rate environment. The path of the expected interest rates having adjusted, the introduction of NIRP affects the entire treasury bond yield curve shifting and even flattening in the case term premium drops (Figure 4.4). The foregoing contrasts with the influence of interest rates in below zero environment. It is because the empirical literature shows that normally under such circumstances the yield curve steepens as the adjustment of long-term interest rates is proportionally lower than the scale of central bank's interest rate reduction (Bottero et al., 2019). In addition, in the environment of positive interest rates, it is the short-term bonds that reflect the scale of the changes the most. In contrast, the eurozone example shows in turn, that in the case of NIRP, it is the medium-term interest rates that adjust to ECB's deposit rate reduction the most (Figure 4.5). Consequently, NIRP proves to be approximating unconventional monetary policy tools (as compared to the effect of QE on bond yields) more rather than the conventional interest

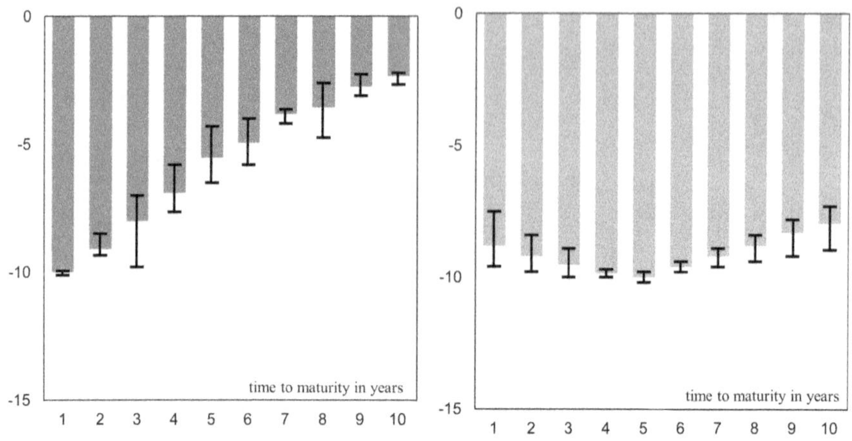

Figure 4.5 Standardized impact of change in ECB's deposit rate by 10 basis points on sovereign yield curve in the regime of positive rates (left panel) and in negative interest rates environment (right panel)

Note: Columns denote an average short-term reaction to interest rate changes (in basis points), while black lines represent min-max range.

Source: Own work based on Rostagno et al. (2019).

rate policy (Altavilla et al., 2015; Gambetti and Musso, 2017). In particular, NIRP may be considered as a major form of strengthening the central bank's communication with respect to future interest rates.

Owing to the decision's expansionary character and to the strengthening of signalling channel, the zero lower bound was crossed also for treasury bond yield even up to long term to maturity (Figure 4.5). As mentioned earlier, the long-term interest rate, next to the expectations for what levels short-term interest rates will be reaching, draws from many components associated with risk valuation, including credit risk or the risk of future macroeconomic uncertainty (e.g., in the case of Italy, see Figure 4.6). Thus, although the short end of the yield curve dropping below zero is a natural alignment with the central bank's rates, long-term interest rates show that the term premium component may also hit all-time low. In the case of diversification of bond issuers by risk, despite the uniform central bank interest rate in the euro area, the transmission of NIRP policy to long-term government bond yields also varied, mainly through the country credit risk component incorporated in the valuations of these securities (e.g., Italy). However, it should be noted that in many NIRP economies, the transmission of negative interest rates to treasury bond yields proved relatively effective.[5, 6] The foregoing is substantiated by the entire yield curve (i.e., even with 30 years term to maturity) of German, Danish or Swiss bonds remaining in the negative territory in some periods.[7] In addition, what becomes conspicuous is the phenomenon of long-term treasury bond

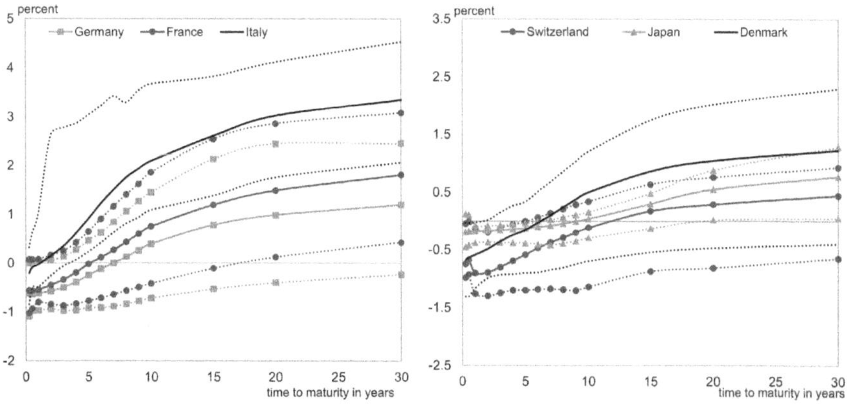

Figure 4.6 Sovereign yield curves for selected Euroarea NIRP countries (left panel) and in other NIRP economies (right panel)

Note: Solid lines represent a median curve during the NIRP period in analysed economies, while dotted lines denote minimal and maximal level of the curve over that respective period.

Source: Own work based on Bloomberg data.

yields of some countries (e.g., Germany) dropping below the central bank's short-term rate. It was probably associated with a major reduction of the eurozone expected interest rates component.

Much as the credit risk component normally matters more for the valuation of corporate bonds, still the yields of the securities in the environment of negative interest rates also reached negative values.[8] Notwithstanding, because of the differentiation by risk premium, in the case of corporate bonds, the phenomenon was much less popularized (approx. 8% of the securities on the market reached negative yields; see Figure 4.8) and confined mainly to the eurozone and Switzerland. The change structure of the bond market contributed to a significant decline in the cost of capital for business entities (both equity and debt). For the eurozone, it was a scale comparable to the impact of ECB's corporate bond purchase programme (EC, 2017; Santis et al., 2018)[9] (Figure 4.7).

NIRP pursued by the central banks and the aforementioned adjustments of yields gave rise to a considerable growth in the volume of bonds quoted by negative yield – up to almost one-fourth of all the bonds on the market and, in particular, to almost half of all the treasury bonds globally (see Figure 4.9). The geographical structure of negative yield bonds shows, in turn, their distinct geographical concentration. It is the Japanese bonds that make up almost three-fourths of the group (Figure 4.8). In addition, almost half of the bonds are held by the Bank of Japan,[10] which is due the asset purchase programme. It should be noted that the growth dynamics of the volumes of negative yield bonds is closely correlated not so much with the

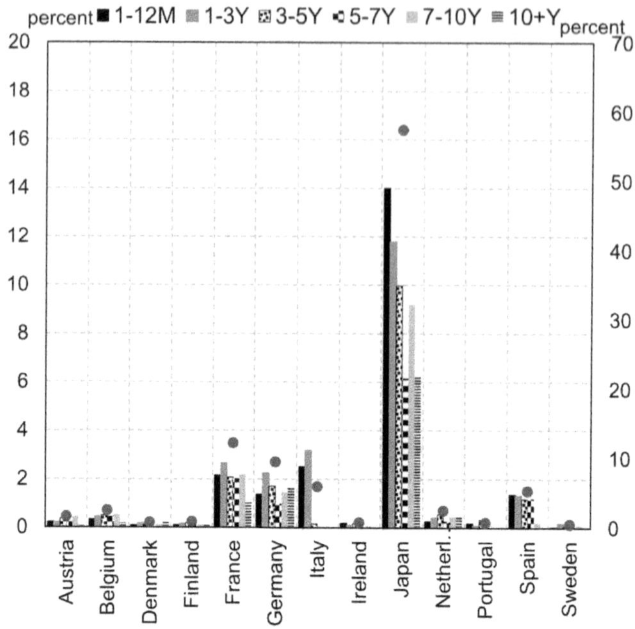

Figure 4.7 Geographical and term structure of sovereign bonds with negative yield

Note: The structure based on the outstanding amount as of August 2019; dots represent the share of each economy in the total outstanding amount of bond with negative yields (right scale).

Source: JP Morgan (2019d) and Bloomberg data.

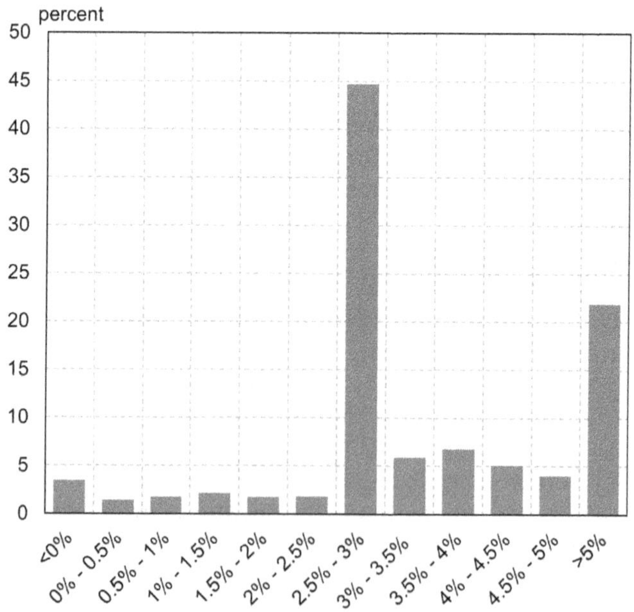

Figure 4.8 Yield distribution of sovereign corporate bonds (as of August 2019)

Source: Bloomberg data.

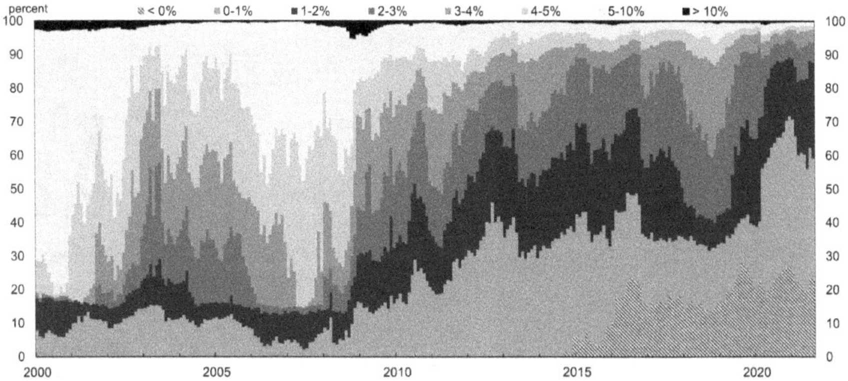

Figure 4.9 Yield distribution in the global fixed-income market

Note: Calculations based on outstanding amount of fixed income included in the *ICE BofAML Global Fixed Income Markets Index;* composition of index evolving over time, calculations at the end of each month.

Source: Own work based on Bloomberg data.

very period in which NIRP was introduced, as with the expectations for the interest rates to remain in the negative territory.[11]

Simultaneously, it should be pointed out that the above tendencies are but a part of a medium-term tendency to change the yield structure of debt instruments. Whereas just two decades ago, more than half of all bonds in the world had an annual yield of at least 5% (Figure 4.9), during recent years, that ratio has declined to barely 3% and has thus reached a historic low. At the same time, structural changes commencing to affect bond yields may be directly attributed to the period of the GFC. In such an event, the macroeconomic factors and ultra-expansionary monetary policy of the major central banks gave rise to a demonstrable pressure on treasury bond yields globally.

Thus, the aforementioned conclusions show that the change in yield structure observed was not only attributable to NIRP. The structure of global bond yields does not imply a shift in their entire range with the advent of negative interest rates, but rather a push effect observed among those securities with yields oscillating at low levels, particularly the 1% level (Figure 4.9). Consequently, much as average investment yield has undoubtedly gone down, the negative interest policy has not significantly expanded the reservoir of bonds offering a rate of return below 1%. Both before and after introduction of NIRP, it approximated 40% of debt instruments spectrum. It suggests that NIRP may have contributed to the search for yield phenomenon to a lesser extent than the zero-interest rate policy paired with the central bank's unconventional instruments.

At this point, the impact of NIRP on bond yield should be distinguished from that on the bond interest rates, i.e., the coupon rates. Much as the yields of a vast majority of treasury bonds in NIRP economies reached negative levels, their interest determining coupon payment for bond holders remained positive (Figure 4.10). It is because the payments are zero bound[12]

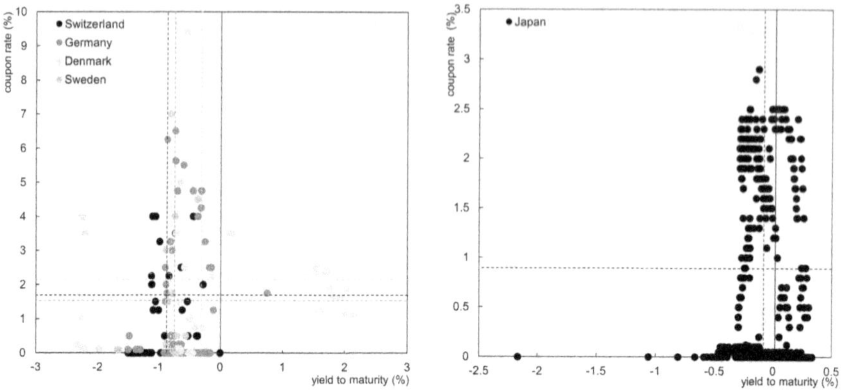

Figure 4.10 Relationship between yields and coupon rates of sovereign bonds in NIRP economies

Note: Dashed lines represent averages weighted with the outstanding amount; calculations as of August 2019; only publicly traded bonds are included.

Source: Own work based on Bloomberg data.

(for the so-called zero-coupon bond) and their range, to give treasury bonds as an example, is markedly broader in the European economies than in Japan. What needs to be emphasized, however, is that whenever the market structure of coupon payments clearly shifts downwards (down to the zero bound) along with rising primary market issue in negative interest rates environment, so does the impact of NIRP on this component gradually fade. It means that, in medium term, such a phenomenon shifts a larger portion of negative interest rate policy transmission to bond yield components, mainly the term premium. Consequently, in short term, yield reaction to NIRP introduction may be weaker, while it may strengthen in medium term, that is, whereby negative interest rates and structural changes on part of business entities become entrenched.

The mentioned difference between yield and interest is of particular relevance for corporate bonds. It is because both the values should incorporate the issuer' risk credit component which is typically higher for business entities than countries. The experience to-date confirms that also in the case of corporates, bonds with negative yields still bear positive interest. As for corporate bonds, it is partly down to a relatively small scale of the negative character of interest rates. Still, their continued reduction by the central banks which translates into offering negative interest for bonds on the primary market may impede the assessment of creditworthiness, with corporate bonds being affected the most (Assenmacher and Krogstrup, 2018). It is because negative interest on corporate bonds means that the issuer will not have to bear financial costs attributable to coupon payments, hence generating funds to this aim. Under such circumstances, particularly in the case of long-term bonds, whether there is a capacity to repay a portion of capital borrowed under the issue of bonds will not be subject to the assessment by market participants. This issue may be defined as a specific characteristic of NIRP and – if materialized – may limit the informational content of market pricing in a form of yield curves. Importantly, this does not refer solely to the corporates but it is also given a broader context, also with respect to treasury bonds (Barr et al., 2016; Eisenschmidt and Smets, 2018; JP Morgan, 2019a).

It should be noted that the aforementioned dependencies chiefly referred to fixed-income type of bonds as they definitely prevailed in this market.[13] However, variable coupon bonds for which negative interest rate is the reference rate may, in theory, yield negative coupon payments in case the issuer's idiosyncratic risk level is relatively low. Notwithstanding, a large portion of companies entering the primary bonds market during NIRP period legally set the lower bound for coupon payments at zero[14]. In addition, the clearing agents make it clear they will not be charging the bond holder (on account of a negative coupon) and transferring the payment to the issuer (JP Morgan, 2019b). However, such a scenario does not mean that if the central banks continue to reduce interest rates, the transmission to business entities' cost via corporate bond market will be limited. There is a prevalent belief that, if necessary, the structure of corporate bond issue may be transformed from fixed (with a zero lower bound) to variable coupons (e.g., Barclays, 2015).

4.1.2.3 Specific Factors of the Bond Market under NIRP Conditions

The question why investors hold bonds with negative yield seems to be what naturally comes out of the observations of the mentioned tendencies. After all, in nominal terms (and in real terms, given the current inflation conditions) they may seem to experience a loss. The question is all the more reasonable given the fact that the lower yield on bonds did not translate into any reduction of investor demand for these securities, both on the secondary and the primary market (HSBC, 2017). Two main reasons behind that can be mentioned here apart from the factors the investors cannot control (the supply factor or the central bank's direct influence through QE). The first one shows that for some entities, profitability is not what counts the most. They include entities which – regardless from the profit motive – will maintain a relatively stable treasury bond portfolio: (i) central banks which, notwithstanding monetary policy goals and the yield on bonds will try to keep a diversified geographical structure of foreign currency reserves, (ii) pension funds which purchase long-term securities so as to align the maturities with their liabilities, (iii) commercial banks – so as to meet, *inter alia*, the regulatory liquidity requirements as well as to provide hedge in certain operations (e.g., with the central bank), and (iv) money market funds – to meet their statutory investment goals.

The second, counterintuitive reason points to the profit motive in line with which – in spite of negative yield on bonds – such an investment remains profitable. As shown before, the investment scope for long-term securities with respect to their yield clearly shrank in the post-crisis period (Figure 4.9). Under such circumstances, the investors who are reasonable and maximize their rate of return on investment have in fact two scenarios to choose from: to search for more profitable investments (which carry a markedly higher risk than in the pre-crisis period) or to retain the safe asset and manage it more actively for higher return. Importantly, the return on such investment in bonds can be analysed from three perspectives: (i) the rate of return in the term to maturity, which is equated with a yield on bond (ii) total rate of return or (iii) total rate of return on hedged investment.[15]

Analysing the second of the aforementioned rates of return, it should be noted that it can be decomposed into two elements – one associated with interest payments and the other with valuation change. In this case, the price component is very important as investment horizon for a majority of investors is shorter than the term to bond maturity.[16] Thus, in contrast to yield, in the present macroeconomic environment translating into a significant rise in treasury bond prices worldwide (see, e.g., Figure 4.14), the price component represents the major portion of the total rate of return on investment. Consequently, and in spite of negative yields, this rate of return remains positive across numerous NIRP economies (JP Morgan, 2019a). It means that an investor who purchases negative yield bond and sells it when the yield becomes even more negative, attains in fact a positive rate of return on account of the price component.[17] In addition, whenever negative yield bond is a foreign investment and the investor is not hedged against FX risk, it is also the appreciation premium that matters a lot for the total rate of return (Kowalewski, 2014; Hameed and Rose, 2016).[18] It should also be noted that the price component of the rate of return is of relevance mainly for short- and medium-term investors, while negative yield on bonds remains the main risk factor for long-term investors, such as pension funds and insurance companies.

In turn, the profit from a hedged foreign investment in a bond should be perceived from the perspective of domestic investment's profit. In such an approach, profit lends itself to being split into: (i) the component of the difference between the direct interest income and the cost of financing the investment position (so-called *carry*) and (ii) the component of a change in valuation as the term to maturity shortens (so-called *roll*). Since bonds offering negative yield typically carry low credit risk and a low susceptibility to a change of market perceptions, the influence of the latter component remains relatively stable over time. This factor boosts the demand for this

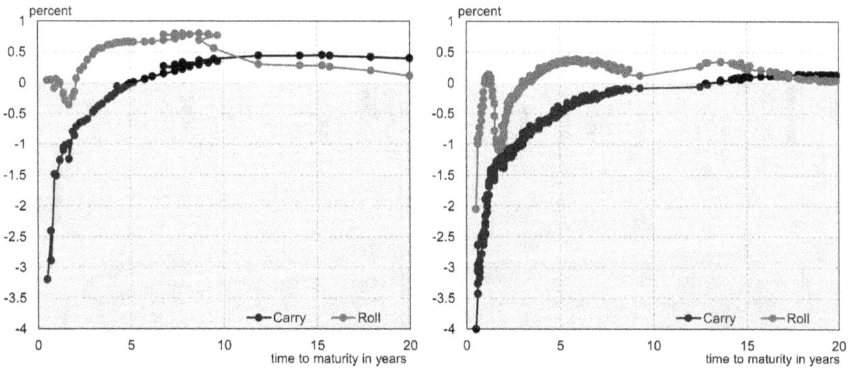

Figure 4.11 Decomposition of investment return on German (left panel) and US (right panel) sovereign bonds into a roll and hedged carry components

Note: Calculations based on all publicly traded sovereign bonds (as of August 2019) for an annual investment position, in line with the methodology proposed by Koijen et al., (2018). *Carry* refers to return that arises from the convergence of spot yield curve to that implied by forward rate, while *roll* represents the return that arises from to moving over the yield curve as time elapses.

Source: Own calculations based on Bloomberg data.

bond type, be it in relation to risk factors which offer a positive rate of return, yet at a higher risk and portfolio value being volatility-susceptible.

In order to portray the logic of the above argumentation, an econometric decomposition of return on investment in treasury bonds has been conducted along with contrasting the metrics for negative and positive yields (Figure 4.11).[19] The analysis shows that an investment in short-term bond comes at a nominal loss, yet a similar situation takes place (as a result of relatively higher investment financing costs) also in the case of economies with positive interest rates. It follows that, from international perspective, a short-term investment in debt securities, whether in the environment of negative or positive interest rates, offers the investors a relatively similar return. Simultaneously, investing in long-term bonds provides a foreign investor with a positive and a higher rate of return versus a corresponding security with a similar risk quoted with a positive yield. Summing up the considerations on the profit motive of investments in treasury bonds prevalent among NIRP economies, it should be noted that, in spite of negative yields, they still generate a positive rate of return for both hedged and non-hedged investment positions, with price component being a material factor.

Ultimately, risk hedging motive may be identified as the third reason behind investing in bonds in spite of their negative yield. It is particularly pointed out that in the environment of secular stagnation, entities treat treasury bonds not as a form of investment, but rather as a hedge against long-term uncertainty. Consequently, the entities are willing to accept a

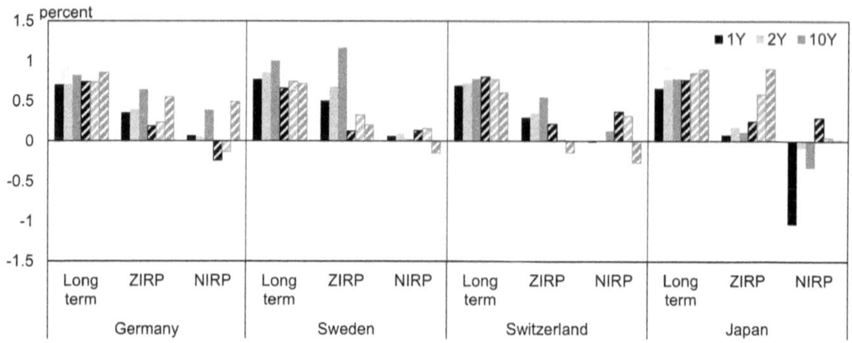

Figure 4.12 Impact of key economic data releases on sovereign bond yields differentiated by rates regimes

Note: For Germany, ZIRP period denotes X.2008-VI.2014, for Sweden: VII.2009-II.2015, for Switzerland: XII.2008-I.2015 and for Japan: IV.2013-II.2016. Estimates for daily data frequency (filled columns) and for monthly frequency (striped columns)

Source: Own work based on Bloomberg data and Fatum et al., (2019) methodology.

nominal loss which is relatively minor versus the assets hedged (Fletcher, 2019; The Economist, 2019). The aforesaid motive of hedging may play an important role also in the context of macroeconomic risk. Namely, one essential characteristic of the yield on bonds in the economies under scrutiny during NIRP comes to the surface. For all the economies in question, the immediate reaction to the publication of macroeconomic data is markedly less pronounced that in the long term as well as in case of positive, albeit low interest rates (Figure 4.12). Thus, another observation may be added to the conclusion referred to earlier on in that the environment of negative interest rates "rigidifies" the macroeconomic component of yield curve while the monetary policy being communicated directly gains in importance.

Summing up the analyses of the bond market in the context of NIRP, it seems natural to ask whether the factor of NIRP introduction is a prerequisite for negative bond yield to emerge. The phenomenon of negative yields for short-term treasury debt instruments under the conditions of positive central banks' interest rates was first recorded in Japan, right at the very end of the last century (Kowalewski, 2014), and nowadays, including the eurozone during the sovereign debt crisis (Figure 4.13).[20] In the latter case, the phenomenon was due to increased demand on the part of financial markets' participants and was not directly attributable to the central bank's actions. It may suggest that NIRP is not a prerequisite for negative yields to affect the financial markets, still it is necessary that at least one of the following conditions is met: (i) so that the level of the yield is conspicuously negative, (ii) so that it is observable, at least in medium term or (iii) so that negative yields are also observable for long-term instruments.

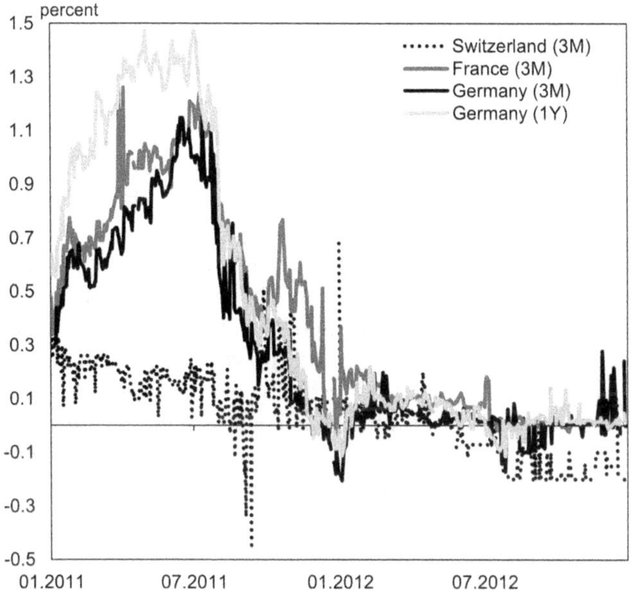

Figure 4.13 Selected yields in pre-NIRP regime
Source: Eikon data.

Figure 4.14 Price of selected longest-term sovereign bonds in the euro area (as a percentage of nominal value)

On the other hand, potential for contributing to a speculative bubble is viewed as one of *ex-ante* risks arising from the introduction of NIRP. Normally, however, such a risk is identified in the context of stock or real estate prices. Still, the debate among investment banks is increasingly pointing out that the bond market, especially long term, starts to show the hallmarks of a speculative bubble (see, e.g., Claeys, 2016; Horne, 2019; JP Morgan, 2019a; Bloomberg, 2019). It particularly refers to the price criterion for the assessment of how the phenomenon developed.[21] The importance of this phenomenon has been noticeable since the beginning in 2019, chiefly on the treasury bonds market of eurozone economies (Figure 4.14). It is therefore indirectly inferred that NIRP may have contributed to this, especially as the impact from central banks' asset purchase programmes gradually faded during that period. On the other hand, however, it is emphasized that the observed phenomenon does not probably confirm the fundamental criterion to identify a speculative bubble has been met (e.g., JP Morgan, 2019c).[22] It is because there are factors which partly substantiate the negative yields, much as they do not account for the varying change in the prices of long-term bonds separately from medium-term securities.

4.1.3 Stock Market

The monetary policy affects stock market valuation through two major mechanisms. Interest rates' cut translates into expected economy boost and hence higher expected profits and dividends in the corporate sector. Moreover, the discount factor used in the estimated valuation of company theoretical value, thus, the theoretical stock price, goes down (see, e.g., Elton and Gruber, 1998). In the environment of negative interest rates, this mechanism may give rise to irrational conclusions regarding the determination of stock price theoretical value. In order to illustrate this phenomenon with the use of a dividend discount model (DDM), stock prices for the largest European companies have been estimated based on the interest rate level.[23] Their potential change has also been analysed with respect to the theoretical value obtained for an average level of interest rates in the eurozone since the outbreak of the GFC. Such a simulation yielded several important conclusions.

First, a clearly asymmetrical effect of monetary policy on the change in stock valuation is visible depending on the interest rate environment (Figure 4.15). A minor alteration of the interest price alone in the negative rate environment allows to increase company theoretical valuation by 80–100% with unchanged assumption as for the future company financial performance or their dividend stream. In extreme cases, whenever interest rates drop down to heavily negative levels (-5% in this case), even a tenfold rise in company theoretical value ensues.[24] For comparison, in the environment of positive rates, the same absolute level corresponds to a reduction in the company market value by about a half.

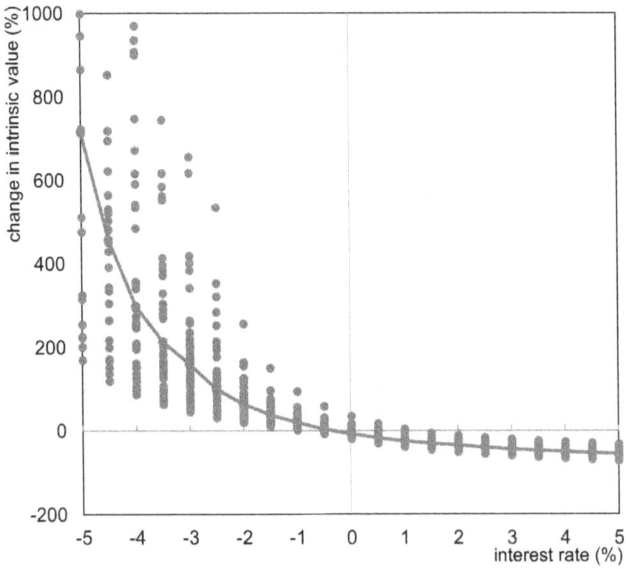

Figure 4.15 Reaction of stock intrinsic value in response to a simulated change in central bank interest rate – a case of European market

Note: Simulation carried out for actual financial data of publicly listed companies that are included in Eurostoxx stock market index; simulation with the use of discounted dividend model (DDM) assumed change of only one specific parameter (risk-free rate) in steps amounting to 25 basis points. Dots represent each company, while solid line denotes median.

Source: Own calculations based on Bloomberg data.

Second, the environments of positive and negative interest rates are told apart by the spread magnitude of the effect on the valuation of respective entities. While in the case of positive rates the dispersion of the risk-free rate effect, *ceteris paribus*, is relatively slight, it rises significantly under NIRP (Figure 4.15).[25] It suggests that with negative interest rates the consequences of monetary policy impact on the economic environment are difficult to estimate. This, in turn, translates into higher uncertainty in business operations.[26] It particularly holds for the valuation of financial sector companies whose potential to generate positive cash flow in NIRP environment may be weaker. Therefore, it can be expected that the change of market valuation of these entities in negative interest rates' environment will differ from that for the non-financial sector (Jobst and Lin, 2016). Moreover, while the impact of negative interest rates on the banking sector may vary under the monetary policy pursued, e.g., with the use of direct cost burden levelling (*tiering*), such a mechanism does not apply for other than non-financial sector stock valuation. As a result, also in the case of stock market (just as for the debt instrument market), the mechanism of assessing the actual risk as early as per entity is supposedly disrupted.

Notwithstanding the above model relations, the character of the monetary policy impulse in NIRP environment observed in the experience of the central banks under scrutiny has remained expansionary and supporting companies' market valuation (Figure 4.15). As the change in interest rate level was a relatively small alteration, the scale of valuation reactions did not vary much from that observed historically for positive rates environment.

4.1.4 Exchange Rates

Taking into account NIRP's particular character, the exchange rate channel may be one of the key channels of its impact on the real economy, particularly from the global perspective. Lower interest rates contribute to a decline in return on risk-weighed investments in domestic assets and they may, as a result, encourage investors to relocate capital abroad, which fosters exchange rate weakening. On the one hand, weaker exchange rate bolsters exports by improving price competitiveness, though it drives up the prices of imported goods (e.g., Chmielewski et al., 2018). It should be emphasized, however, that for interest price reduction below zero to entail the said "conventional" economic effects, it is necessary that they are smoothly transmitted onto the remaining interest rates in the economy. As mentioned before, the experience of NIRP economies to-date shows that the changes of central

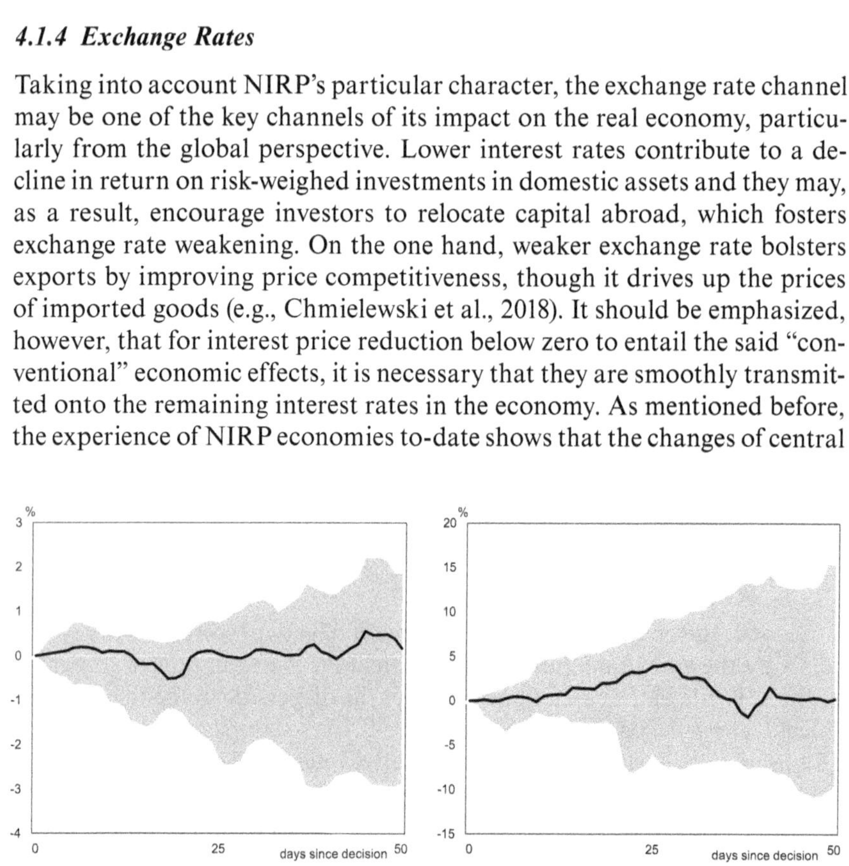

Figure 4.16 Cumulative change in nominal effective exchange rate (left panel) and main stock market index (right panel) since the lowering of central banks' interest rates in NIRP environment

Note: Solid black line denotes median for the cumulative change in the case of 17 monetary policy decisions in Denmark, Sweden, Switzerland, Japan and the euro area (Germany) during period of NIRP policy; grey area indicates range between 10th and 90th percentiles of mentioned changes; for NEER, increase means appreciation of local currency; for stock market representation, MSCI indices are employed.

Source: Own work based on Bloomberg data.

bank's rates are still transmitted to short-term rates on the money market. In this way, the central bank upholds its ability to affect the size of rate disparity on the money market in a given economy versus the international markets and, thus, to affect the development of exchange rate.

The experience of the central banks in question shows, however, that the reduction of interest rates below zero across the entire group of central banks under scrutiny had a relatively neutral effect in short term on the exchange rate (Figure 4.16). However, what should be emphasized is that the effect of NIRP varied across the economies. It proved relatively effective in countering currency appreciation for small open economies such as Denmark or Switzerland. In turn, in the case of large economies (such as the eurozone), the effect of interest rate decline on the exchange rate – including in the context of NIRP – may be weakened by interest rate adjustments in the economy's environment.

4.2 Macroeconomic Effects of NIRP

The above considerations should also be given a broader, macroeconomic context. However, the assessment of macroeconomic consequences, next to difficulties to identify common tendencies, is yet additionally impeded by delays affecting the monetary policy transmission mechanism. As a result, given the period necessary for economic entities to adapt to the new surroundings, macroeconomic consequences of NIRP have not been markedly reflected in the literature. It is for the same reason that only the most important and directly observable macroeconomic effects will be identified with an important reference to the main topic of this study.

- Cash in Circulation

  The level of cash in circulation in the context of NIRP should undergo a twofold analysis: first, as one of the indicators of risk materializing of the lower bound being reached by nominal interest rates and second, as a structural determinant for NIRP, i.e., a factor which enables broadening the scope of negative interest rates.

  With respect to the first issue, it should be noted that so far negative interest rates have not been observed to give rise to a sharp increase of cash in circulation. Even in the case of Denmark where interest on deposit for financial institutions and non-financial entities was pushed down below zero, the rise in the use of cash was only moderate (Figure 4.17). Concomitantly, the experience of Switzerland may show that the said effect did take place. Namely, immediately after the introduction of NIRP, the dynamics of cash in circulation accelerated along with a change in its structure, i.e., with a sharp rise in the number of highly denominated banknotes in circulation (UBS, 2016). Much as ultimately this effect

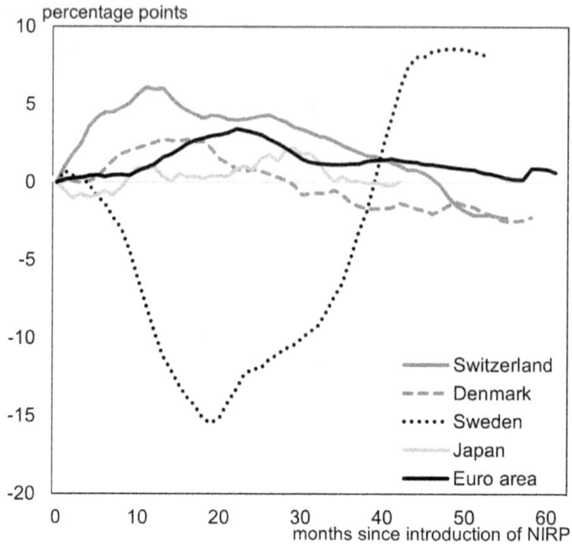

Figure 4.17 Cumulative change in growth of cash in circulation since the introduction of NIRP in respective countries

Note: Positive values in the left figure indicate acceleration of growth rate of cash in circulation as compared to the dynamics observed when NIRP was introduced – negative values indicate slowdown.

Source: central banks data, own calculations.

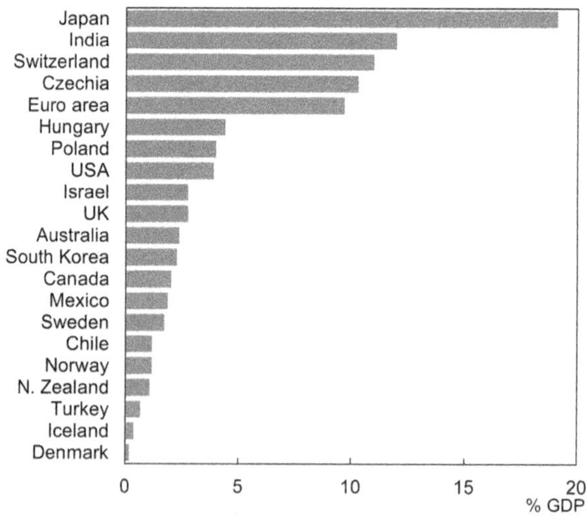

Figure 4.18 Currency in circulation in selected economies

Note: Positive values in the left figure indicate acceleration of growth rate of cash in circulation as comparing to the dynamics observed when NIRP was introduced; respectively – negative values indicate slowdown.

Source: central banks data, own calculations.

faded, it persisted in medium term. At the same time, judging by the relative level of cash in circulation, Switzerland was also an economy with relatively most difficult structural determinants as regards the introduction of NIRP (Figure 4.18).[27]

- Household Savings

  The impact of NIRP on savings in the economy, especially households, is ambiguous and it arises from two counteracting mechanisms. The first one identifies a negative dependence between the interest rate level and the savings rate. As a result, NIRP environment should work to reduce the level of savings (versus income). On the other hand, however, low interest rates may give rise to, quite paradoxically, higher savings. Amid very low interest on deposits and a low rate of return on relatively safe assets, it is necessary to increase current savings to provide for a fixed-income stream in the future (e.g., at retirement). In addition, in the environment of negative interest rates, the effect of the second mechanism intensifies as a result of the monetary policy itself affecting the financial sector. The fact that the central bank's rates are not fully transmitted to the interest on households' deposits (in comparison to interest on loans) exerts pressure on the banks' interest income in the environment of NIRP. Such an asymmetry of NIRP transmission

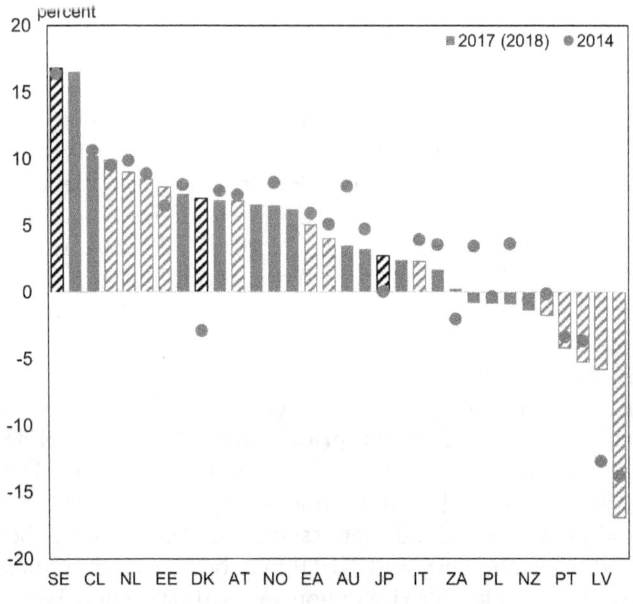

Figure 4.19 Household saving rates in selected economies

Note: Saving rate is defined as the percentage of disposable personal income that a person prefers to save rather than spend on consumption; striped columns indicate selected NIRP economies.

Source: OECD data.

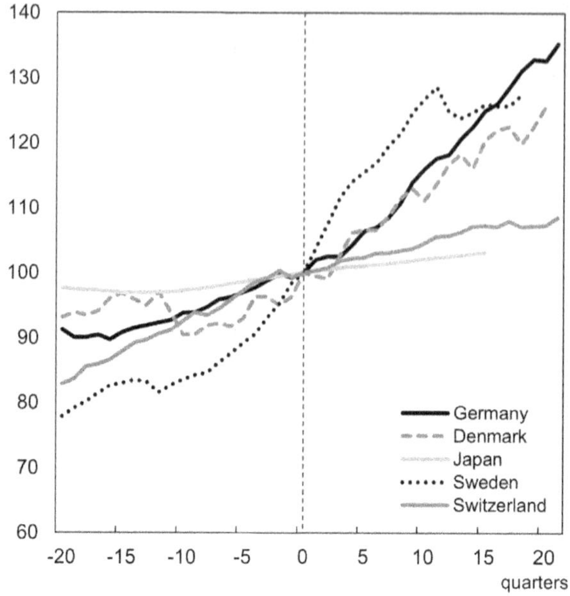

Figure 4.20 Residential property prices in NIRP countries
Note: Introduction of NIRP = 100.
Source: Own calculations based on BIS data.

adds up to the relative attractiveness of deposits versus other investment forms available for households. It may also strengthen the already mentioned economic mechanism of NIRP driving the savings up.[28] Accordingly, the experience to-date of NIRP economies points to a possible balancing of the two identified mechanisms. This can be borne out by the absence of sharp changes in the household saving rate in a large portion of these economies, unjustified by other fundamental factors (Figure 4.19).

- Real Estate Market
  The increase in house prices observed in the NIRP economies is part of the long-term trend present prior to the introduction of negative interest rates; however, in many of them (Sweden, Germany, Denmark), it clearly intensified in this environment (Figure 4.20). On the one hand, it should be borne in mind that assigning a clear causality between the observed price tendency and NIRP may be an oversimplification. It is because the considerable rise in housing real estate may be attributable to structural reasons (for instance, rising demand caused by housing shortage, see Sweden; Aspegren, 2018), to an international factor (e.g.,

real estate prices rising in economies other than NIRP) as well as to the use of other central bank tools rather than negative interest rate policy.[29] On the other hand, though, whatever the causal relationship, the dynamics of housing prices in the environment of negative nominal interest rates has accelerated, both with respect to the earlier periods and other economies with low, albeit positive nominal interest rates.[30]

- Fiscal Policy
  As shown before, cutting central bank's interest rates below zero deepened the decline in treasury bond yield (in many cases the bonds also entered the negative territory). Such a market environment may affect the fiscal policy in NIRP economy via two mechanisms. On the one hand, it may give rise to lower costs of sovereign debt service as well as the scale of necessary fiscal adjustments. It encourages to lessen restrictive (or to deepen the expansionary) character of the fiscal policy. Notwithstanding, the experience of NIRP economies shows that the effect only partly materialized for just some of them (mainly in the eurozone; e.g., Figure 4.21), while in Sweden or Denmark, the scale of fiscal policy's restrictive character broadened in the period NIRP was employed.

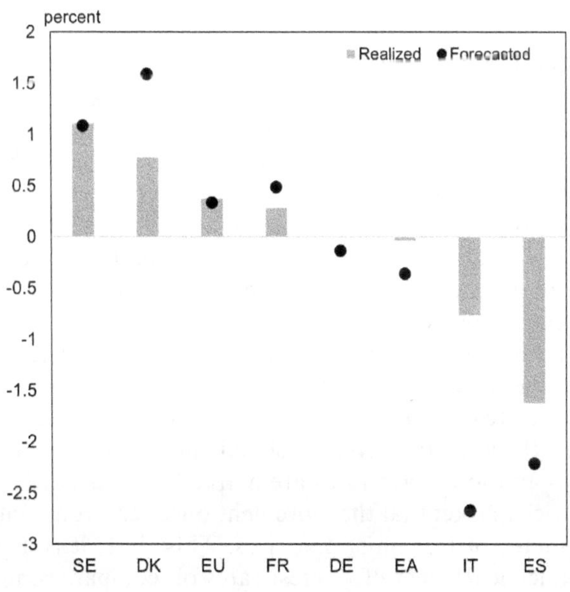

Figure 4.21 Change of fiscal policy position since the introduction of NIRP

Note: Fiscal policy position is approximated by a change in structural primary balance (in relation to potential GDP); positive values indicate more restrictive fiscal policy, negative values – more accommodative. 'Realization' stands for a change since 2014 up to the end of 2019, while 'forecast' indicates projection for 2021.

Source: Own calculations based on Bloomberg and AMECO data.

Such fiscal policy conditions may, by definition, somewhat constrain the macroeconomic effectiveness of NIRP by encouraging the curb on economic growth. On the other hand, though, owing to the aforesaid reduction in treasury bonds yield, the maturity of bonds may be extended, in some economies at a significant scale. In this way, future borrowing needs are reduced or extended over a longer time span. Consequently, the debt-refinancing risk may be mitigated.

Summing up, it should additionally be noted that the above mechanisms are not new tools which emerge in the environment of negative interest rates. They are rather intensified amid low, albeit positive interest rates. Accordingly, their stronger impact may have worked still before NIRP was introduced. It is also the measures taken by central banks along with the negative interest rate policy that may have contributed to these mechanisms arising. Consequently, the dependencies identified in this chapter should be considered the determinants for NIRP analysis in the context of systemic risk presented later on in this book rather than the underlying reasons.

Summary

A review of the NIRP economies' experience shows that in the short term, the transmission of central bank's negative interest rates at the first stage of transmission mechanism (i.e., the interbank market) remained undisturbed. Across all the economies under scrutiny, the interbank rates fully aligned with the changes of central bank's rates, no matter how much the implementation processes varied. The reduction of central banks' interest rates below zero also exacerbated the decline in treasury bonds yield. In many cases, the yields also went down below zero, thus reducing sovereign debt service costs and the scale of necessary fiscal adjustments, particularly in the eurozone. At the same time, however, this market highlights transmission varying between positive and negative interest rates environments. In the former case, changes of the central bank's interest rates mainly concentrate on a short end of yield curve. Conversely, in NIRP environment, as the monetary policy's signalization channel grows stronger, also medium- and long-term rates are markedly adjusted. It is also in the case of the stock market that the aforementioned, environment-dependent, varying character of transmission arises. This time, it is attributed to a clearly asymmetrical effect of interest rates on companies' market valuation. In turn, with respect to the possible unintended consequences of rate cuts, the experience of NIRP economies suggests that the policy has so far not contributed to a strong increase in the amount of cash in circulation, except for the effect observed in Switzerland in the period immediately following the central bank's decision.

The motives guiding the introduction and the effect of NIRP on individual categories analysed in this chapter are captured in Table 4.1.

Table 4.1 An overview of major consequences of negative rates

	Euro area	*Sweden*	*Denmark*	*Switzerland*	*Japan*
Objective of introduction	Support of inflation return to target	Support of inflation return to target	Mitigation of currency appreciation pressure	Support of inflation return to target; mitigation of currency appreciation pressure	Support of inflation return to target
Objective realization assessment	Supportive effect on credit activity and inflation processes, jointly with other central bank activities	Increase of inflation expectations, closure of output gap, support of credit activity	Effective preserve of fixed exchange rate	Increase of inflation expectations; appreciation pressure on currency maintained after the floor abandonment	No inflation pressure, low inflation expectations
Effect on interest rate market	Full transmission to money market rate; compression of term premium (joint effect with QE); parallel shift of yield curve; negative bond yields evidenced	Decline of bond yields but steepening of the yield curve	Full transmission to money market rate	Full transmission to money market rate; entire yield curve evidenced below zero	Full transmission to money market rate; decline of bond yields and flattening of the curve (joint effect with QQE)
Effect on FX market	Currency depreciation, but due to non-NIRP factors	Relative stabilization of exchange rate	Appreciation pressure limited	Appreciation pressure limited, but other factors outweighed the NIRP effect	Potential effect not identified due to the range of other factors
Effect on currency in circulation	Not identified	Not identified	Not identified	Significant acceleration of growth immediately after the NIRP introduction; effect was diminishing over time	Not identified
Other effects	Concerns about banking sector profitability	Not identified	Property prices growth; negative interest on deposits of non-financial sector	Concerns about stability of pension funds and insurance companies; negative interest on deposits of non-financial sector	Concerns about banking sector profitability; decay of liquidity in interbank market

Source: own work based on reports of central banks, IMF and World Bank.

Notes

1 In the case of the euro area, the money market rate is currently anchored to ECB's deposit rate.
2 The liquidity in the interbank market should be distinguished from excess liquidity in the banking sector, at least the level of definitions. The former, like in other segments of financial market, denotes an ease with which an asset or security can be converted into cash without affecting its market price.
3 The literature has defined theoretical problems for transaction settlements in the interbank market, which was originally designed for positive interest rates (see Fleming and Garbade, 2004 – for the case of negative repo rates). In reality, however, such a problem has not been identified for any of NIRP economies (BIS, 2016).
4 Forward guidance is a monetary policy communication strategy that is used to inform the public about the likely future course of monetary policy. It is kind of verbal commitment that is aimed to influence the financial decisions of households, business and financial market investors.
5 Although originally, when the NIRP was introduced, a widely spread scepticism and uncertainty dominated, in particular, with respect to the transmission of negative rates to longer horizons than short-term money market rates (see, e.g., Barclays, 2015).
6 With respect to the transmission of central bank negative rates to the bond yields in Japan, it should be noted that other monetary policy tool counteracts this effect. Namely, the Bank of Japan has introduced a framework of yield curve controlling, under which a greater deviation from 0% than ±20 bps (or ±10 bps till July 2018) is not allowed.
7 This period should be associated with two important factors – with significant rise in market risk aversion and with strengthening of market expectations on further easing of monetary policy by major central banks (JP Morgan, 2019b).
8 At the point of NIRP introduction, negative yields on corporate bonds were perceived as 'highly unlikely' (e.g., Barclays, 2015).
9 ECB was buying corporate bonds under its CSPP (ang. Corporate Sector Purchase Programme) from June 2016 until end of 2018. However, the overall amount of securities bought was relatively small as compared to the size of the market as well as to the portfolio of sovereign bonds purchased (Santis et al., 2018).
10 As of first quarter of 2019, Bank of Japan held as much as 46.3% of all issued Japanese governmental bonds (Morgan Stanley, 2016).
11 Interestingly however, the mentioned correlation can be easily evidenced with respect to ECB's monetary policy, but – unlike the geographical concentration would suggest – not with respect to monetary policy of Bank of Japan
12 The zero lower bound for cash flow payments arises to a greater extent from market practices rather than from economic limitations (HSBC, 2018).
13 According to the Bloomberg data, about 96% of all outstanding sovereign bonds and about 80% of corporate bonds are issued as fixed coupon securities (as the end of 2019).
14 About 40% of all bonds issued in 2016–2018 have a contractual guarantee on non-negative coupon payments (HSBC, 2018)
15 Yield to maturity (YTM) should not be equated with return on investment in bonds. There are at least three reasons. First, the former implies that the investment position will be held to maturity. Such an approach enables comparison with, e.g., bank deposit but does not account for a price component of a bond, particularly important when the holding horizon is shorter than the maturity. Second, the former assumes that the coupon payments are reinvested at the yield that equals to YTM. This might be difficult to achieve, particularly in a changing interest rate environment over the long-term investment horizon. Third,

although the former takes into account the credit component of investment, it simultaneously assumes that all payments are made in full; thus, no credit event takes place (see more in Fabozzi, 2000, 2015).

16 Moreover, due to the greater effectiveness of the signalling channel after crossing zero lower bound, the speculative aspects of an investment in bonds have also gained in importance (BoAML, 2019) and were evidenced in the shortening of an investment horizon of such.

17 On the basis of a hypothetical example, 1-year investment in 10-year bond at spot rate of -0.1% that ends at rate of −0.4% will bring a return on investment of 2.6% (ceteris paribus).

18 This premium assumes a depreciation of currency in which bond was issued, which might arise due to the economic factors (e.g., further easing of monetary policy) or risk factors (e.g., risk of bankruptcy). Regardless of the causes, this translates into an effective rise in the expected return on investment.

19 Due to a relatively small number of issued bonds by other NIRP economies (i.e., Denmark, Sweden, Switzerland), comparable estimates cannot be conducted for them. Thus, the described findings, yet probably appropriate for other NIRP economies, should not be directly assigned to them.

20 More information about eurozone debt crises can be found, e.g., in NBP (2013).

21 A price-driven criterion for an identification of asset bubble assumes a rapid and continuous rise in asset prices that create expectations of further continuity of such a dynamic (Kindleberger, 1999).

22 A fundamental criterion for an identification of asset bubble points that the price dynamics is not associated with a change in fundamental characteristics

23 In DDM models, risk-free rate (alongside the risk premium) is a major component of discount rate employed to calculation of intrinsic value of future cash flows.

24 This impact in some cases was evidenced to be even stronger; however, due to the axis scaling, it was not presented in the figure.

25 For the analysed extreme scenario, this range amounts to around 50% for positive interest rates environment and as much as about 3500% for NIRP environment.

26 Interestingly, the conducted simulations pointed that the impact of negative rates is weaker for riskier entities (i.e., those with greater risk premium).

27 Eurozone was characterized by a relatively high share of cash in circulation, in particular, higher than in Denmark or Sweden. This might suggest that the lower bound for nominal rates is greater in that particular economy.

28 This mechanism might be evidenced even despite the fact that negative interest rates for households with mortgages might indicate lower credit payments and thus greater disposable income. In the long run, however, such policy might translate into heightened demand for mortgages, a rise in property prices and finally lower disposable income.

29 In some of NIRP economies, the heightened demand for residential and commercial properties arose from searching for yield activity and instability of the stock market (see JP Morgan, 2016).

30 The problem of rising prices of residential properties was pointed out by the European Systemic Risk Board in 2019 (see, e.g., ESRB, 2019).

Bibliography

Altavilla, C., Carboni, G., Motto, R., (2015). *Asset Purchase Programmes and Financial Markets: Lessons from the Euro Area*, Technical report, ECB Working Paper.

Anderson, R., Baba, C., Danielsson, J., Das, U.S., Kang, H., Segoviano, M., (2018). *Macroprudential Stress Tests and Policies: Searching for Robust and Implementable Frameworks*, IMF Working Paper no. 18/197.

Aspegren, H., (2018). *Sweden's Housing Market: Structural Challenges*, DG Economic and Financial Affairs European Commission, 23 October.

Assenmacher, K., Krogstrup, S., (2018). *Monetary Policy with Negative Interest Rates: Decoupling Cash from Electronic Money*, IMF Working Papers 18/191, International Monetary Fund.

Barclays, (2015). *A Brave New (Negative Yield) World*, Credit Research, European Credit Focus, 8 May.

Barr, M., Kasman, B., Mackie, D., (2016). *Negative Policy Rates: The Bound is Lower than You Think*, Special Report, JP Morgan, 9 February.

Barth, M., Davies, Z., Pascual, A., G., Keller, C., Maraffino, G., (2016). *Negative Ascent: Life amid Negative Nominal Interest Rates. Equity Gilts Study*, Barclays, 3 March.

Bech, M., Makhozov, A., (2016). *How Have Central Banks Implemented Negative Policy Rates?* BIS Quarterly Review.

BIS, (2016). *Quarterly Review*, Bank for International Settlements, March.

Bloomberg, (2019). *This Might Be the Bond Market's Dot-Com Moment*, John Authers, 8 August.

BoAML, (2019). *NIRP manias are back. The European Credit Strategist*, Bank of America Merill Lynch, investment note, 4 April.

Bottero, M., Minoiu, C., Peydro, J.L., Polo, A., Presbitero, A., Sette, E., (2019). *Negative Monetary Policy Rates and Portfolio Rebalancing: Evidence from Credit Register Data*, IMF Working Papers 19/44, International Monetary Fund.

Chmielewski, T., Kapuściński, M., Kocięcki, A., Łyziak, T., Przystupa, J., Stanisławska, E., Wróbel, E., (2018). *Monetary transmission mechanism in Poland. What do we know in 2017?* NBP Working Papers no 286, Narodowy Bank Polski.

Claeys, G., (2016). *Low Long-term Rates: Bond Bubble or Symptom of Secular Stagnation?* Policy Contribution, no. 15.

De Groot, O., Haas, A., (2018). *The Signaling Channel of Negative Interest Rates*, Unpublished manuscript. [available online: http://www.europarl.europa.eu/cmsdata/153241/DIW_final.pdf]

Draghi, M., (2017). *Press Conference Introductory Statement. Introductory Statement at ECB Press Conference*, Frankfurt am Main, 27 April.

EC, (2017). Quarterly Report on the Euro Area (QREA), European Commission's Institutional Paper, vol. 16, no. 3.

Eisenschmidt, J., Smets, F., (2018). Negative Interest Rates: Lessons from the Euro Area, Presentation at *XXI Annual conference of the Central Bank of Chile*, forthcoming.

Elton, E.J, Gruber, M.J., (1998). *Nowoczesna teoria portfelowa i analiza papierów wartościowych*, WIG-Press, Warszawa. [available only in Polish]

ESRB, (2019). *ESRB Issues Five Warnings and Six Recommendations on Medium-term Residential Real Estate Sector Vulnerabilities*, 23 September.

Fabozzi, F.J., (2000). *Rynek obligacji: analiza i strategie*, Wydawnictwo WIG-Press.

Fabozzi, F.J., (2015). *The Handbook of Fixed Income Securities*, 7th Edition, McGraw-Hill.

Fatum, R., Hara, N., Yamomato, Y., (2019). *Negative Interest Policy Rate and the Influence of Macroeconomic News on Yields*, Institute for Monetary and Economic Studies, Bank of Japan, Discussion Paper no. 2019-E-2.

Fleming, M.J., Garbade, K.D., (2004). *Repurchase Agreements with Negative Interest Rates*, Current Issues in Economics and Finance, Federal Reserve Bank of New York, vol. 10, no. 5.

Fletcher, L., (2019). How Hedge Funds are Thriving in a World of Negative-yielding Debt, *Financial Times*, 15 August.

Gambetti, L., Musso, A., (2017). *The Macroeconomic Impact of the ECB's Expanded Asset Purchase Programme (APP)*, Working Paper 2075, European Central Bank, Frankfurt.

Hameed, A., Rose, A.K., (2016). *Exchange Rate Behavior with Negative Interest Rates: Some Early Negative Observations*, CEPR Discussion Paper No. 11498.

Horne, P., (2019). Investors Need to be Aware of the Other Bond Bubble, *Financial Times*, 21 June.

HSBC, (2017). *Rates Today. Stuck with Negative Yields*, HSBC Global Research, Fixed Income Rates, 11 April.

HSBC, (2018). *Credit Telegram. Negative Yields, Negative Coupons*, Investment note, HSBC Global Research, 19 March.

IMF, (2017). *Negative Interest Rate Policies – Initial Experiences and Assessments*, IMF Policy Paper.

Jobst, A., Lin, H., (2016). *Negative Interest Rate Policy: Implications for Monetary Transmission and Bank Profitability in the Euro Area*, IMF Working Paper WP/16/172.

JP Morgan, (2016). *Flows & Liquidity: The Unintended Consequences of Very Negative Rates*, investment note, 24 February.

JP Morgan, (2019a). *ECB: Is a Tiered Reserve Charging System an Option?* Europe Economic Research, 20 February.

JP Morgan, (2019b). *Flows & Liquidity, Negative Rates Are Neither Necessary Nor Unavoidable*, Global Markets Strategy, JP Morgan, investment note, 16 August.

JP Morgan, (2019c). *The Limits to Japanization as a Global Investment Theme. Nine presumptions Worth Rethinking.* Investment report, 30 July.

JP Morgan, (2019d). *Negative Yield Index Monitor*, Global Index Research, 12 September 2019.

Kindleberger, Ch., (1999). *Szaleństwo, panika, krach. Historia kryzysów finansowych*, WIG, Warszawa. [available only in Polish]

Koijen, R., Moskowitz, T., Pedersen, L.H., Vrugt, E., (2018). Carry, *Journal of Financial Economics*, vol. 127, pp. 197–225.

Kowalewski, P., (2014). Ujemne stopy procentowe to nic nowego. *Obserwator finansowy*, 17 March. [available only in Polish].

Morgan Stanley, (2016). *BoJ Surprise: Implications for Macro, Equities, Fixed Income and Foreign Exchange. Japan Economics and Strategy*, investment note, 29 January.

NBP, (2013). *Kryzys w strefie euro. Przyczyny, przebieg i perspektywy jego rozwiązania*, Narodowy Bank Polski. [available only in Polish]

Rostagno, M., Altavilla, C., Carboni, G., Lemke, W., Motto, R., Guilhem, A.S., Yiangou, J., (2019). *A Tale of Two Decades: The ECB's Monetary Policy at 20*, ECB Working Paper Series, no. 2346.

Santis, R., Geis, A., Juskaite, A., Vaz Cruz, L., (2018). *The Impact of the Corporate Sector Purchase Programme on Corporate Bond Markets and the Financing of Euro Area Non-financial Corporations*, ECB Economic Bulletin, nr. 3/2018.

Szpunar, P., (2000). *Polityka pieniężna. Cele i warunki skuteczności*, Polskie Wydawnictwo Ekonomiczne.

Tan, G., (2019). *Beyond the Zero Lower Bound: Negative Policy Rates and Bank Lending*, DNB Working Paper no. 649.

The Economist, (2019). As Yields Turn Negative, Investors are Having to Pay for Safety, *The Economist*, 8 August 2019.

UBS, (2016). *Global Macro Strategy. Switzerland Looking Up*, investment note, 4 March.

Woodford, M., (1999). *Optimal Monetary Policy Inertia*, NBER Working Paper Series, nr 7261.

5 Financial Sector and Negative Interest Rate Policy

5.1 Channels of NIRP Impact on the Banking Sector

One of the fundamental risk categories identified in the previous chapters is a deterioration of the banking sector's condition. The risk itself may be traced back to the negative nominal interest rate policy and it may be one of the threats to financial stability.[1] The literature on monetary policy impact (more precisely, interest rate policy) on the banking sector's profitability provides evidence that a positive and relevant interplay does exist (Genay and Podjasek, 2014; Alessandri and Nelson, 2015; Busch and Memmel, 2015; Borio et al., 2017; Claessens et al., 2017). It shows that the rise in the central bank's interest rates (which may additionally give rise to a larger scale of long-term rates) drives the bank's short-term profitability viewed through the lens of interest profitability. Concomitantly, in analysing environment effect on this sector, low interest rates in particular, the literature attests to profitability erosion observed as interest rates go down and as they remain relatively low over a longer time-span (Bikker and Vervliet, 2017). It should be emphasized, however, that in the case of relatively low interest rates, the vulnerability of the banking sector's profitability to their subsequent changes is non-linear. That is to say, it intensifies as interest rates go down while it is the net interest margin that remains the main factor of the central bank's interest rates transmission to the banks' overall profitability (Borio et al., 2017). Notwithstanding, empirical experience shows that some banks (e.g., American entities) are able to restrain the adverse effect by growing other than interest income (Bikker and Vervliet, 2017). In addition, also the reaction of credit dynamics to interest rates decline is getting increasingly weaker as the zero lower bound draws closer (Borio and Gambacorta, 2017), with the bank's risk tolerance to increase (Delis and Kouretas, 2011). Consequently, the literature emphasizes that a lengthy period of the banks' low profitability in low interest rate environment impedes their capacity for capital accumulation necessary to cover potential future losses (Claessens et al., 2017). In this way, the entities become more vulnerable to shocks arising from macroeconomic disruptions, including those monetary policy generates.

DOI: 10.4324/9781003312116-5

Based on literature, NIRP transmission to the banking sector may be expected to employ channels similar to those applicable for low, yet positive interest rates. It should be emphasized, however, that in the environment of negative nominal interest rates, commercial banks may take up or intensify measures to-date aiming to contain the potentially adverse effect on their profitability. Such measures include first and foremost: higher lending volume or reducing interest costs (Scheiber et al., 2016), increasing interest on loans or the central bank's changes in interest rates not being fully transmitted to commercial lending (Sääskilahti, 2018), higher margin and fees or engaging in more risky and, thus, potentially more profitable investments (Heider et al., 2017; Albertazzi et al., 2018) or operating costs reduction. What is more, lower profitability of banks may not be purely an aftermath of NIRP as it emerged in the environment of low, still positive, interest rates (Borio and Gambacorta, 2017). What is interesting is that some empirical studies show that this phenomenon (e.g., in the eurozone) did not intensify in negative interest environment at all (Horvath et al., 2018).

Still, it is difficult to provide a clear-cut assessment of negative interest rates affecting the financial sector (banking in particular) for a number of reasons. First, negative interest rates are accompanied by other central banks' measures which do have an effect on the standing of commercial banks, including their profitability. Second, the effect varies on several levels, including the bank-specific characteristics (such as business model, type of business operations, policy regarding interest rates transmission, structure of fees and commissions, structure and quality of assets and liabilities, size of equity) as well as country-specific traits. Third, negative interest rates impact banks' income statement not only (albeit mainly) via interest income but also the profit or loss on the sales of financial assets or their revaluation.

Notwithstanding the above factors, however, there are some main channels passing NIRP influence to the banking sector. In the broadest terms, they may be classified as indirect and direct, i.e., for which adjustment mechanisms are necessary or not, accordingly (see Figure 5.1).

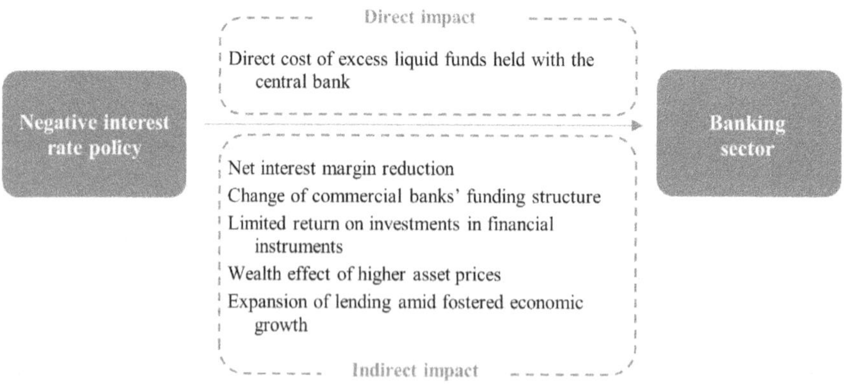

Figure 5.1 Channels of possible NIRP impact on the banking sector
Source: Own work.

- Direct burden of the cost of excess liquid funds held with the central bank (Basten and Mariathasan, 2018; Demiralp et al., 2019) – commercial banks which deposit their excess liquidity with the central bank in case the interest rate on reserves is negative are required to pay interest to the central bank. If the excess liquidity is relatively non-substantial, so may the direct burden be modest. However, in case the scale of excess liquidity grows markedly (e.g., as an aftermath of central banks' non-standard activity in a form of purchase of financial assets), the scale of the said burden on the banking sector will considerably grow.
- Net interest margin reduction – in the NIRP environment commercial banks may be inclined to holding household deposits on other than negative levels, which – paired with the adjustment (i.e., reduction) in credit interest to the changes of central bank's rates – may contribute to pushing a pressure on interest income and may entail lower net interest margin and the banking sector's profitability likewise (Bech and Makhozov, 2016; Heider et al., 2017). This channel is of major importance particularly for banks with a large variable interest rate credit portfolio.
- Change of commercial banks' funding structure – low interest on deposits may encourage the savers to move their funds to other assets, which would give rise to a lower growth dynamic (or even a lower size) of the deposit base, that is, a change in the banks' funding structure aiming to increase the share of the less stable market funding.
- Limited income from investments in financial instruments amid negative yield on treasury bonds – although this mechanism works also for very low (still positive) interest rates, the introduction of NIRP may be expected to further intensify it. It is because bringing interest rates below zero contributes to the yield on treasury bonds reaching negative levels. Thus, the range of available, relatively low-risk assets with positive rates of return shrinks, particularly for entities with a long-term investment horizon. Under such circumstances, banks and other financial institutions increase their exposure in assets with positive rates of return, albeit carrying higher risk.
- Wealth effect of higher asset prices – unlike the medium-term effect of the said factor, in the short-term NIRP – due to its expansionary character – directly supports the market valuation of financial assets in the portfolio of both banks and non-financial entities. It follows that, in the banks' case, it may build up the sector's capital base, while in the second case (via the macroeconomic wealth channel), it indirectly boosts creditworthiness of entities which hold specific financial instruments in their portfolios.
- Expansion of lending amid fostered economic growth – by lowering credit cost, NIRP also bolsters demand for credit (for both consumption and investment purposes) on the part of non-financial entities and households; thus, it fosters economic growth in the medium term.

5.2 Direct Effect of Negative Interest Rates on the Banking Sector

The first stage of transmitting negative interest rates to the banking system should, as in the positive rates' case, take account of the direct cost of short-term deposit or loan (typically, the overnight standing facilities) for the commercial bank. Such funds derive, on the one hand, from the interbank market (at market rates) or the central bank offering a deposit or a loan bearing interest set by the bank at a higher or lower interest rate. As central banks' deposit rates go down below zero followed by interbank rates behaving accordingly, depositing excess funds above the minimum reserve (i.e., excess liquidity of the banking sector[2]) comes with an additional direct cost charged to the entire banking sector the distribution of which among the individual banks varies (Pyka, 2010; Pietryka, 2016)[3].

It needs to be emphasized that, unlike other mechanisms with an indirect impact, the mechanism of negative interest rates directly affecting the banking system will work only when the banking system overflows with liquidity. In the opposite case, the mechanism may be an advantage in the form of a stable and highly liquid investment with the central bank. However, all the economies in which the central banks introduced NIRP did experience or have been experiencing excess liquidity. Although such a monetary policy generates an extra cost for the commercial banks, there is clearly limited room for action in order to reduce it. It is because the scale of excess liquidity cannot lend itself to an easy reduction on a macroeconomic scale as it is a result of medium- and long-term processes in real economy. It means that, at an aggregate level – but for a minor exception mentioned below – effective charging of NIRP cost is independent from the reaction of commercial banks to such a situation (Eisenschmidt and Smets, 2018).[4] In turn, from microeconomic perspective, the phenomenon of negative interest rates creates a so-called *hot potato effect* whereby individual banks attempt to shift a portion of excess liquidity to other commercial banks to reduce their own individual cost (Ryan and Whelan, 2019). In addition, as with the analysis of motives behind holding negative yield treasury bonds, the regulatory framework should also be brought up in this context as being an important factor in accepting the direct cost of a deposit with the central bank (Baldo et al., 2017). In this case, it may be the banks seeking to increase the share of other instruments with higher yield that could limit the scale of a direct effect of NIRP.[5]

By way of applying a multi-level interest system for commercial banks' deposits (tiering), the central banks attempt to reduce NIRP's direct cost and to meet monetary policy goals at the same time. The mechanisms largely varying among the respective central banks employing NIRP were reflected in a like differentiation of effective interest rate charging excess liquidity of the banking sector (Figure 5.2). However, notwithstanding the model employed, the cost is effectively lower than the nominal interest rate across all the central banks using such a mechanism. For comparison, the

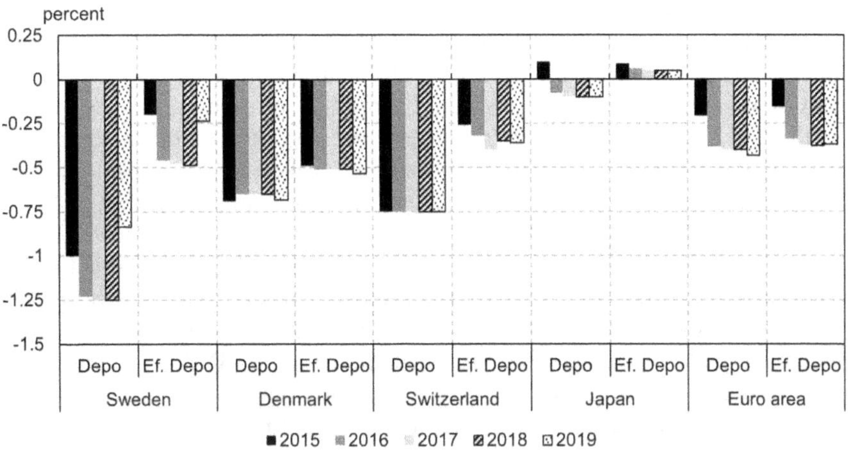

Figure 5.2 Nominal and average effective interest rate on overnight deposit with central banks that implemented NIRP

Note: Effective deposit rate on excess liquidity in the banking sector calculated as a weighted average nominal rates across implemented tiering schemes.

Source: Own calculations based on central banks data.

effective level of the lowest, in nominal terms, deposit rate (Swedish central bank) is comparable with that of other central banks using NIRP, while for ECB – which did not use the differentiation mechanism for most part of the analysed period – both interest rates were practically on the same level.[6] In other words, in spite of markedly different levels of nominal interest rates across NIRP economies, the effective interest rate for deposits with the central bank varies much less (except for Japan). In the case of the Bank of Japan, due to the multi-layered system of interest rates for assets deposited with the central bank, it is possible to maintain the assets' effective interest positive amid the central bank's negative rate and the negative yields of treasury securities (Figure 5.2).[7] Thus, the Japanese banking sector is the only economy classified as one which pursues NIRP, yet does not experience its direct adverse effect via the channel under scrutiny which concerns the interest on excess liquidity with the central bank's account.

In analysing NIRP direct costs, its endogenous character should be noted as well. It would particularly materialize if the introduction of NIRP by the central bank was commonly expected by business entities (including banks) in medium-term perspective. This issue is directly related to the aforesaid multi-level character of the mechanism implementing negative interest on deposits with the central bank. Therefore, if commercial banks were to expect that the deposit with the central bank would be renumerated at negative interest, they could (artificially) affect the funds they hold (on macroeconomic level) in excess of the minimum reserve so that the expected negative interest rate mechanism could – as much as possible – release a given bank from this obligation (i.e., qualify for a zero and non-negative interest group, for instance). In line with the empirical evidence, as the introduction of NIRP was not – partly due to its novelty character – expected, the above situation was not observed, and the distribution of excess liquidity among individual banks in the system right before the decision on negative interest was made did not differ much from the long-term average (Hiroshi, 2018).

The above conclusions imply, however, an important difference with respect to NIRP as opposed to positive interest rate policy. Namely, it is argued in the literature that the impact of the central bank on expectations regarding the future monetary policy adds up to the latter's effectiveness in the monetary transmission mechanism. Thus, the policy is able to reach its goals at a relatively lower cost. Still, in the case of NIRP, this mechanism is distorted at the structural level. It is because raising expectations for NIRP introduction, including as part of central bank communication or forward guidance, could entail lower effectiveness of this policy in real life assuming that the negative interest mechanism will be multi-layered.

As regards the implications for NIRP's direct cost, a clear interaction between two simultaneously employed central bank tools should be noted, that is, between financial asset purchase programme and NIRP. Namely, the first

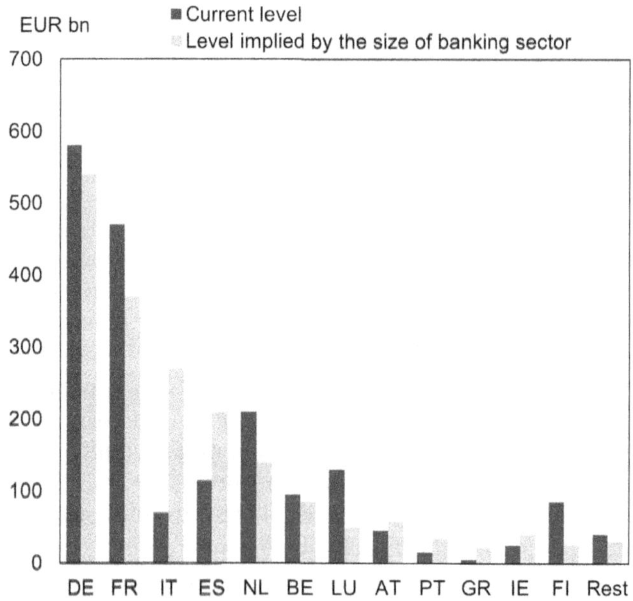

Figure 5.3 Geographical structure of excess liquidity in the banking sector of euro area

Note: The level in proportion to size of the banking sector calculated with respect to annual data for 2019.

Source: ECB, Baldo et al. (2017) and JP Morgan (2019).

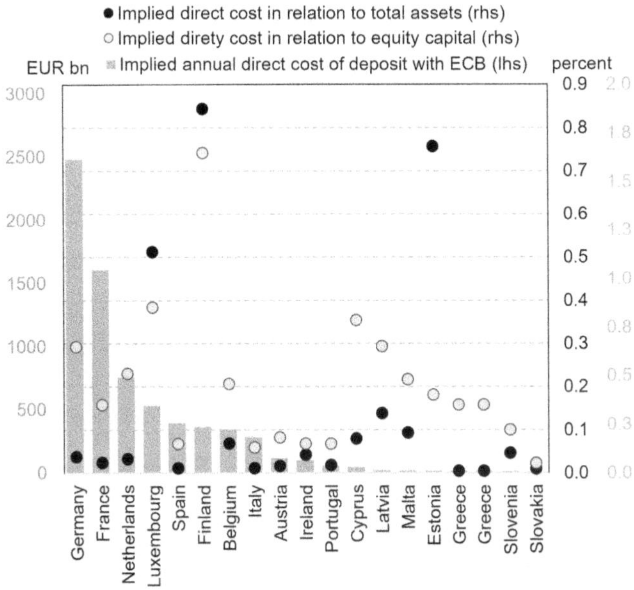

Figure 5.4 Geographical structure of NIRP-caused direct cost for banking sector in the euro area, as implied from the distribution of excess liquidity

Note: Calculations on the basis of average excess liquidity in banking sector for period of 2015–2018 with respect to average sum of assets or net income; we assume that the total excess liquidity is deposited with ECB under no tiering mechanism.

Source: Own calculations, ECB data.

tool affects the scale of excess liquidity in the banking sector, whereas the other has a direct effect on its cost. That is to say that, with limited transmission of these measures to real economy (as the case has been in recent years including the eurozone or the United States), if the asset purchase programme continues, it will only aggravate the direct burden on banking on account of negative interest rate (Altavilla et al., 2018; Figures 5.3 and 5.4).

The European Central Bank has been identified as the only one which did not introduce tiering scheme at the onset of NIRP. However, almost five years after the policy was introduced, in a debate surrounding the future monetary policy of ECB, the issue of introducing a multi-level system for the interest on deposits with the central bank was given much prominence (EBC, 2019a). Given considerable differences in the implementation schemes and thus the direct cost varying among NIRP economies, an attempt to simulate this cost may be made in case a similar mechanism is employed in the eurozone (Figure 5.5). The fundamental principle of tiering holds that all of its construction varieties reduce the direct cost of NIRP for the banking sector. In the case of ECB, such an effect would be important scale-wise both if a mechanism similar to that employed by the central bank

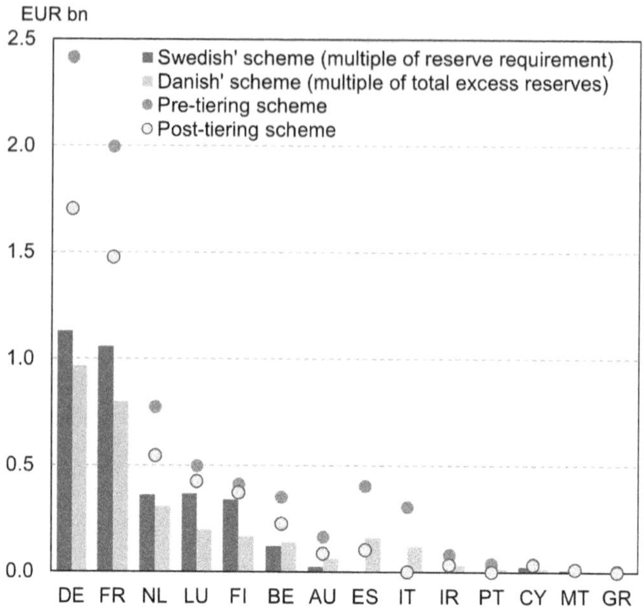

Figure 5.5 Simulated geographical distribution of annual direct cost for banking sector due to deposit with central bank depending on the tiering scheme

Note: For comparability reasons, calculations are made for the ECB deposit rate as of pre-introduction of tiering mechanism; other assumptions as with Figure 4.3.

Source: Own calculations, ECB data.

of Sweden or Denmark came into play. In both cases, the direct cost on an aggregate basis would be approximately cut by half. In absolute terms, this would primarily apply for the major economies (Germany, France). Given the entire eurozone, the Swedish solution effectively gives rise to the lowest aggregate direct cost of NIRP (apart from the model set out by BoJ). The above solutions, however, entail diverse redistribution effects. For the Swedish variant, the direct cost is to a greater extent confined to the largest banking sectors of the eurozone, whereas the opposite effect can be identified for the second of the presented variants (Figure 5.5).

More than five years into NIRP, ECB finally introduced a two-level mechanism of varying the cost of deposit with the central bank which followed, for the most part, the Swedish model. Consequently, the direct cost associated with the central bank's deposit went down across all the eurozone economies, albeit to a lesser extent than a similar mechanism employed to deal with the experience of other NIRP would have suggested (Figure 5.5). Once the mechanism was introduced, the said cost clearly declined for the banking sectors of peripheral economies (Spain, Italy). Still, definitely most of the cost – as in the period before the differentiation mechanism – remained confined to the banking sectors of the eurozone's major economies.

Accordingly, it should also be mentioned that in the empirical literature analysing the direct effect of NIRP on the banking sector the level of excess liquidity in banking is used to discriminate between the effect of this tool alone and that of the central bank's other tools used simultaneously (Demiralp et al., 2019). It is because, in microeconomic terms, banks which do not hold excess liquidity are only indirectly burdened with an extra factor in a form of negative nominal interest rates. It means that in identifying changes in the banks' behaviour in the environment of negative versus positive interest rates, the level of excess liquidity in the sector is of vital importance. Accordingly, Demiralp et al. (2019), based on standalone data of the eurozone's banking sector, confirmed that commercial banks take up measures to limit their use of the deposit held with the central bank. In particular, the effect of rising exposure in treasury bonds with a concomitant drop in the bank's excess liquidity is both statistically and economically relevant during the NIRP period. Such an effect, in turn, is not observed for positive interest rate periods nor for the economies which never drove the rates below zero (including the United States; Ennis and Wolman, 2015). Moreover, the effect is non-linear, which means that the entities carrying a larger burden of excess liquidity will be more than proportionally willing to increase their exposure in treasury bonds. These findings confirm that a bank considers the direct cost economically relevant only after a certain level has been exceeded. The cost may also identify potential implications if interest rates are moved further below zero. It should also be emphasized that the mechanism is an additional demand factor which contributes to treasury bonds yield compression up to relatively long term to maturity.

5.3 Indirect Impact of NIRP on the Banking Sector

The indirect impact of negative interest rate policy on the banking sector is based on the medium-term character of monetary policy transmission which is due to the adaptation of respective entities to the new environment. However, it should be noted that while NIRP's direct effect on the banking sector markedly differs from that in positive rates environment, the indirect influence is – at least theoretically – largely similar in both environments. It may complicate both theoretical and empirical research as for to what extent the phenomenon under scrutiny simply continues or intensifies earlier observed risk categories and to what extent it reflects the new ones materializing. The indirect impact analysis provided in this sub-chapter will chiefly be presented in the context of an effect on the banking sector's profitability.

5.3.1 Interest Rate Channel – Impact on the Banks' Funding Sources

From the perspective of the aforesaid overall impact of interest rate policy on the banking sector, the influence of NIRP on banks' profitability is largely reliant on two factors: the lower bound for interest on both deposits and loans as well as the structure of the banks' funding sources. The literature shows that slightly negative interest rates will not have a significant impact on the profitability of universal banks in which the predominant source of funding is so-called wholesale funding or international funding (Bernanke, 2016), and the impact will be relatively greater with respect to entities whose major source of funding derives from retail deposits. In this context, such a banking sector may, due to the first of the aforesaid factors, experience more acute adverse consequences of NIRP.

The first of the factors named above gives rise to a conflict between the profitability of the banking sector and the effectiveness of monetary transmission into the real economy. If negative interest rates are entirely reflected in the adjustment of interest on credit for the non-financial sector and of bond yield, banks will expect their profitability to drop in case interest on deposits is not adjusted accordingly, that is, if it does not go below zero. The said effect is constrained by the downward stickiness of interest rates which is due to a number of factors (see, e.g., Lowe and Rohling, 1992; Valadkhani et al., 2013). First, whenever banks cross the zero interest bound for deposits of the non-financial sector, lower growth dynamics of the deposit base (or in extreme scenario even withdrawing the deposits away from banking and holding them as cash) may represent a substantial risk source for banks.[8] In case this risk materializes on a large scale and with respect to numerous banks, what may ensue is higher liquidity risk in banks, and ultimately, the entire sector's financial stability may be affected. This mechanism approximates the bank run phenomenon, however, it would most probably be spread over an extended period of time. This risk pertains more to household deposits (and small firms), which is due to a lower cost of holding cash than in the case of big corporates, as well as to a greater significance of the psychological zero interest barrier (Alsterlind et al., 2015; Jobst and Lin, 2016).[9] Although in theory there are methods of charging negative interest also to cash (thus, mitigating this risk), implementation-related and social problems cause these methods to become marginalized in business practice (IMF, 2017). In other words, while the direct cost of NIRP, as shown before, is distorted by the central banks affecting liquidity in the banking sector (Figure 5.6), it is the share of non-financial deposits in the structure of banks' funding that matters much in the analysis of indirect cost. Consequently, commercial banks with a significant share of high-value deposits or the core deposit remaining low are more inclined to charge the deposits with negative interest out of concern for profitability. Next to the very funding structure of banks, what matters is also their ability to estimate the lower bound for interest on deposits at which the adjustments mechanism of the depositories intensify. In this context, the banks which are unable to precisely estimate the lower bound for interest rates will not be willing to lower interest on deposits, and the entire process will be spread over time and divided into minor gradual adjustments much as it will be possible to

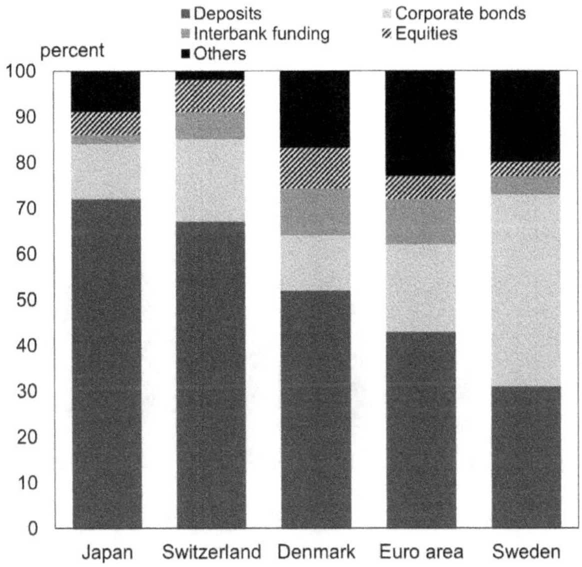

Figure 5.6 Funding structure of banks in NIRP economies
Source: Central banks data and BoAML (2019).

boost other than interest income on deposits (such as, for instance, account maintenance or debit card fees; see, e.g., Altavilla et al., 2018; Heider et al., 2017; Lopez et al., 2018).

Accordingly, deposits still represent the main liability of commercial banks for all the NIRP economies concerned. Although the banking sector of the eurozone in this respect has a relatively lower share of deposits in the funding structure (Figure 5.6), it is vital to bear in mind that, at the same time, the sector is affected by the direct NIRP cost more than others. Concomitantly, as NIRP was pursued in the eurozone, the share of banks with a relatively high representation of deposits in the funding structure clearly lost to those with a lower representation (Figure 5.7).[10] On the one hand, the foregoing may reflect the activity of the central bank which propelled the rise in other funding sources, but also the measures taken by the commercial banks alone to reduce the indirect cost. In this context, some academics emphasize that the introduction of NIRP may – unlike the conventional interest rate policy – reverse post-crisis tendencies regarding the evolution of banks' funding structure (Henriques et al., 2019). It is wholesale funding in particular that may prove clearly cheaper than deposit-based funding on condition of a "sticky" character of the interest on deposits. Much as being conspicuous, the changes are limited by perceiving deposits as a stable source of long-term funding. Such is the perception of both banks (e.g., Drechsler et al., 2017a, 2017b) as well as of macroprudential bodies

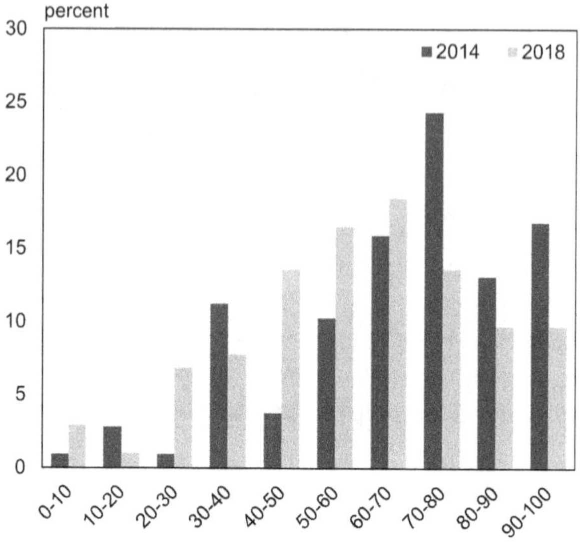

Figure 5.7 Distribution of banks' deposit-to-assets ratio in euro area
Note: Calculations for the sample of 100 banks with the largest total assets.
Source: Own calculations, Bloomberg data.

which view deposit-based funding as weighing more in terms of commercial banks' exposure to financial risk.

The second factor which adds up to the banks' unwillingness to fully transmit negative interest rates to interest on deposits – quite independent of the relevance of cash – is the strive to keep a competitive advantage (Jobst and Lin, 2016). Namely, the banks which are the first to introduce negative interest on deposits will be exposed to a risk of transferring customers' funds to other banks which offer higher (i.e., other than negative) interest. Consequently, banking sectors characterized by lower competition on the deposit market, particularly in retail, can faster transmit the cost of negative interest on deposits to their clients.

The third factor increasing the lower "stickiness" of interest in the NIRP environment may be of legal character (i.e., country regulations), which in some jurisdictions curb the transmission of negative interest rates to interest on deposits or on loans.[11] It is not only such limitations exist but also their varying character across individual eurozone countries that implies differentiation (directly attributed to legal background) of this stage of monetary policy transmission. In particular, in a majority of judicatures, the general law states that the commercial banks are bound to return to the depository no less than the initial value of the deposit (e.g., France, Germany).[12] In other economies (e.g., Austria, Portugal, Spain), the general law does not make a reference to negative interest on bank deposits, so there are no restrictions on its use.

5.3.2 Interest Rate Channel – Impact on Interest on Credit

In the context of nominal interest rigidity analysis, the literature shows that this phenomenon applies not only for deposits but also for credit (IMF, 2016). Still, it may be noted that while for deposits the interest rigidity distinguished between the environments of positive and negative interest rates, in the case of loans, it may have not sufficiently intensified in a new surrounding to tell these two environments clearly apart. It also means that it may be more difficult to identify the effects of both environments given this particular characteristic. A negative pressure on banks' profitability brought on by maturity transformation had been there before, i.e., since financial assets purchase programmes had been introduced by the central banks. Under such circumstances, NIRP experience to-date shows that the policy has a similar (albeit weaker) impact also on banks' profitability in that its effect on the yield curve approximates that of QE programmes (IMF, 2017).

A share of variable interest rate loans in the structure of commercial banks' assets may be one of the structural determinants that varies the impact of NIRP on credit interest, that is, further transmission of negative interest rates.[13] As the share rises, so does NIRP transmission to interest proceed faster and largely independently in the short term from the commercial bank. Unlike the above-mentioned case of deposits, the transmission does not only follow the terms of new loan agreements being adapted, but it also takes place through the ones already in existence. In view of the conclusions regarding the restraint on deposit negative interest, the pressure on bank's profit or loss in the environment of negative interest rates may become stronger and it may emerge relatively earlier than in the case of positive rates and those remaining markedly higher than zero, the household loans in particular (EBC, 2017a).

Accordingly, the eurozone seems to be clearly much exposed to the magnitude of NIRP's indirect effect. The evidence for this is a high share of household loans based on variable interest rates (Figure 5.8). Yet again, the scale of these phenomena greatly varies among eurozone countries. Consequently, during NIRP, in a vast majority of eurozone economies, commercial banks markedly reduced their share of variable interest rate loans (Figure 5.8). Further, so as to evade interbank-based negative rate, some banks introduce a zero lower bound for interest in new loan agreements (Bech and Makhozov, 2016). On the one hand, it means curbing pressure on the banking sector's profitability by diminishing the vulnerability of interest income to possible further monetary policy loosening at a relatively rigid constraint for interest costs. On the other hand, though, as emphasized before, it is one of the direct reasons to weaken NIRP transmission owing to a less pronounced reaction of interest on credit and thus impact on the real economy. Still, it has to be recalled that a relatively evenly distributed scale of reducing the share of variable interest rate loans among individual eurozone economies implies that the risk of monetary policy transmission being heterogeneous on account of NIRP introduction has not increased so far.

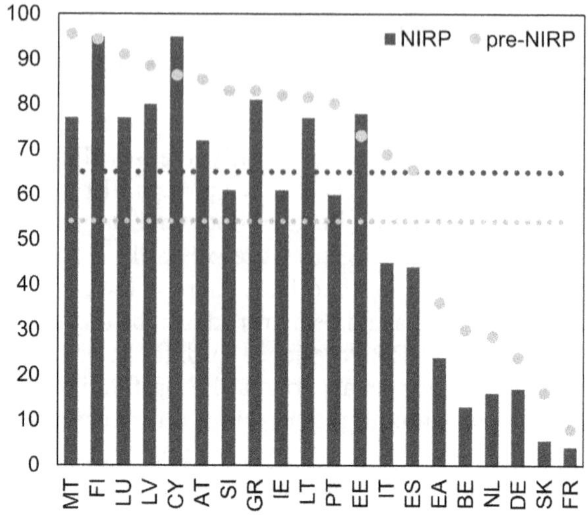

Figure 5.8 Share of floating-rate loans in newly granted loans to households in the euro area

Note: *Pre-NIRP* stands for a 4-year period preceding the NIRP introduction, while *NIRP* refers to period from June 2014 to August 2019; dotted lines denote average for all countries.

Source: Own work, ECB data.

5.3.3 Interest Rate Channel – NIRP Economies' Experience

The above-presented structural determinants and the channels of NIRP's potential impact, given "stickiness" of interest on credit and deposits, as well as banking sectors' structural determinants may be analysed twofold – at the macro- and microeconomic levels.

On an aggregate basis, there are several major conclusions. First, across all the NIRP economies the interest both on loans and deposits markedly lowered, which reflects an expansionary character of the monetary policy (Figure 5.9). The magnitude of interest cuts on loans (both households and non-financial firms) surpassed in a vast majority of cases (but for the eurozone) the decline in interest on deposits. At the same time, however, only some economies (i.e., Denmark and Switzerland) drove the interest on new deposits down to negative values (Figure 5.9). It gave rise to a relatively unchanged difference in interest versus the interbank rate in positive and negative interest rate environment. In both cases, the adjustment followed a gradual fashion and it was somewhat forced by the NIRP period becoming extended. Namely, given the entire NIRP period, both in Denmark and Switzerland the interest on household deposits remains, on average, positive. Notwithstanding, the example of Denmark and Switzerland shows that the zero lower bound for interest rates – next to interbank and bonds – does not hold also for the later stages of monetary transmission mechanism (i.e., for non-financial entities' deposits and loans).

Second, it took commercial banks in Denmark and Switzerland – so where negative interest was applied also to bank products – to adjust interest on products for businesses faster than for households.[14] It means that banks estimate the cost of holding household deposits as being markedly lower than in the case of businesses. Thus, a smaller or slower scale of interest adjustments by the banks in NIRP environment mitigates the risk of crossing the lower bound for interest rates which the banks most probably identified as placed higher for the household sector. Yet another incentive strengthening the economic factor manifesting itself in avoiding nominal loss (especially for retail clients) may be behavioural determinants. In particular, the retail clients' belief is that a deposit with a commercial bank should entail positive interest. Consequently, the opposite case whereby it is the client that pays interest to the bank for depositing funds may be viewed as irrational. It is especially because most of the society considers the propensity to save as an advantage (Guin, 2017). Thus, negative interest on deposit is viewed, in turn, as a type of wealth tax (Gafrikova, 2016). In addition, the effect is clearly more pronounced in the case of negative (and real positive) than in real negative interest rates (Horioka and Terada-Hagiwara, 2012).

Furthermore, implications for the eurozone banking sector should be brought up. Positive interest on deposits lingering in spite of a relatively highest direct cost of NIRP may show that the eurozone commercial banks are potentially the least willing to transmit central bank's interest rates to the retail market. This consequently translates into potentially most solid reasons for monetary transmission weakening among NIRP economies. On the other hand, though, the effect of NIRP on eurozone banking sector's profitability remains weaker than on the other economies under scrutiny. It is because – judging by the deposit side – the reduction of interest on deposit versus the interbank rate (that is, the indicator of the banks' cost of funding; Figure 5.9) was the highest for the eurozone itself. Across all the remaining economies concerned, the reduction of interest on the banks' assets side (loans) did not have a corresponding adjustment on the liabilities side. It means that, in spite of the highest direct cost, eurozone banking sector may be charged with an indirect cost to a relatively lesser degree than in the other economies concerned. Accordingly, empirical analyses show that if the direct cost is mitigated by the differentiation mechanism, in order to push interest on retail deposit down below zero, the ECB's nominal rate should be twice as lower as today (providing the technical lower bound has not been reached yet, Barr et al., 2016). Therefore, importantly, the reduction in direct cost may overproportionately increase the indirect cost.

As shown above, the structural specificity of the eurozone – similarly to the case of the direct cost burden – is of relevance also for the indirect cost. Amid the above-mentioned rigidity of interest on deposits, NIRP may also encourage greater differentiation of common monetary policy transmission

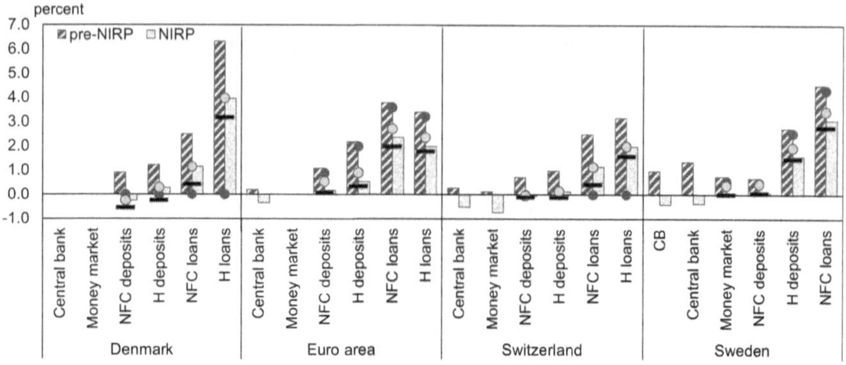

Figure 5.9 Average level of interest rates in NIRP economies

Note: Dots denote spread to central bank interest rate (in percentage points); dark grey stands for pre-NIRP period and light grey for NIRP period; black lines mark the lowest identified level; *pre-NIRP* refers to an average over period from 2009 to the introduction of NIRP; *NIRP* denotes period up to August 2019; NFC – non-financial corporations, H – household; calculations based on interest rates for new deposits and loans only.

Source: Own calculations based on central banks data.

among individual eurozone countries. It is partly attributable to a clear differentiation in the structure of credit interest, thus, its varying – both with respect to the scale and pace – adjustments to monetary impulses in respective economies (Jobst and Lin, 2016). Given the previously mentioned distribution of direct cost in the eurozone, it may further aggravate the risk of deepening profitability disproportions among the respective country-level banking sectors of the eurozone. Thus, it should be noted that the level of interest on loan and deposit also largely varies across respective economies of the eurozone (Figure 5.10; EBC, 2019a). It means that in some of the economies (e.g., in Spain or Italy), interest on deposit had definitely more room for reduction than in the others (e.g., in Germany or France). In that context, the empirical literature highlights particularly the German case given its particular character in the environment of negative interest rates. Specifically, as already mentioned, in Germany, the yields of government bonds are the lowest, the banking sector has the highest NIRP direct cost and the interest on deposit approximated zero even before the policy was introduced by the ECB (Eisenschmidt and Smets, 2018). Consequently, the German example is considered to be the most representative for a NIRP analysis in the eurozone, particularly in the context of risk factors to emerge.

A weaker NIRP transmission to deposit interest may especially be confirmed at the level of individual banks. The eurozone's structure of deposit interest comes as a good example (Figure 5.11). As NIRP was introduced by the ECB, a noticeable flattening of the interest distribution as well as its concentration around low (albeit positive) levels can be evidenced, for

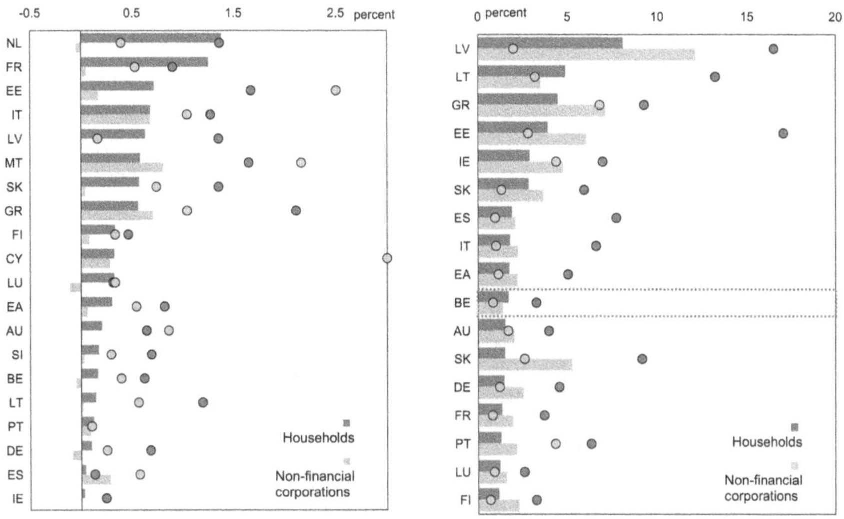

Figure 5.10 Average level of interests on deposits (left panel) and loans (right panel) in selected euro area countries

Note: Columns refer to short term deposits (up to 1-year, left panel) and mortgage loans (for households, right panel) or small-amount loans (up to EUR 1 million, for corporates, right panel); dots denote interest on long-term deposits (longer than 2 years, left panel) and consumer credit (for households, right panel) or large-amount loans (for corporates, right panel); statistics as of August 2019.

Source: ECB data.

both households' and businesses' deposits. This may suggest that banks are unwilling to reduce interest on deposit. Namely, what a complete NIRP transmission to deposit interest would imply is that the interest distribution remains relatively of comparable shape, but it is only parallelly shifted to the negative territory. In line with such a deterministic assumption, around half of all eurozone deposits should bear negative interest within, approximately, two years from ECB's introducing NIRP. Such a phenomenon was not in fact observed and the sharp narrowing of deposit interest distribution resulted in only a minor part of it being shifted to the negative territory. At the same time, it should be noted that – as in the case of aggregate perspective – this factor is more pronounced for households' than businesses' interest on deposit.

The experience of NIRP economies provides evidence for interest rigidity applying also to credit. In particular, the literature points to a counterintuitive reaction of commercial banks in Switzerland, which in response to interest rates cut by the central bank into negative levels and probably extrapolating the expectations for their potential impact on their profitability, in fact increased interest rates, e.g., for mortgage loans (Bech and Makhozov, 2016; Borio and Zabai, 2016). Such a scenario, albeit extended over

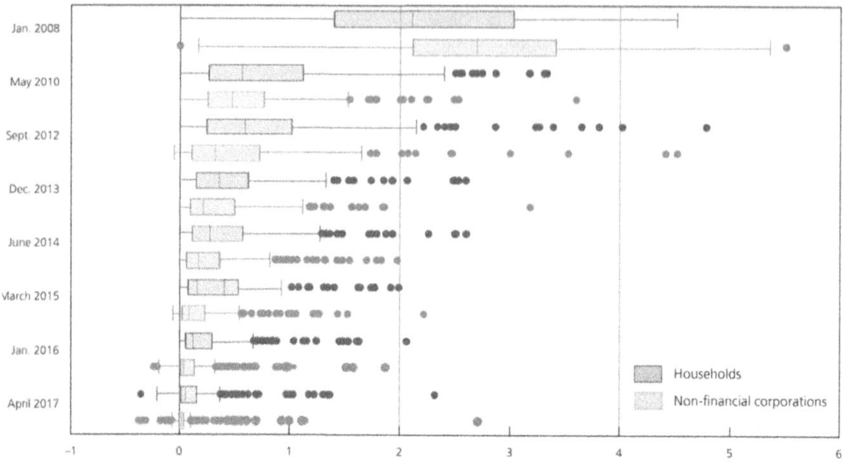

Figure 5.11 Distribution of interest rates on deposits if households and non-financial corporations offered by euro area banks

Note: The rectangle contains the values between the lower and upper quartile; the vertical line in the rectangle indicates the median; the horizontal lines comprise the values between the lower quartile less 1.5 times the interquartile range and the upper quartile plus 1.5 times the interquartile range; the dots indicate the extreme values; data for a sample of 283 banks.

Source: Perea and Kashama (2017).

the entire banking sector, was also evidenced in Sweden (Eggertsson et al., 2017). In the environment of low (near zero) interest rates, the interest on credit demonstrated, admittedly, a weaker reaction to the change of central bank's interest rates; however, it was still consistent with the expansionary stance of this monetary policy. On the contrary, importantly, in NIRP environment this relationship reversed (Figure 5.12). What additionally stands out is a relatively wide distribution of this relation estimates in NIRP environment, which implies a sharp rise in the banking sector's heterogeneity (Figure 5.12). It is because some banks still align their interest on loans to the changes in the central bank's interest rates, albeit on a smaller scale, similarly as in the environment of interest rates approximating zero. Notwithstanding, the majority of entities react to a decline in the policy rates by raising the interest on bank loans, similarly as in the aforementioned Swiss example. A higher dispersion may be attributable to several reasons, out of which the most important may yet again be a relative importance of deposits as a source of funding. Eggertsson et al. (2017) confirmed that there is a significant negative relationship between deposit share on the bank's balance sheet and interest on credit. Banks with a higher share will be less willing to transmit monetary policy in the NIRP environment.

As the commercial banks' unwillingness to fully transmit central bank's rates to interest on deposit has been corroborated, a pressure to withdraw

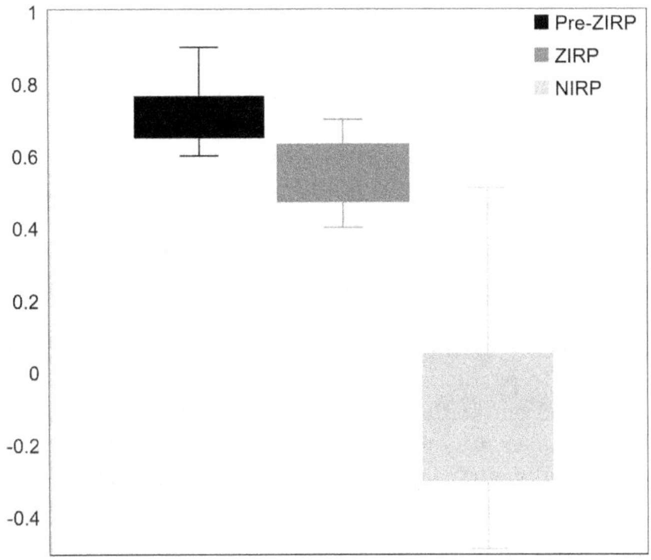

Figure 5.12 Distribution of correlation coefficients for linear relation of interest rate on loans and central bank policy rate – a case of Sweden

Source: Eggertsson et al. (2017).

funds from banks has receded. In result, the risk of excessive rise of cash amount in circulation has not materialized for any of the economies using NIRP. Hence, it may be inferred that the lower technical bound for interest rates has not been reached yet either and – other risk factors aside – there may still be room for central banks' interest rates going deeper into negative territory (Cœuré, 2016). It may force the commercial banks to intensify their measures undertaken with the aim to reduce pressure on their profitability (e.g., by a reduction in overhead and administrative costs). It should also be noted that the extent of NIRP transmission to interest on deposits may have implications for the commercial banks' satisfying the regulatory norms, that is, for one of the tools of macroeconomic policy. It is particularly in the realm of liquidity norms (aiming to improve a bank's short-term resistance to a shock scenario; BIS, 2013) that the banks are required to, *inter alia*, meet the liquidity coverage ratio, i.e., to hold adequate liquid high quality assets to cover the foreseeable net cash outflow. In turn, in the environment of negative interest rates, an important part of the component which defines cash outflow is the direct cost of a commercial bank's holding a deposit with the central bank. The cost may be offset by the commercial bank charging the customer's deposit with negative interest. Consequently, owing to the transmission of central bank's rates to interest on non-financial sector's deposit in NIRP environment, the liquidity norms may be satisfied to a higher extent, albeit probably only slightly (Henriques et al., 2019).

5.3.4 Credit Channel

Unlike the positive interest rate policy, the influence of NIRP on lending has been identified in the literature as ambiguous. Namely, some empirical research studies indicate NIRP's expansionary character (Rostagno et al., 2016; Demiralp et al., 2019), other findings emphasize only a moderate influence or no relationship between this policy and the banks' lending (Borio and Gambacorta, 2017), whereas in several cases the influence is identified as restraining the pace of credit supply growth (Heider et al., 2017). One of theoretical approaches of NIRP's impact on lending shows that the policy is perceived as a type of tax. Accordingly, in spite of such a monetary policy being commonly viewed as expansionary, the empirical research for Japan points to a different lending reaction (Hiroshi, 2018), i.e., to a restrictive impact of NIRP. In particular, this effect was identified as the strongest for smaller banks and markedly lesser for international institutions. A similar relationship, however, was not empirically proved for other economies in which central banks pursue NIRP. It should be noted here that it is within the credit channel – jointly with observations of limited transmission of negative interest rates to interest on loans – that the economic bound on interest rates can be reached. Thus, the above ambiguity of NIRP impact may suggest that this interest rate's limitation is gaining in importance and it might be gradually approached.

Owing to the presented above mechanism, the environment of negative interest rates (and primarily its indirect effect) came to be perceived as structurally different from those of positive (albeit low) rates. It means that from the lending perspective, the negative interest rate may change the policy of commercial banks in favour of increasing the balance-sheet share of assets free from direct NIRP influence. Given the structure of the eurozone's banking sector, the literature shows that credit supply (especially for the corporate sector) was markedly increased first and foremost by the banks which had a higher international exposure (hence, a high level of excess liquidity; see, e.g., Bottero et al., 2019). This finding distinguishes between the credit channel working amid NIRP and positive rates environment. Namely, in the consensual economic view, the expansionary monetary policy has a stronger effect on banks whose share of liquid assets in balance-sheet structure is lower (Kashyap and Stein, 1995; Jiménez et al., 2012). In contrast to the interest rate channel, however, the literature does not provide evidence for the degree of funding credit with deposits to have any impact on the strength of the credit channel in the NIRP environment. In other words, it was not confirmed that a higher level of deposits among banks' liabilities may considerably drive credit supply higher (Bottero et al., 2019). In this context, one may become more willing to diversify the currency composition of a commercial bank's balance sheet. Consequently, the interest rate risk may also become more heterogeneous, i.e., the vulnerability to the effects of changes, both domestic and foreign interest rates, may strengthen. Such a hypothesis was empirically proved for Denmark whereby commercial banks' preferences for growing domestic asset versus foreign asset portfolio were analysed (Khayat, 2018). Notwithstanding, such an implication of NIRP should mainly be perceived as a specific case of the Danish economy. It is a small open economy with a monetary policy to be restrained by an exchange rate regime. It means that for a large economy (that the eurozone is) similar tendencies for the local banking sector may not be observed; however, the literature has not furnished any empirical evidence so far.

5.3.5 Risk-Taking Channel and Portfolio Channel

What particularly characterizes the environment of low interest rates, especially NIRP, is intensification of a tendency among financial institutions to seek positive rates of return (search for yield phenomenon). As a result, commercial banks may enhance their tolerance and appetite for risk within the risk-taking channel. The contemporary literature, however, does not provide any exhaustive theoretical model accounting for how the channel works nor showing all economic mechanisms which spur on its expansion (Chmielewski et al., 2018). For these reasons, this channel is relatively most difficult to be empirically identified. As a result, also we present only a tentative analysis of it. The literature that identifies the existence of the risk-taking channel in the environment of low interest rates manifest themselves by, *inter alia*, lower lending standards (Delis and Kouretas, 2011; Maddaloni and Peydro, 2011; Angeloni and Faia, 2013; Abbate and Thaler, 2015), higher financial leverage (Adrian and Shin, 2014; de Groot, 2014) or a portfolio expanded so as to include less liquid assets and/or assets carrying higher risk (Angeloni et al., 2015).[15]

Starting with the last of the above factors, it may be shown that NIRP has not contributed to a considerable "shift" of banks' lending portfolios either among non-financial entity categories or towards financial institutions (Figure 5.13, upper panel). That is to say, the foregoing does not identify any lending focus on a given sector that could entail the system's impeded immunity to a potential contagion effect. However, banks' exposure to debt financing is indicative of a significant expansion of their portfolios to include treasury bonds. It is overproportionate in relation to other debt instruments and also to the scale of the banks' own securities issued (Figure 5.13, lower panel). This factor is partly attributable to the banks willing to reduce NIRP direct cost. It may, in turn, aggravate interest rate risk and market risk and, consequently, give rise to banks' losses in case of a rapid revaluation of these bonds.

Accordingly, it may be assumed that the manifestation of a bank risk-taking is its higher exposure to relatively more risky types of loans (given the borrowers' capacity for the loan repayment). This phenomenon may be signalled by a relaxation of standards[16] and terms[17] in its credit policy.

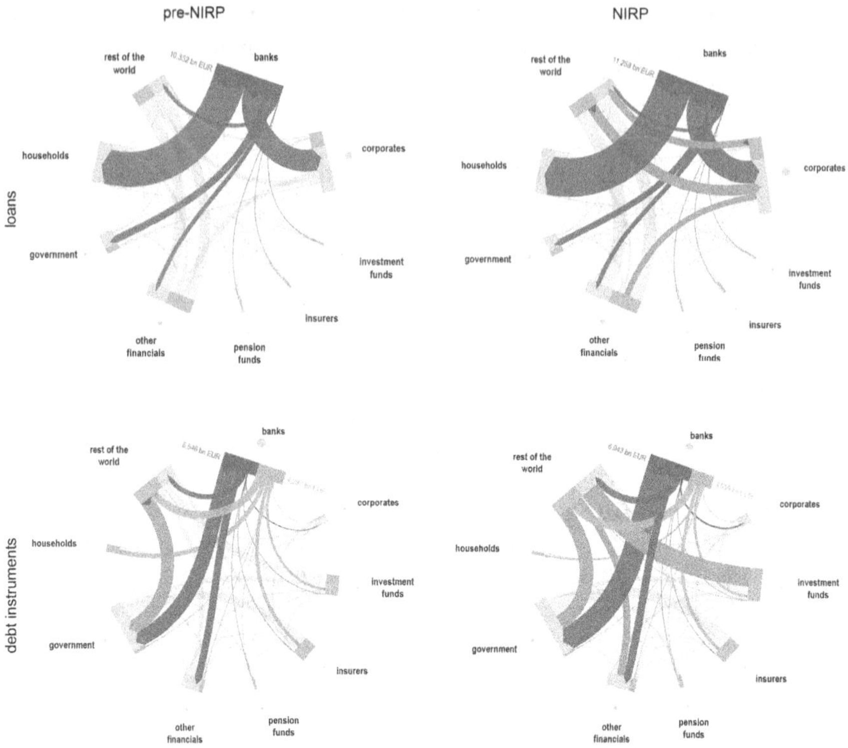

Figure 5.13 Network of balance-sheet long-term relations across selected entities in the euro area

Note: Pre-NIRP refers to the relations as of the end of 2013, while NIRP to ones as of the end of 2018; based on balance-sheet data.

Source: EBC.

Consequently, in affecting loan standards and terms, monetary policy – assuming no significant demand limitations – may affect the credit supply in the economy (with such a mechanism missing on an aggregate basis; Figure 5.13, upper panel). Indeed, since the onset of NIRP, banks in the eurozone have been seen as more inclined to relax lending standards in more risky credit categories, in particular, loans for small and medium enterprises (Figure 5.14). Since a similar tendency did not hold for low (albeit positive) interest rates in the eurozone, this rationale may corroborate the thesis of the risk-taking channel strengthening in NIRP environment.

Under the search for a yield mechanism, financial entities may seek to expand their portfolios to include more risky instruments, which is consistent with the above conclusions on the changes in the links among economic sectors. For a bond market, this mechanism particularly manifests itself in financial institutions' rising demand for more risky bond types, more specifically, collateralized loan obligations (Figure 5.15). This thesis may be

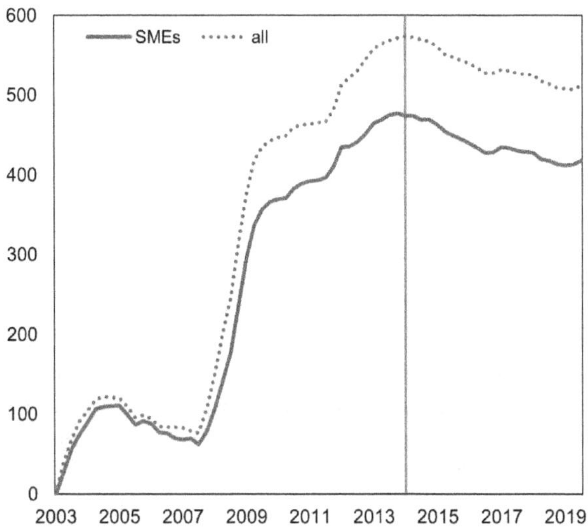

Figure 5.14 Cumulative change in credit standards applied to the approval of loans or credit lines to enterprises in the euro area

Note: Vertical line point out the introduction of NIRP in the euro area, and SMEs denotes small and medium enterprises.

Source: ECB data (Bank Lending Survey).

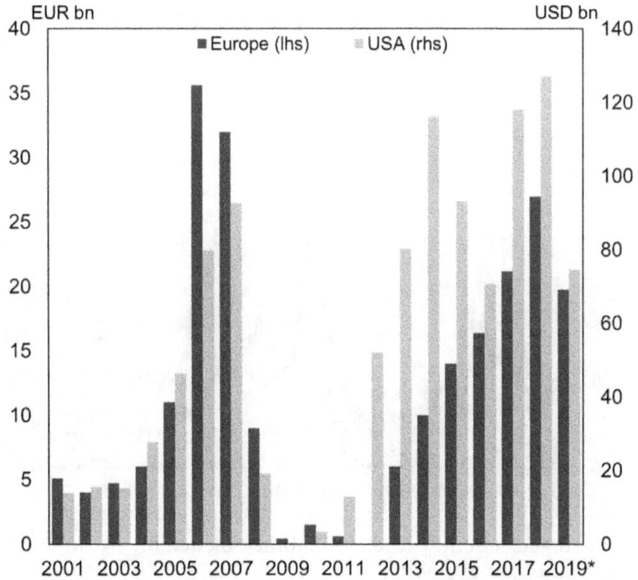

Figure 5.15 Annual issuance of collateralized loan obligations (CLOs) in the USA and the euro area

Source: JP Morgan and Bloomberg data.

supported by an increased net issuance of these financial instruments in recent years – first in the United States (in the environment of low interest rates), followed by their rapid, almost threefold rise in NIRP-driven Europe. However, it should be noted that a demand for such instruments among financial institutions is probably to a greater extent generated by investment firms (hedge funds, investment funds) rather than banks or insurance companies. Reasons for that include clearly varying regulatory frameworks (e.g., capital requirements) among these types of entities (ESRB, 2016).

Finally, another approach to empirical analysis of the risk-taking channel – employed in the literature and encompassing the whole spectrum of the bank's activity on an aggregate basis – is total risk of the institution that may be approximated by the probability of its default (see, e.g., Altunbas et al., 2009, Gambacorta, 2009). Apart from the aforesaid advantage which shows that this indicator takes account of all the measures of a commercial bank (not requiring that they are precisely differentiated), one of its obvious drawbacks is that it takes into consideration also exogenous factors, which may reflect an impact of broadly understood economic environment on the level of risk taken by a given commercial bank. Consequently, the conclusions of such an analysis should not directly identify a causal relation between NIRP and the indicator analysed. Notwithstanding, it should be emphasized that across all of NIRP economies under scrutiny (except for

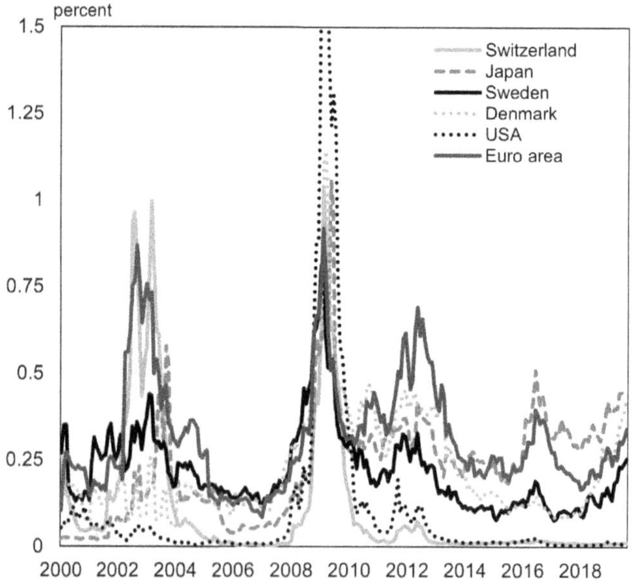

Figure 5.16 Aggregate country-level probability of default in the banking sector over a 1-year horizon.

Note: The country-level aggregation is based on weighted average with respect to total assets of banks; the scaling of the vertical axis underreports the numbers for the United States which in the extreme case amounted to around 2.7%.

Source: Own work based on Bloomberg data and Moody's KMV methodology.

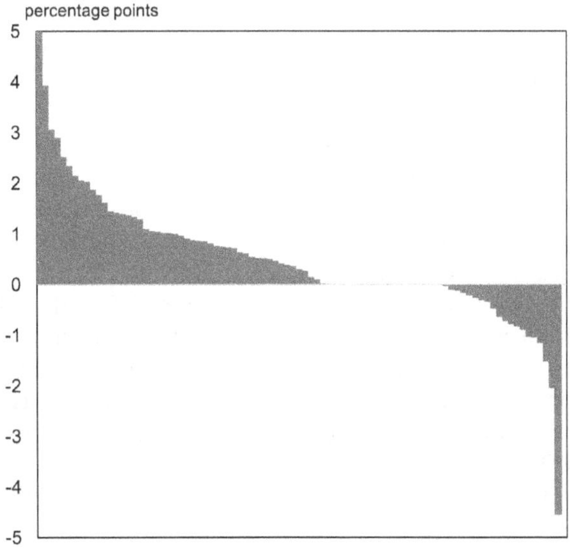

Figure 5.17 Distribution of changes in 1-year probability of default in the banking sector in the euro area during NIRP period

Note: Each column describes a change in an average probability of default of each bank; changes calculated as average level from years 2014 to 2019 in comparison to average level from 2010 to 2014; calculations for 100 biggest banks.

Source: Own work based on Bloomberg data and Moody's KMV methodology.

Switzerland), this indicator (estimated on an aggregate basis) went up in value as NIRP was introduced (Figure 5.16) and then rise again as the expectations for further loosening of monetary policy intensified. Although this might seem just a minor increase given its scale (as compared to the GFC episodes), it is worth noting that for Sweden or Denmark, this indicator approximated the level evidenced during the eurozone debt crisis. For the eurozone, in turn, what is visible is high heterogeneity of indications for individual commercial banks, with a clear predominance of those which record higher likelihood of an event of default during NIRP (Figure 5.17). On the one hand, it may reflect, as already pointed out, a higher risk the banks take, and a higher pressure on the banking sector to generate profit on the other.

5.3.6 Profitability and Wealth Effect of the Banking Sector

The common element for all of the aforementioned mechanisms is the negative interest rate policy affecting the banking sector's profitability. It is namely down to commercial banks being reluctant to fully transmit NIRP to interest on deposit while adjusting interest on credit (particularly in the case of a large share of variable rate-based loans) that may contribute to shrinking profitability of the banking sector. Simultaneously, it should be taken into account that it is empirically more difficult to conclusively identify the nature of links since some of the mechanisms indicated as applying for NIRP may arise from other unconventional monetary policy tools.[18]

The impact of negative interest rates on the banks' profitability should be analysed twofold – with respect to interest margin (that is, the difference between interest revenue and costs) and overall profitability. In the environment of negative nominal interest rates, banks experience a statistically and economically relevant drop in interest revenues. The decline is partly mitigated by a reduction in interest costs (Lopez et al., 2018). However, due to the earlier referred to "stickiness" of interest on deposits, it is mitigated on a relatively small scale. Further, lower costs of wholesale funding in the NIRP environment also drive interest costs down. For a vast majority of banks in the environment of negative rates, the interest margin went down (Figure 5.18). This impairs a bank's capacity for generating profit on core operations and thus may particularly entail lesser ability to build the capital base to secure absorption of adverse future economic shocks affecting the institutions (Avalos and Mamatzakis, 2018).

Banks, however, were not just a passive observer of the said circumstances and they took up measures to offset the negative effect of NIRP

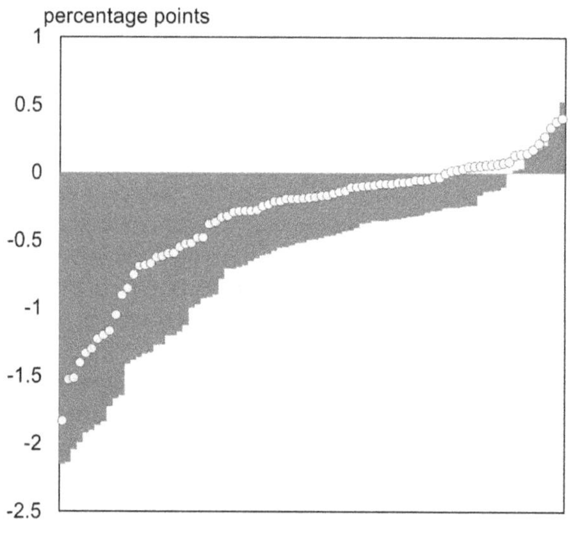

Figure 5.18 Distribution of changes in gross and net interest income of banks from NIRP economies

Note: Each column describes a change in the net interest income of each banks, while each dot represents gross interest income; changes calculated as average level from years 2014 to 2019 in comparison to average level from 2010 to 2014; calculations for 100 biggest banks from the euro area, Sweden, Denmark and Switzerland which total assets represent around 70% of the whole banking sector.

Source: Own calculations based on Bloomberg data.

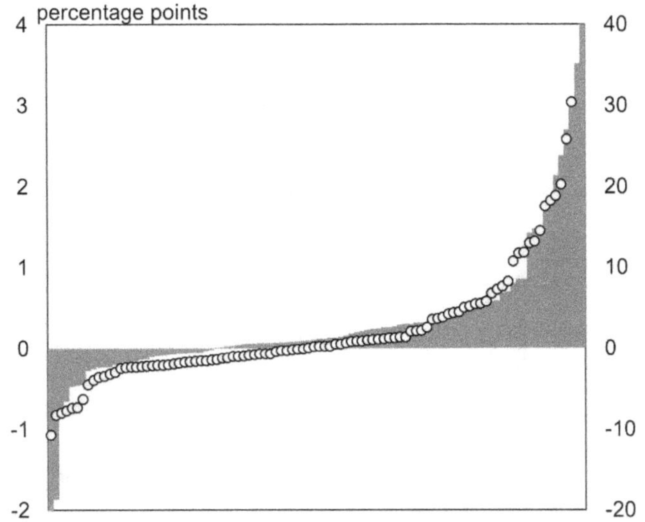

Figure 5.19 Distribution of changes in return on equity (ROE, right axis) and return on assets (ROA, left axis) of banks from NIRP economies.

Note: Each column describes a change in ROA of each banks, while each dot represents a change in ROE; changes calculated as average level from years 2014 to 2019 in comparison to average level from 2010 to 2014; calculations for 100 biggest banks from the euro area, Sweden, Denmark and Switzerland which total assets represent around 70% of the whole banking sector.

Source: Own calculations based on Bloomberg data.

on their profitability (e.g., by increasing the lending to more profit-yielding entities, raising fees and other revenue sources, e.g., Cœuré, 2016). In addition, NIRP is expansionary by definition. Thus, in the medium term and paired with other simultaneously introduced central bank's tools, it should work to bolster business activity and foster the banking sector's profitability by a rising lending volume and an improved credit portfolio quality. In the short term, such a positive effect of NIRP is observable in the rising prices of financial assets.

The phenomena concerned were corroborated by a clear differentiation of changes in bank profitability categories – interest-based (Figure 5.18) and overall (Figure 5.19) – in the NIRP period. For the first category, the effect of NIRP was definitely negative. At the same time, however, the return on both asset and equity increased during NIRP. The above observations are also evidenced in the literature, which shows NIRP has either a minor effect on the banking sector overall (Denmark, Switzerland) or does not have it at all (eurozone) with a major pressure on interest profit or loss (Lopez et al., 2018). As mentioned before, it is because banks attempt to counter the decline in interest margin (Basten and Mariathasan, 2018).

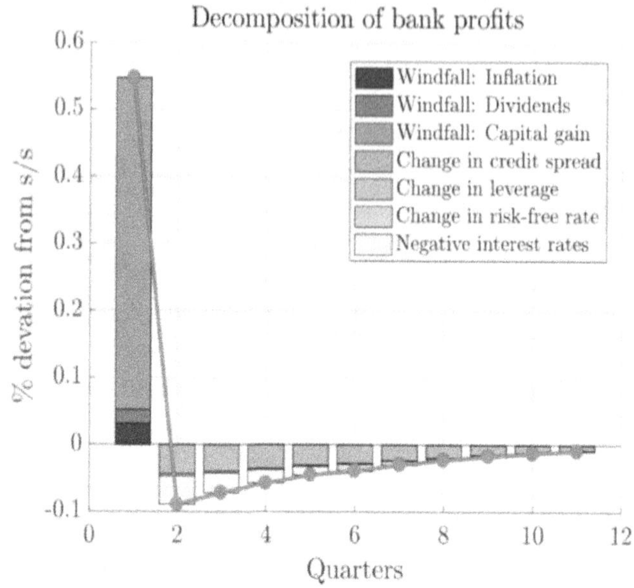

Figure 5.20 Decomposition of bank profits response to monetary policy in NIRP environment

Source: de Groot and Haas (2018).

The multi-dimensional character of NIRP effect on the overall profitability of the banking sector may also be examined by a model analysis of the effect of monetary policy impulse. Based on theoretical models, a medium-term magnitude of this effect is shown as neutral (e.g., de Groot and Haas, 2018). A positive initial effect manifested in a rise in valuation of instruments held in the banks' portfolios (in this chapter understood as an immediate wealth effect attributable to a security held) increases a short-term return on assets. Similarly, the effect spurs on a medium-term credit volume growth amid economic upturn attributable to expansionary character of the monetary policy (EBC, 2017b), and reserve costs are driven down by an improved quality of credit portfolio. The effects are, however, systematically contained by narrowing credit spreads and NIRP direct cost, until the initial effect is entirely neutralized (Figure 5.20). Also in empirical terms – for the to-date experience – the cumulative NIRP effect on eurozone banks' profitability remained limited. Still, the effect slightly varied with respect to individual countries – not so much for the scale, rather more structure-wise (Figure 5.21).

The impact of NIRP on the banking sector's profitability identified as close to neutral entails two further conclusions. First, a neutral magnitude

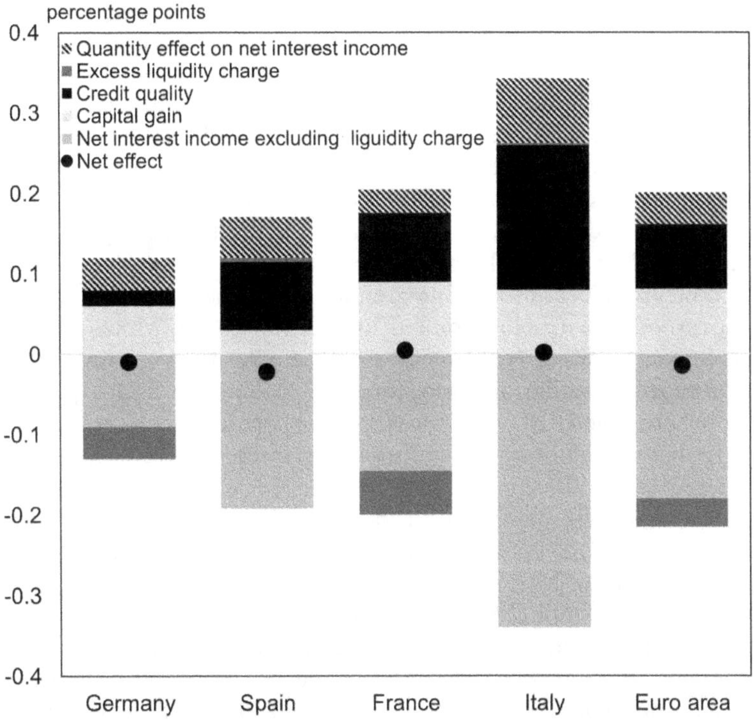

Figure 5.21 Decomposition of aggregate non-standard monetary policy effect on banks' return on assets in selected economies

Note: Total cumulative effect for the 2014-2017 period; contribution of each category in percentage point to total return on assets; net interest income excludes the cost of deposit in central bank and quantity effect; capital gains based on data on a consolidated basis for 68 euro area banking groups; calculates of euro area figures represents the weighted average.

Source: EBC (2017b), Altavilla et al. (2019).

of the medium-term impact does not imply a similar long-term effect as the measures taken by commercial banks may not produce a comparable outcome and a negative pressure on revenues from banks' core operations is consistently settled. Second, what is of particular importance for our research topic, is that such a relationship with respect to profitability does not mean the effect on the systemic risk in NIRP economies will not materialize.

5.4 The Results of Banks' Survey on the Effect of Negative Nominal Interest Rates

To summarize the impact of NIRP on the banking sector, in addition to the data analysis presented above, it is also worth looking at the views of commercial banks themselves (in a form of so-called "soft data"). In its quarterly survey to the credit committees of the largest banks in the eurozone (*Bank Lending Survey*), ECB asked for an opinion on the impact (both direct and indirect) of NIRP on credit parameters and profitability. According to them, since the introduction of negative interest rates, a vast majority of banks have systematically pointed out the rates' adverse effect on interest margin (Figure 5.22). Notwithstanding the credit category, the banks also note a pressure on credit interest decline which is mainly attributable to margins shrinking versus the market interest rates. In order to reduce the impact of decline in average income on credit affecting profitability, the banks declare they will increase the scale of lending (e.g., by loosening credit policy). Indeed, most banks report NIRP impact on higher lending volumes, the highest being pointed for housing loans. Much as the scale of this impact is rather moderate, it is still greater than – notwithstanding the loan type – a similar indicator for the assessment of ECB's quantitative easing programme (EBC, 2019b). What is more, banks claim that the QE measures have a definitely weaker impact on interest margin than the negative interest rate policy.

Arce et al. (2018), based on an in-depth microeconomic analysis (microdata) of the Bank Lending Survey, found that the banks which report an adverse effect of NIRP on their interest margin are characterized (on average) by lower capital ratios than the banks which report positive influence. It means that the aforesaid mechanism of mitigating the adverse effect of NIRP by growing lending volumes by banks with lower capital ratios may not work and the impact of NIRP on such banks' profitability may be greater due to macroprudential restrictions. This mechanism is a source of heightened risk – as central banks keep interest rates low or negative, banks' ability to accumulate capital is limited by persistent pressure on their profitability. In turn, growing profitability in the case

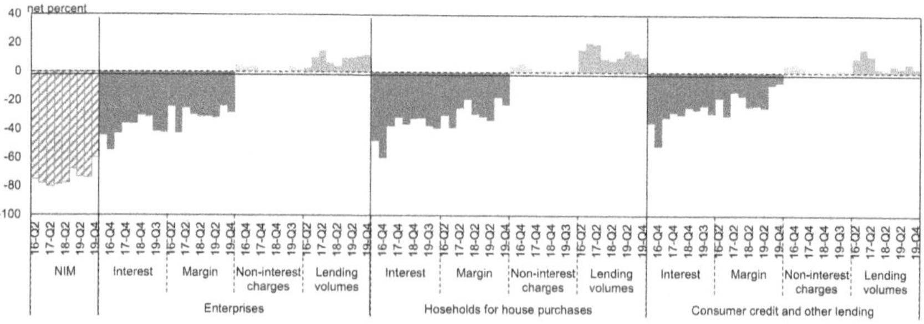

Figure 5.22 Banks' self-assessment of NIRP impact on their profitability and credit policy

Note: The columns represent a net effect, e.g., the difference between the sum of the percentages of banks responding "considerably positive" and "somehow positive" and the sum of the percentages of banks responding "somehow negative " and "considerably negative"; NIM – net interest margin.

Source: Own work based on ECB data (Bank Lending Survey).

of low capital ratios may be constrained by macroprudential regulations. Consequently, with a specified low level of interest rates or in keeping them low for considerably long time, monetary policy which is viewed as expansionary, starts to grow restrictive from the financial perspective and given the effect it has on the banking sector. In the literature, this phenomenon is referred to as reversal interest rate, and the above indications may also suggest that it is of empirical nature. Nevertheless, the said level has not been reached for any of the NIRP economies so far, including in the eurozone in particular. Such a statement is corroborated by no significant difference being identified between credit supply by banks reporting a significant adverse impact of NIRP and those which deny it (Arce et al., 2018). Somewhat in contrast, Altavilla et al. (2018), based on the above survey, showed that the banks which reported a major influence of NIRP also experienced a proportionately higher credit growth dynamics during this period than the banks which indicated no such impact, as in the case of quantitative easing (Figure 5.23).

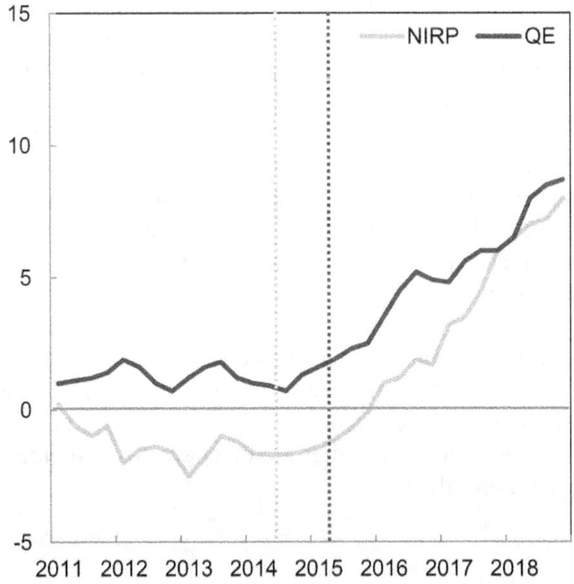

Figure 5.23 Cumulative difference between credit growth of banks reporting significant impact of unconventional monetary policy in comparison to those reporting no effect

Note: NIRP denotes the difference across banks reporting significant effect of negative rates on their net interest income in comparison to those reporting no effect; QE – comparable measure across banks reporting effect on their liquidity measures; positive values indicate that in the first group (considerable effect) relatively faster pace of credit growth was observed; vertical lines indicate moments of introduction of respective monetary policy instrument.

Source: Altavilla et al. (2018).

Summary

One of the fundamental risk categories identified in the context of the negative nominal interest rate policy and being one of the major threats to financial stability, is a deterioration of the banking sector's financial condition. Such an impact works at two levels which may be classified as direct (i.e., bearing directly on monetary policy implementation mechanism) and indirect effects (i.e., requiring adjustment mechanisms). Unlike other mechanisms with an indirect impact, the mechanism of NIRP directly affecting the banking system will work only when the banking system overflows with liquidity. It somewhat unveils a conflict between monetary policy tools used concomitantly, i.e., NIRP and quantitative easing programmes. It is also the channel of impact that is most subject to differentiation across NIRP economies and, what is crucial, within an economic area covered by a common monetary policy, i.e., the eurozone in our case. In turn, an indirect effect of NIRP is chiefly confined to the interest rate channel. The channel highlighted the mechanisms which implied that the central bank's interest rates are not entirely transmitted to interest on deposit and that the mechanism is asymmetrical in the balance-sheet structure of commercial banks. The scale of this effect, however, largely varies among NIRP economies. In particular, the lingering positive level of interest on deposits, in spite of a relatively highest burden of NIRP direct effect, may imply that the eurozone's commercial banks will potentially be the most reluctant to transmit central bank's interest rates to retail deposits. It also shows potentially most solid reasons for monetary transmission to weaken among NIRP economies precisely for this economic area. What further characterizes the environment of low interest rates, especially negative rates, is intensification of a tendency among financial institutions to seek positive rates of return. In the end, commercial banks, along with the other monetary policy channels, may enhance their tolerance and appetite for risk within the risk-taking channel. What these actions entail is curbing the ensuing pressure on commercial banks' results, albeit with a higher risk over the sector. Consequently, in the medium term and in case multiple channels of the said mechanisms coincide, the financial stability may be jeopardized.

Notes

1 The concept of financial stability will be defined in Chapter 6.
2 Excess liquidity in the banking sector is defined in this book as total bank liquidity remaining in the sectors after meeting or required bank liquidity (e.g., in a form of reserve requirement). The volume of central banks' open market operations may be a proxy for excess liquidity in the banking sector.
3 Excess liquidity in the banking sector can be low or high regardless of the liquidity of each selected commercial bank. Some banks might exhibit overproportional holdings of liquid assets, while the others might suffer shortages.

However, what matters for the monetary policy purposes is the overall aggregate level of sectoral liquidity.

4 In the case of small open economy, large banks may try to avoid negative remuneration by placing deposits with central bank that conducts positive rate policy – e.g., through their subsidiaries (Gostomski, 2015). However, in the case of a large economy – like euro area – this mechanism would not work, given the size of the European banking sector.

5 Literature points out several reasons why banks may hold portfolio of bonds regardless of the return on such. Among them the ability to absorb liquidity squeeze (Holmström and Tirole, 1993; Gennaioli et al., 2013), preferential treatment by prudential (Popov and van Horen, 2013; Bonner, 2016) or tax (Gambacorta et al., 2017) regulations can be mentioned.

6 In case of ECB's monetary policy, the introduction of tiering scheme in late 2019 allowed the effective short-term rate to remain unchanged despite lowering of the nominal deposit rate. Assuming no changes in the nominal deposit rate but still implementing the tiering scheme, the effective rate would increase the effective rate by around 10 bps.

7 Assuming current tiering scheme of Bank of Japan, in order to lower the effective interest rate below zero, the BoJ deposit rate should be set at level of −1.25%.

8 Such risk is confirmed, e.g., by a survey conducted by ING shortly after NIRP introduction by the ECB. According to it, almost 80% of households declared that would withdraw money from bank deposits if it was remunerated with negative interest rate. The answers were, however, differentiated by countries in the euro area – from as much as 92% of respondents in Austria, 80% in Germany to 75% in France and Italy (see ING, 2015).

9 Empirical studies confirm that households have strong preference to gravitate towards cash if their bank accounts or deposits are charged with additional – in their opinion overproportional – costs. A good example of that is Denmark, where it was allowed to charge households' deposits with a cost for cashless payments that was proportional to the amount of deposited money. From economic perspective, this approach can be understood as negative interest rates. As a result, however, number of transactions and deposits have shrunk significantly (Abildgren et al., 2010), which may implicate high households' vulnerability to NIRP also in the current circumstances.

10 Over the period of 2014–2018, the share of banks in which deposits constitute above 70% of all financial sources has shrunk significantly.

11 Most likely, however, this factor is in greater importance for interest on credit (see IMF, 2017 and further in the book).

12 Nevertheless, the legislative changes that will allow German banks to charge households' deposits with negative interest were proposed in June 2019 (Arnold, 2019).

13 Negative interest on loans – unlikely in case of negative coupon rate on bonds – does not mean reversal cash flow stream. Specifically, the borrower still need to pay off the incurred loan, usually on regular monthly basis. Thus, the capital share of amount to be paid is reduced by the amount of interest rate. In case of bond, in turn, a usual regular payment comes down to sole interest one.

14 It is important to point out that banks started to introduce negative interest on new credit with a significant lag. In August 2019, one of Danish banks (Jyske Bank A/S) granted a new mortgage loan with annual interest of −0.5% (The Guardian, 2019).

15 The latter mechanism refers directly to portfolio rebalancing channel (see, e.g., Albertazzi et al., 2018).

16 Credit standards in this book refer to banks' internal guidelines or loan approval criteria.
17 By credit terms and conditions, all actual terms and conditions agreed in loan contracts should be understood.
18 In particular, bank's profitability does not exclusively depend on central bank's interest rate but it is also affected by range of other factors, both macroeconomic (e.g., phase of business cycle) and microeconomic (e.g., cost management policy).

Bibliography

Abbate, A., Thaler, D., (2015). *Monetary Policy and the Asset Risk-Taking Channel*, Deutsche Bundesbank, Discussion Papers, no. 48/2015.

Abildgren, K., Andersen, B.N., Thomsen, J., (2010). *Monetary History of Denmark 1990–2005*, Danmarks Nationalbank.

Adrian, T., Shin, H.S., (2014). Procyclical Leverage and Value-at-Risk, *Review of Financial Studies, Society for Financial Studies*, vol. 27, no. 2, pp. 373–403.

Albertazzi, U., Becker, B., Boucinha, M., (2018). *Portfolio Rebalancing and the Transmission of Large-Scale Asset Programs: Evidence from the Euro Area*, ECB Working Paper, no. 2125.

Alessandri, P., Nelson, B.D., (2015) Simple Banking: Profitability and the Yield Curve, *Journal of Money Credit and Banking*, vol. 47, pp. 143–175.

Alsterlind, J., Armelius, H., Forsman, D., Joensson, B., Wretman, A.L., (2015). *How Far Can the Repo Rate Be Cut?* Economic Commentaries, No. 11, Stockholm: Sverige Risksbank.

Altavilla, C., Boucinha, M., Holton, S., Ongena, S., (2018). *Credit Supply and Demand in Unconventional Times*, ECB Working Papers, no. 2202.

Altavilla, C., Desislava, C.A., Boucinha, M., Holton, S., (2019). *Monetary Policy, Credit Institutions and the Bank Lending Channel in the Euro Area*, Occasional Paper Series no. 222, European Central Bank.

Altunbas, Y., Gambacorta, L., Marques-Ibanez, D., (2009). *An Empirical Assessment of the Risk-taking Channel*, SSRN Electronic Journal.

Angeloni, I., Faia, E., (2013). Capital Regulation and Monetary Policy with Fragile Banks, *Journal of Monetary Economics*, vol. 60, no. 3, pp. 311–324.

Angeloni, I., Faia, E., Lo Duca, M., (2015). Monetary Policy and Risk Taking, *Journal of Economic Dynamics and Control*, vol. 52, pp. 285–307.

Arce, O., García-Posada, M., Mayordomo, S., Ongena, S., (2018). *Adapting Lending Policies When Negative Interest Rates Hit Banks' Profits*, Banco de España Working Papers no. 1832.

Arnold, M., (2019). German Banks Wade into Negative Rate Debate, *Financial Times*, 26 August.

Avalos, F., Mamatzakis, E., (2018). *Euro Area Unconventional Monetary Policy and Bank Resilience*, BIS Working Papers no. 754.

Baldo, L., Hallinger, B., Helmus, C., Herrala, N., Martins, D., Mohing, F., Petroulakis, F., Reinek, F., Vergote, O., Usciati, B., Wang, Y., (2017). *The Distribution of Excess Liquidity in the Euro Area*, Occasiona Paper Series, European Central Bank, no. 200, November 2017.

Barr, M., Kasman, B., Mackie, D., (2016). *Negative Policy Rates: The Bound is Lower than You Think*, Special Report, J.P. Morgan, 9 February.

Basten, C., Mariathasan, M., (2018). *How Banks Respond to Negative Interest Rates: Evidence from the Swiss Exception Threshold*, CESifo Working Paper No. 6901.

Bech, M., Makhozov, A., (2016). How Have Central Banks Implemented Negative Policy Rates? *BIS Quarterly Review.*

Bernanke, B., (2016). *What Tools Does the Fed Have Left? Part 1: Negative Interest Rates*, Brookings Institution (blog), 18 March.

Bikker, J., Vervliet, T., (2017). *Bank Profitability and Risk-Taking Under Low Interest Rates*, DNB Working paper no. 560, July.

BIS, (2013). *Basel III: The Liquidity Coverage Ratio and Liquidity Risk Monitoring Tools*, Bank for International Settlements.

BoAML, (2019). *Back to the Negative Rates Lending Debate*, Japan Economic Viewpoint, Bank of America Merill Lynch, 27 August 2019.

Bonner, C., (2016). Preferential Regulatory Treatment and Banks' Demand for Government Bonds, *Journal of Money, Credit and Banking*, vol. 48, no. 6, pp. 1195–1221.

Borio, C., Gambacorta, L., (2017). Monetary Policy and Bank Lending in a Low Interest Rate Environment: Diminishing Effectiveness? *Journal of Macroeconomics*, vol. 54(B), pp, 217–231.

Borio, C., Gambacorta, L., Hofmann, B., (2017). The Influence of Monetary Policy on Bank Profitability, *International Finance*, vol. 20, pp. 48–63.

Borio, C., Zabai, A., (2016). *Unconventional Monetary Policies: A Re-appraisal*, BIS Working Papers, no. 570.

Bottero, M., Minoiu, C., Peydro, J.L., Polo, A., Presbitero, A., Sette, E., (2019). *Negative Monetary Policy Rates and Portfolio Rebalancing: Evidence from Credit Register Data*, IMF Working Papers 19/44, International Monetary Fund.

Busch, R., Memmel, C., (2015). *Bank's net interest margin and the level of interest rates.* Deutsche Bundesbank Discussion Paper no. 16/2015.

Chmielewski, T., Kapuściński, M., Kocięcki, A., Łyziak, T., Przystupa, J., Stanisławska, E., Wróbel, E., (2018). *Monetary transmission mechanism in Poland. What do we know in 2017?* NBP Working Papers no 286, Narodowy Bank Polski.

Claessens, S., Coleman, N., Donnelly, M., (2017). "Low for Long" Interest Rates and Banks' Interest Margins and Profitability: Cross-country Evidence, *Journal of Financial Intermediation*, Elsevier, vol. 35, pp. 1–16.

Cœuré, B., (2016). *Assessing the Implications of Negative Interest Rates, Speech of Member of the Executive Board of the ECB at the Yale Financial Crisis Forum*, Yale School of Management, New Haven, 28 July.

De Groot, O., (2014). The Risk Channel of Monetary Policy, *International Journal of Central Banking*, vol. 10, no. 2, pp. 115–160.

De Groot, O., Haas, A., (2018). *The Signaling Channel of Negative Interest Rates*, Unpublished manuscript. http://www.europarl.europa.eu/cmsdata/153241/DIW_final.pdf

Delis, M., Kouretas, G., (2011). Interest Rates and Bank Risk-Taking, *Journal of Banking and Finance*, vol. 35, pp. 840–855.

Demiralp, S., Eisenschmidt, J., Vlassopoulos, T., (2019). *Negative Interest Rates, Excess Liquidity and Bank Business Models: Banks' Reaction to Unconventional Monetary Policy in the Euro Area*, European Central Bank Working Paper Series, no. 2283.

Drechsler, I., Savov, A., Schnabl, P., (2017a). The Deposit Channel of Monetary Policy, *Quarterly Journal of Economics*, vol. 132, no. 4, pp. 1819–1876.

Drechsler, I., Savov, A., Schnabl, P., (2017b). *Banking on Deposits: Maturity Transformation without Interest Rate Risk*, SSRN.

EBC, (2017a). *Financial Stability Review*, European Central Bank, November.

EBC, (2017b). *Annual Report,* European Central Bank.

EBC, (2019a). *Heterogeneity and the ECB's monetary policy*, Speech by Benoît Cœuré at the Banque de France Symposium & 34th SUERF Colloquium on the occasion of the 20th anniversary of the euro on "The Euro Area: Staying the Course through Uncertainties", Paris, 29 March.

EBC, (2019b). *The Euro Area Bank Lending Survey*, European Central Bank, 2019.

Eggertsson, G.B., Juelsrud, R.E., Wold, E.G., (2017). *Are Negative Nominal Interest Rates Expansionary*? NBER Working Paper no. 24039.

Eisenschmidt, J., Smets, F., (2018). *Negative Interest Rates: Lessons from the Euro Area*, Prezentacja na *XXI Annual conference of the Central Bank of Chile*, forthcoming.

Ennis, H.M., Wolman, A.L., (2015). Large Excess Reserves in the United States: A View from the Cross-section of Banks, *International Journal of Central Banking*, vol. 11, pp. 251–289.

ESRB, (2016). *Macroprudential Policy Issues Arising from Low Interest Rates and Structural Changes in the EU Financial System*, Joint Task Force of ESRB Advisory Technical Committee (ATC), ESRB Advisory Scientific Committee (ASC), and ECB Financial Stability Committee (FSC), November 2016.

Gafrikova, V., (2016). *Ujemne stopy procentowe. Doświadczenia europejskie*, Przedsiębiorczość i Zarządzanie, Wydawnictwo SAN, ISSN 1733–2486, tom XVII, pp. 73–84. [available only in Polish]

Gambacorta, L., Ricotti, G., Sundaresan S., Wang, Z., (2017). *The Effects of Tax on Bank Liability Structure*, BIS Working Papers, no. 611.

Genay, H., Podjasek, R., (2014). What is the Impact of a Low Interest Rate Environment on Bank Profitability? *Chicago Fed Letters*, vol. 321, pp. 1–4.

Gennaioli, N., Martin, A., Rossi, S., (2013). Sovereign Default, Domestic Banks, and Financial Institutions, *Journal of Finance*, vol. 69, no. 2, pp. 819–866.

Gostomski, E., (2015), *Konsekwencje stosowania w strefie euro ujemnych stóp procentowych*, Bank Spółdzielczy, nr 1/578, luty-marzec. [available only in Polish].

Guin, B., (2017). *Culture and Household Saving*, ECB Working Paper Series, no. 2069.

Heider, F., Saidi, F., Schepens, G., (2017). *Life Below Zero: Bank Lending Under Negative Policy Rates*, Working Paper.

Henriques, R., Finsterbusch, A.J., Sharma, D., (2019). *Don't Be So Negative. Potential Impact of Negative Yields on European Bank Funding and Liquidity Strategies*, European Credit Research, JP Morgan, 9 September.

Hiroshi, G., (2018). *Did BOJ's Negative Interest Rate Policy Increase Bank Lending? Research Institute of Economy*, Trade and Industry Research Paper, no. 18-E-086.

Holmström, B., Tirole, J., (1993). Market Liquidity and Performance Monitoring, *Journal of Political Economy*, vol. 101, no. 4, pp. 678–709.

Horioka, Ch., Terada-Hagiwara, A., (2012). The Determinants and Long-term Projections of Saving Rates in Developing Asia, *Japan and the World Economy*, vol. 24, no. 2, pp. 128–137.

Horvath, R., Kotlebova, J., Siranova, M., (2018), Interest Rate Pass-through in the Euro Area: Financial Fragmentation, Balance Sheet Policies and Negative Rates, *Journal of Financial Stability*, vol. 36, pp. 12–21.

IMF, (2016). *Global Financial Stability Report*, International Monetary Fund.

IMF, (2017). *Negative Interest Rate Policies – Initial Experiences and Assessments*, IMF Policy Paper.

ING, (2015). *Negative Rates, Negative Reactions. Survey Suggests Sub-zero Deposit Rates Might Not Boost Consumer Spending*, ING Economic and Financial Analysis, Global economics.

Jiménez, G., Ongena, S., Peydró, J., Saurina, J., (2012). Credit Supply and Monetary Policy: Identifying the Bank-balance Sheet Channel with Loan Applications, *American Economic Review*, vol. 102, no. 5, pp. 2121–2165.

Jobst, A., Lin, H., (2016). *Negative Interest Rate Policy: Implications for Monetary Transmission and Bank Profitability in the Euro Area*, IMF Working Paper WP/16/172.

JP Morgan, (2019). *ECB: Is a Tiered Reserve Charging System an Option?* Europe Economic Research, 20 February.

Kashyap, A.K., Stein, J.C., (1995). The Impact of Monetary Policy on Bank Balance Sheets, *Carnegie-Rochester Conference Series on Public Policy*, vol. 42, pp. 151–195. Elsevier.

Khayat, G., A., (2018). The Impact of Setting Negative Policy Rates on Banking Flows and Exchange Rates, *Economic Modelling*, vol. 68, pp. 1–10.

Lopez, J.A., Rose, A.K., Spiegel, M.M., (2018). *Why Have Negative Nominal Interest Rates had Such a Small Effect on Bank Performance? Cross Country Evidence*, Federal Reserve Bank of San Francisco, Working Paper Series.

Lowe, P., Rohling, T., (1992). *Loan Rate Stickiness: Theory and Evidence*, Research Discussion Paper, Reserve Bank of Australia, no. 9206.

Maddaloni, A., Peydro, J-L., (2011). Bank Risk-taking, Securitization, Supervision, and Low Interest Rates: Evidence from the Euro-area and the U.S. Lending Standards, *Review of Financial Studies, Society for Financial Studies*, vol. 24, no. 6, pp. 2121–2165.

Perea, M., Kashama, M.K., (2017). *The Negative Interest Rate Policy in the Euro Area and the Supply of Bank Loans*, Economic Review issue III, National Bank of Belgium, pp. 42–61.

Pietryka, I., (2016). *Płynność sektora bankowego a skuteczność polityki pieniężnej Narodowego Banku Polskiego na tle Eurosystemu*, Instytut Badań Gospodarczych. Polskie Towarzystwo Ekonomiczne. [available only in Polish]

Popov, A., van Horen, N., (2013). *The Impact of Sovereign Debt Exposure on Bank Lending: Evidence from the European Debt Crisis*, DNB Working Paper 382.

Pyka, I., (2010). *Bank centralny na współczesnym rynku pieniężnym*, Warszawa: C.H. Beck. [available only in Polish]

Rostagno, M., Bindesil, U., Kamps, A., Lemke, W., Sugo, T., Vlassopoulos, F., (2016). *Breaking through the zero line: The ECB's negative interest rate policy*, Presentation at Brookings Institution, 6 June 2016, Washington, DC.

Ryan, E., Whelan, K., (2019). *Quantitative Easing and the Hot Potato Effect: Evidence from Euro Area Banks*, CEPR Discussion Paper, no. DP13499, Central Bank of Ireland.

Sääskilahti, J., (2018). Retail Bank Interest Margin in Low Interest Rate Environments, *Journal of Financial Services Research*, vol. 53, pp. 37–68.
Scheiber, T., Silgoner, M., Stern, C., (2016). The Development of Bank Profitability in Denmark, Sweden and Switzerland during a Period of Ultra-low and Negative Interest Rates, [in:] *Focus on European Economic Integration Q3/16*, pp. 8–28.
The Guardian, (2019). Danish Bank Launches World's First Negative Interest Rate Mortgage, Patrick Collinson, *The Guardian*, 13 August.
Valadkhani, A., Anwar, S., Arjomandi, A., (2013). Downward Stickiness of Interest Rates in the Australian Credit Card Market, *Journal of the Asia Pacific Economy*, vol. 9, no. 1, pp. 52–65.

6 Concept and Measurement of Systemic Risk

6.1 The Idea and Properties of Systemic Risk

Systemic risk is a particular risk category as it spans the entire financial system. Hence, in order to understand it, it is necessary to present both the ideas of risk and of financial system. First, this category is defined in terms of risk, not uncertainty, so it bears some specific characteristics vital for further analysis, including the capacity for being measured or managed (see, e.g., Knight, 1921). Financial risk may also be viewed from two perspectives – negative (interpreted as a negative deviation from the expected result) and neutral (as any deviation from the expected result; Jajuga et al., 2017). In this context, systemic risk is a disturbance to financial stability. With respect to the definition of the financial system, it is regarded in this study as a mechanism which enables rendering services that trigger purchasing power in the economy (Pietrzak et al., 2004). Thus, economic growth may be fostered by financial institutions and non-financial entities, i.e., firms and households.[1] The financial system is composed of financial institutions (i.e., banks, non-bank financial institutions, including investment firms and insurance companies), financial instruments, financial markets and financial system infrastructure (Szczepańska, 2008).

In combining the ideas of "risk" and "financial system", ECB (2010) comes up with a twofold definition of systemic risk whereby it is referred to as an occurrence of a systemic event, i.e., one affecting all the entities in a financial system. From this perspective, systemic risk may bear some characteristics of credit risk, since the latter may also be explicitly defined – as credit risk event. However, a systemic event is broadly understood as a manifestation of financial instability giving rise to a material adverse effect on the economy's macroeconomic and financial sphere. In turn, in a narrow understanding, it is an event which causes shock to the entire economy, disrupts the financial system and may negatively affect economic growth (Blundell-Wignall and Roulet, 2013). From the perspective of the empirical analysis, a systemic event bears characteristics of a tail event to which a relatively minor (some calling it substantially underestimated) likelihood is assigned, the materialization of which, however, results in large-scale losses (Kemp, 2017).

DOI: 10.4324/9781003312116-6

Hence, inextricably connected with the idea of systemic risk is financial system stability (also referred to as financial stability). Consequently, some scholars define systemic risk as a collection of such phenomena which jeopardize financial stability (e.g., ECB, 2009; IMF, 2009). In turn, social sciences often identify stability with static or dynamic equilibrium (see, e.g., Bertalanffy, 1984:156). Whether it is possible to attain such equilibrium or not, the academics agree that a system drifting away from a state of equilibrium evokes instability (Bernaciak, 2012). Therefore, financial stability may be presented as a property of a financial system which involves restoring equilibrium after the disruption which upset the system's balance ceased. In this context, it is a major scale of the disruption and the system's susceptibility to this risk materializing that would be labelled systemic risk. In contemporary business practice, financial stability is defined through the lens of a financial system's capacity for performing functions it has been assigned, in particular, effective allocation of funds across the economy (Smaga, 2014b). In numerous cases, financial stability is equated with a banking system stability, which is, in turn, a reference to financial system models, especially in countries whereby it is the banks that occupy the most prominent position in the financial system.[2] In this study, financial stability will also be understood in multiple ways. On the one hand, the ability to perform its functions will be emphasized, and its ability to counter shocks or to easily absorb them, on the other. Accordingly, a financial system which performs its functions, yet it is vulnerable to even minor disturbances which require a long-term recovery, should not be referred to as stable.

Hence, the very definition of financial stability may imply a comprehensive character of systemic risk concept. Thus, on the one hand, it may be perceived as a consequence of financial stability missing, that is, a social cost attributable to a properly working system being interrupted. On the other hand though, systemic risk may be a reason for financial instability viewed by the likelihood of losing stability due to rising imbalances and the scale of interconnections in the system or the financial system's shrinking capacity of absorbing shocks.

It follows that a broad conceptual scope of systemic risk renders it difficult to being classified as a risk category (next to credit, liquidity or operational risk) as systemic risk may have characteristics of each of the categories manifesting themselves throughout the financial system. At the same time, the risk should not be considered as a aggregation of individual risk categories identified for individual institutions in the system, as these institutions' interconnections are what matters too. In this way, the macroeconomic essence of systemic risk appears. Namely, the costs associated with its materialization are borne by all of the financial system and real economy participants and not, as in the case of other financial risk categories, only by the entities concerned. In other words, systemic risk applies when the entire financial system is exposed to the particular disturbance (Nier, 2009). At the same time, however, it may be construed as having microeconomic character, viewed through the lens of bankruptcy of the systematically important financial institutions, i.e., SIFIs (Smaga, 2014a). Further, it is not possible to interpret systemic risk as a negative deviation from the expected result being sort of a state of equilibrium, as there is no "optimum" nor "desired" systemic risk level (Smaga, 2014a).

Although it is not possible to come up with one precise and simple definition of systemic risk, it is crucial to understand its essence and dynamics. A review of the literature on the essence of systemic risk provides several major conclusions (Figure 6.1, see more: Smaga, 2020). All definitions of systemic risk are intertwined, and it is not possible to assign each definition to a specific group on an exclusive basis. The majority of definitions pertain

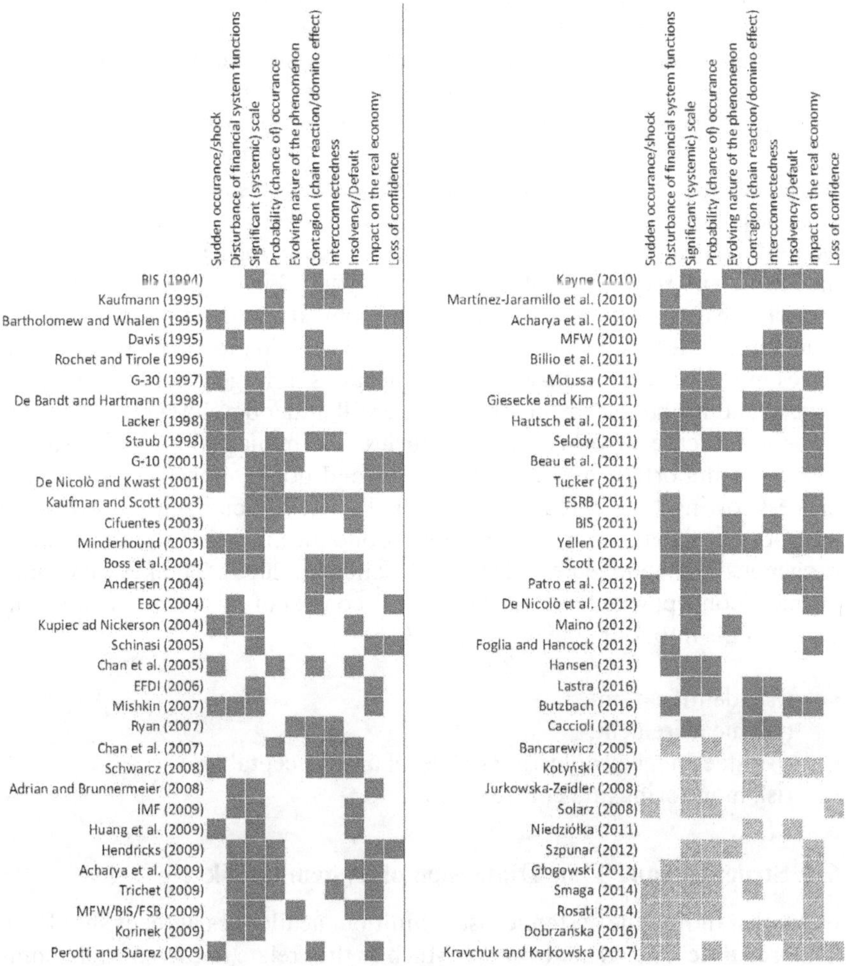

Figure 6.1 An overview of systemic risk definition in literature

Note: The painted squares mean that the respective characteristic has been considered in definition of systemic risk; the hatched squares refer to Polish-language academic literature.

Source: Own work based on Smaga (2014a, 2020).

directly to the financial system. They emphasize that whenever this risk materializes, first and foremost financial system disturbances ensue which are generated by disturbing some of its, not always explicit, functions. The key element is the likelihood of these disturbances migrating among the interconnected system elements. The definitions bring out the significance of the contagion effect and a large scale of connections, predominantly in the period before the global financial crisis (Smaga, 2014a). Thereafter, attention was shifted in the literature to the disturbances in the financial system performing its functions (Figure 6.1). Whatever the approach to how the concept is defined, it cannot be denied that systemic risk, whenever materialized, produces threats to financial stability by spurring on the spread of disturbances into other entities, markets or countries (Ostalecka, 2012).

Concluding the definition-related considerations, a line should also be drawn between systemic versus systematic risk. Systematic risk stems from the core foundations of every economy and it is attributable to market participants influencing asset prices (Karkowska, 2015). Much as this risk is of macroeconomic or aggregate nature (Hansen, 2013), it may be managed and mitigated, albeit not microeconomically (e.g., by diversification). In addition, as opposed to systemic risk, the systematic risk enjoys a relatively long and well-established tradition, both theoretical and empirical, with respect to modelling and measurement (Jajuga et al., 2017). Further, as this risk often materializes, it is easily measurable. In this context, systemic risk has a clearly much broader scope reflected in structural determinants manifesting themselves in the scale of intra-sectoral connections, a largely non-materialized aspect, and its measurement methods are still under development.

As is the case of other risk categories, the manageability of systemic risk is an important aspect. What is beyond doubt, however, is that the process, owing to a complex nature of this very phenomenon, should be multi-dimensional, incorporating both economic and other than economic, exogenous and endogenous elements (Flejterski, 2006). The key risk management concept which can be put into the context of this phenomenon concerned, falls into four stages (Jajuga, 2008):

- risk identification;
- risk measurement;
- risk steering, i.e., adjusting risk level until acceptable;
- risk monitoring and control.

6.2 Structural and Time Dimension of Systemic Risk

Notwithstanding the systemic risk definition, academics agree it should be analysed time- and structure-wise. Much as they relate to the same phenomenon, these dimensions vary in terms of several characteristics, a comprehensive summary of which is presented in Table 6.1.

Table 6.1 The dimensions of systemic risk

	Cross-sectional dimension	*Time dimension*
Aim of the analysis	Shock transmission mechanism	Build-up of macrofinancial imbalances
Approach	Point-in-time	Over the given period
The main area of analysis	Size of the financial system, its structure and the degree of interconnectedness	Procyclicality
The role of macroeconomic factors	Exogenous	Endogenous
Objective of macroprudential measures	The increase in financial system resilience to shocks	Reducing the rate of imbalances accumulation and mitigating their impact
Examples of risk sources	Interconnectedness and similarities in risk exposures of financial institutions leading to exposure to symmetric shock, excessive concentration	Interlinkages between the financial system and the real economy, financial system regulation

Source: Smaga (2020).

The cross-sectional or structural dimension of systemic risk refers to its distribution across the financial system (i.e., its presence in various parts of the system) at a given moment. What underlies the structural dimension of systemic risk is determining of the scale of interconnectedness among financial systems, institutions and economies of respective countries which may spread risk impulse as part of the contagion effect.

In the structural dimension of systemic risk, SIFIs have a special role. They are institutions which, once unable to meet their commitments to clients and creditors, would bring about significant adverse consequences for the entire financial sector and other areas of the economy (e.g., IMF, 2014). SIFIs are complex, both organizationally and business-wise and their role is critical in the financial sector's infrastructure, which makes them too big to fail (TBTF, e.g., Olszak, 2015). Yet, another particular characteristic of these entities is that, in investors' view, financial safety net institutions are inclined to avoid their bankruptcy as their problems would disrupt the entire banking system. Consequently, SIFIs may be strongly tempted by moral hazard and willing to take up excessive risk. In practice, the status of a systemically important financial institution gives additional benefits, including lower funding costs (IMF, 2014; Santos, 2014). However, SIFI status also entails additional substantial costs arising from macroprudential regulations (e.g., FSB, 2010).

The status of a systemically important financial institution demonstrates a critical influence it has on the level of systemic risk (Masciantonio and Zaghini, 2017). Identification of such an institution should primarily allow to evaluate a scale of potential adverse effects to a financial system evoked by its bankruptcy and not just imminent likelihood of the event happening. Thus, identification criteria for such entities are focused on characteristics, such as, for instance, the extent and degree of interconnectedness, whether the services offered are substitutable, how complicated the operations are (see, e.g., ECB, 2010a; BIS, 2013b, 2018). The status of such an institution, however, is dynamic, so it may change over time as an institution of a minor systemic importance in one phase of a cycle may prove important in another. Further, cross-sectionally, the literature also shows that systemic risk may be chiefly confined to the banking sector; hence, supervision authorities, next to systemically important financial institutions, have coined a term focusing on the banking sector only, i.e., Global Systemically Important Banks (G-SIBs). A comprehensive approach to the analysis, however, often requires that the importance of non-banking financial institutions or the central counterparty be taken into account, hence, that the structural changes across the entire financial sector are covered. What is also crucial to systemic risk analysis is that the risk may materialize not only as an aftermath of a SIFI bankruptcy but also due to problems of entities of smaller size, albeit affected with symmetric shock. In other words, the contagion effect is a phenomenon which may affect any entity, not only the one which is in financial troubles but also those strong at the onset and then affected by a secondary shock attributable to spillover effect (Smaga, 2014a).

The time or cyclical dimension of systemic risk, pertains, in turn, to a collective tendency of market participants to periodically under- or overestimate the risk level (Szpunar, 2012). It means that it is inextricably connected with cyclicality which may be defined as a development of a given economic parameter in deviation from a medium- or long-term level of equilibrium that occurs at given intervals. Systemic risk is particularly connected with cyclicality of financial variables, that is, financial cycles. Such cycles are the result of other component cycles pertaining to credit, real estate and prices of financial assets (e.g. Allen and Gale, 2000a). Notwithstanding, it is the credit cycles that are assigned special importance from the perspective of systemic risk analysis (in particular, credit for the non-financial sector) as well as real estate prices. Of lesser relevance, given their relatively high-amplitude short-term fluctuations and a significant effect of other factors, including psychological, are considered stock market cycles. The empirical literature also defines the features of financial cycles while emphasizing their considerable differences from economic cycles (e.g., Pipień et al., 2018). Namely, financial cycles last much longer; in developed economies, the duration may be measured even in decades with a two- or three-times higher amplitude of fluctuations than the amplitude of an economic cycle. This feature also implies that a cyclical systemic risk accrues gradually in the medium and long terms. Still, it should be noted that in spite of the differences between economic and financial cycles, they interact with each other, which may be evidenced by a relation between a peak in the financial cycle and a significantly longer and deep depression following in the real economy as a result of a crisis (Kollintzas et al., 2011; Claessens et al., 2012).

The foregoing also shows that systemic risk is pro-cyclical, i.e., risk is underestimated during prosperity and overestimated during depression, which strengthens the cyclical fluctuations of financial and real spheres. A pro-cyclical character of systemic risk may be borne out by the tendencies in the behaviour of economic entities. The tendencies work through demand and supply channels of bank credit (e.g., Smaga, 2015):[3]

- demand for credit rises proportionately to economic growth;
- typically, during a period of rising business activity, banks' funding costs behave in inverse way, i.e., they decrease, aiming to increase credit supply;
- banks tend to overly relax credit policy during recovery and to tighten it during recession, thus, strengthening a given phase of economic cycle;
- during prosperity, lenders tend to increase their exposure to the same type of assets, which simultaneously puts them at a higher risk of being affected by a symmetric shock and limits risk diversification capacity;
- risk appetite, condition of the financial system and the business climate in real economy are increasingly dependent on (interacting) externalities.

Accordingly, the empirical literature often considers the credit gap (i.e., a deviation of credit level for the non-financial sector, in relation to GDP, from a long-term trend) to be one of systemic risk time dimension indicators and it also brings up a vital role of this indicator as an early warning indicator (EWI; see, e.g., Borio and Lowe, 2002b, 2004).

6.3 Systemic Risk Sources

The multi-level character and the complexity of systemic risk make it really difficult to point to what really is the timeless and universal cause of this risk emergence. Consequently, the literature provides an analysis of a broad range of systemic risk sources the in-depth analysis of which goes beyond the scope of this study. For this work, what seems to be the most relevant is a three-layer classification of systemic risk determinants into (Bradsen et al., 2006; ECB, 2017; see: Figure 6.2): (i) originating inside of the financial system (i.e., endogenous); (ii) brought on by external factors (i.e., exogenous); and (iii) the contagion effect, that is, a mechanism which intensifies the impact of the previous two.

For endogenous sources of systemic risk, it seems obvious three main issues should be taken into account. First, it is information asymmetry

	Endogenous	Exogenous	Contagion
Cross-sectoral	• Asymmetric information • Moral hazard • Debt accumulation (including FX debt) • Procylicality of banking activity	• Cummulation of aggregate credit risk due to macroeconomic factors (including monetary policy) • Lower market liquidity, fragmented trading, loss of confidence • Liberalisation of capital flows	• Excessive concentration of capital in financial sector • Herding behaviour and irrational activity
Sectoral	• Tendency to clustering of market exposures	• Greater focus of regulatory authorities on complexity and size of financial institutions rather than on tendencies to risk taking	• Bank run • Dense network of interrelations
Individual	• Individual overtaking of financial risk • Inappropriate measurement of financial risk (e.g. model risk) • Automatic transaction systems (e.g. high frequency trading)	• Indirect acceptance of market inefficiences (e.g. moral hazard)	• Behavioral biases (including fear of missing out)

Figure 6.2 General classification of systemic risk sources

Note: The above-mentioned classification may be ambiguous since mutual relations across the factors unable their clear placement.

Source: Own work based on ESRB (2016).

(Bullard et al., 2009) which is inherent in the banking business. In this case, however, the phenomenon rests more on the very relations among the entities in a financial system, ultimately affecting the credit risk level across the entire financial system. Second, as a consequence, an important source of systemic risk may be excessive concentration of credit exposures, excessive financial leverage or unstable financing models, which stems from financial institutions' eagerness to take excessive risk. Such phenomena may also cause inadequate market liquidity which may be painful for the banks as system participants, giving rise to a liquidity crisis in the most extreme cases. Third, an important cause of systemic risk may simply be incorrect risk appraisal on financial markets, i.e., its underestimation versus the scale and potential costs (Alexander et al., 2010).

Some scholars argue that the deregulation of financial crisis and liberalization of capital flows observable before the global crisis caused an excessive debt of the private and public sectors (Ostalecka, 2009), and in more general terms, they significantly drove up the impact of the international environment on the domestic assessment of systemic risk. Finally, the effect of the fiscal or monetary policy on a country's external balance may grow increasingly more difficult. In particular, small open economies have become more vulnerable to external shock. Along with national economies growing increasingly more open, a free flow of money and capital, globalization and liberalization, the danger of systemic risk affecting the global economy has exacerbated (Pyka, 2010). Owing to a strong relationship among international banking systems, the condition of one of them determines the situation of the other. Consequently, systemic risk materializing, for instance, in the United States due to endogenous factors, may at the same time represent an exogenous source of shocks and the contagion effect spreading to other world's economies and financial entities. At this point, the endogenous nature of the systemic risk itself is also worth mentioning (Danielsson and Shin, 2003). Accordingly, certain financial institutions becoming insolvent and thus spurring on a negative primary shock must not be considered as an effect of an external shock, as the insolvency occurs within the financial sector. In other words, risks affecting the financial system are largely generated by how market participants behave (Danielsson et al., 2013), so they are mostly intra-systemic.

From such a perspective, the systemic risk in the strict sense should be considered as principally traceable down to endogenous sources, whereas the exogenous sources identified in this chapter may only affect its level or the scale of amplification. Simultaneously, however, a systemic event itself, treated as a factor triggering materialization of systemic risk, may have both endo- and exogenous roots. Such exogenous factors include primarily impact on the macroeconomic environment which, in extreme cases, may induce a negative liquidity shock. Thus, what belongs to the environment is also monetary policy and its effect on the level of risk taken by financial institutions.

In a nutshell, a classification which discriminates between sources situated inside and outside of a financial system applies, in fact, to a majority of financial risk types. In turn, what directly relates to the particular character of the systemic risk is, hard to identify under this methodology, the contagion effect which will be closely scrutinized in the below sub-chapter.

6.3.1 Contagion Effect in the Systemic Risk Concept

What most of the systemic risk concepts have in common is a contagion effect, an intrinsic, structurally embedded in the first place, element of this risk category. There are mainly three definitions that are to be found in the literature, i.e., a broad, a narrow and a very narrow one (see, e.g., Claessens et al., 2001). The first one says that the contagion effect is an international transmission of shocks or an overall international spillover effect which occurs both in peaceful times and during crisis, whereby it becomes intensified. The second idea holds that contagion is a transmission of shocks onto other markets or a relationship among them going beyond fundamental connections and any consequences of common shocks. In turn, according to the narrowest interpretation, contagion occurs whenever inter-market correlation is substantially higher during crisis than stabilization. Notwithstanding the definition itself, academics agree that the contagion effect will not take place unless the primary shock comes first, that is, an impulse to trigger further adjustments on the part of businesses.

From the empirical perspective, this effect, identified both on intra-systemic and an overall economic levels (Jurkowska, 2018), works on two platforms – economic connections or behavioural factors (Ostalecka, 2009). In the case of the first one a negative impulse is transmitted through fundamental connections, i.e., attributable directly to trade or financial connections. The other one occurs in a situation whereby, although fundamental conditions are missing, transmission does take place and it may be due to economic entities' perception and their embracement of adverse signals. To add more detail, such a distinction is due to three channels of adverse signals' transmission coinciding:

- trade channel (see, e.g., Scott, 2010; Adrian and Shin, 2008; Harrington, 2009) – a result of contracts, especially those made on the interbank market or as part of services within a payment system which derive out of an inability to meet obligations to counterparties, which in turn generates problems for yet other entities (the counterparty-contagion effect);
- price channel (see, e.g., Adrian and Brunnermeier, 2016; Harrington, 2009) – emerges whenever one financial institution or a group of such entities are forced to rapidly sell assets at lower prices in case market liquidity falls (i.e., fire sales), which, next to directly affecting the valuation of an asset on a given institution's balance sheet, translates indirectly into a lower valuation of these (or other, yet correlated in terms of price) assets on the balance sheets of other entities;
- information channel (see, e.g., Helwege, 2009; Harrington, 2009) – arises whenever information on a given financial institution being in a poor condition generates information asymmetry on the market for other, like institutions (informational contagion) which share a common factor.

On the contemporary financial market and given a particular character of its transactions, this mechanism is often expanded to include a fourth channel pertaining to mutual exposures of banks in derivative products (Scott, 2010).

For empirical verification, the literature specifies four criteria classifying a given event in a financial system as a contagion effect (Hartmann et al., 2004; Constancio, 2012):

- shock transmission among entities (including their scale and character) surpasses expectations which are attributable to fundamental conditions, which provides grounds for the impact of the aforesaid information channel;
- the transmission differs from financial system adjustments observed in the periods of stability;
- events making up the contagion effect give rise to negative extremes (e.g., a wave of bankruptcies or rapid revaluation in numerous markets);
- the transmission of contagion effect is sequence-based (e.g., it arises from cause-and-effect relationships).

The analysis of the importance of contagion effect for the structural aspect of systemic risk may produce some kind of a paradox, in particular, if the phenomenon is viewed through diversification. It is because, on the one hand, the classical approach holds that growing diversification of, for instance, mutual exposures in the banking system, may reduce systemic risk level in that the dependence on a segment spawning instability becomes lower (a lower risk of exposure concentration).[4] On the other hand, though, along with a higher number of connections naturally comes a broader range of entities possibly affected by transmission of an adverse effect, so the higher sector-level accumulation, the higher systemic risk. A solution to the riddle can be found in the literature which argues that the more connections, the lesser likelihood of the contagion effect spreading; however, a significant cost comes into play of the scale of the effect being greater when a negative impulse is generated anyway (Gai and Kapania, 2010; Allen and Carletti, 2012).

Some authors also note that there are two types of the contagion effect – a "domino" and a "tsunami" effect (see, e.g., IMF, 2016). Such a differentiation aims to highlight the structure of how shock is transmitted over a financial system and to emphasize exogenous factors. The first type essentially pertains to a cascade-like character of primary shock transmission which gives rise to a gradual accumulation of the results. Given the cascade-like feature, the way the transmission proceeds allows to identify the model of impulse transmission and its sources. In turn, the other of the aforementioned effects focuses on the rapid and parallel character of chaotic, often non-linear events. Typically exogenously driven in this case, the primary shock is transmitted simultaneously on numerous levels, so it is not possible to identify the effect a given path has on a specific institution in the financial system. In extreme cases, the tsunami effect may also be identified as resulting in several domino effects going parallelly (Kemp, 2017). In turn, for both these effects, often just one, a sufficiently important impulse will be enough to launch the entire process of spreading contagion.

6.4 Systemic Risk Assessment Concept

Unlike the idea of financial stability, systemic risk, like any other risk, lends itself to being measured. Accordingly, it is possible to construct such measures to allow for both a sufficiently early identification of systemic disturbances and their scale. However, the multi-dimensional and complicated character of this phenomenon implies that it is necessary to develop a multi-layer approach to measurement. Namely, the measures and models for assessing this risk category depend on how the very phenomenon is defined and what factors are considered to be the main cause behind systemic risk in a given approach. Consequently, over the last dozen years or so, along with a robust growth of interest in the very idea of financial stability, the development of systemic risk analysis methods and their methodological advancement have intensified. Still, a single universal approach to systemic risk measurement has not been devised yet either in the literature or in the practice of central banks.

The vital issue in the process of systemic risk measurement is first and foremost to define the dimension to be measured, which will, in turn, determine the method applied (see Figure 6.3). The time dimension of systemic risk should be captured by methods which enable identification of this risk accruing, whereas the structural dimension – by processes which identify the strengthening of systemic disturbances and how much they spread across the system. Such a specification of needs regarding systemic risk assessment means that the measurement tools in the first case are more supposed to determine the probability of a systemic event, so they should be based on time series empirical models, and use indicator methods, also as early warning indices. In the other case, the focus is primarily on the results of a given event in case it materializes. Consequently, a systemic event may be considered exogenous and incorporated into the systemic risk network models or systemic risk structural models in the narrow sense as construed in our study.

Our approach to estimating systemic risk is broadened to include the endogenous aspects via a three-layer analysis which covers the following perspectives (Benoit et al., 2015; Jajuga et al., 2017):

- measurement of systemic risk scale employing both tension indicators in the financial system and sophisticated methods of estimating the scale of systemic risk (np. Kiyotaki and Moore, 1997; Acharya, 2009; Brunnermeier and Oehmke, 2013);
- transmission of disturbances across the financial system, that is, methods analysing how risk is transferred by identifying channels and entities affected by a systemic event, with a focus on what directions this effect will be heading (Allen and Gale, 2000b; Duffie and Zhu, 2011);

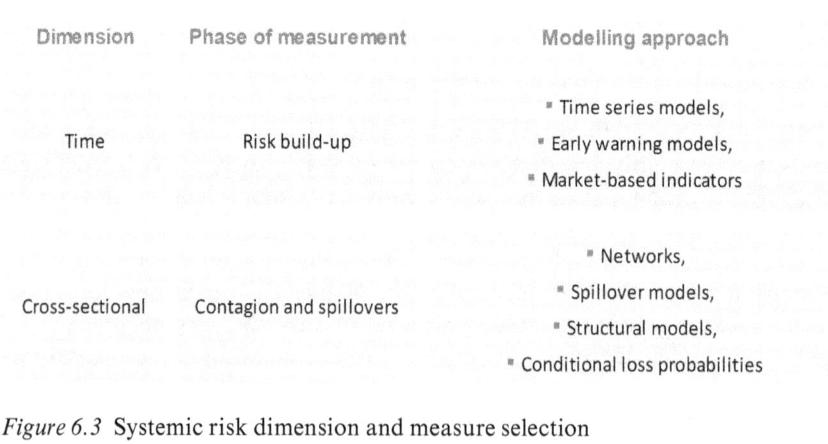

Figure 6.3 Systemic risk dimension and measure selection
Source: Own work based on Smaga (2014a) and ECB (2018).

- impact of systemic risk on the real economy – the use of systemic risk measures so as to incorporate them into the structural macroeconomic models.

The sub-chapters below present the said approaches to the measurement of systemic risk by growing complexity of the method used, concentrating on the measurement methods in the narrow sense as the most important category for the analysis from economic policy perspective.

6.5 Systemic Risk Indicators

The methods of systemic risk assessment include, first and foremost, financial soundness/stability indicators (FSIs) that are commonly used also by supervisory authorities. They are relatively the least complicated, hence their popularity. They may come as sets of variables reflecting financial stability (so-called dashboards) or as aggregate synthetic risk indicators determined on the basis of simple economic or financial variables (Jajuga et al., 2017). This group includes both indicators made from standalone data, mostly from balance sheets (Gadanecz and Jayaram, 2009) as well as sector or macroeconomic data which are applied relatively more often (Illing and Liu, 2003; Nelson and Perli, 2007; Holló et al., 2012). Consequently, the indicators are also used to monitor the stability of a financial system globally, e.g., by the International Monetary Fund (IMF, 2006), and internationally, by, e.g., the European Union or the European Systemic Risk Board. Such a way of monitoring systemic risk, however, may force the use of a set of indicators so as to make them applicable for as many economies as possible, which at the same time precludes these measures from being subject to one universal prudential threshold (Agresti et al., 2008) and it prevents the use of more advanced risk measurement methods.

The phenomenon's very nature impedes systemic risk analysis in the context of its above assessment. As mentioned before, systemic events normally occur in crisis situations which, in turn, occur relatively seldom. It follows that a measure of systemic risk must be resilient to what the characteristic implies, i.e., must not be blurred by the effect of the scale of an already materialized risk. Namely, such a disturbance may show that there are no grounds whatsoever for the non-materialized risk to rise, because, in contrast to the materialized risk, this parameter may be so negligible that it is ignored in analyses. The argument is raised most often by the advocates of simple, and not advanced, measurement methods (Rodríguez-Moreno and Peña, 2013).[5] It is possible to assess risk only by comparing how these two indicators develop over time. It follows that necessary historical data should be at hand as the current absolute value of an indicator has only a small information value. In addition, the "risk boards" referred to earlier are not one synthetic measure (much as they perform their overseeing function), so they may not be implemented into broader economic analyses, for instance, in the analysis of transmitting risk disturbance. A further defect of macroeconomic systemic risk indicators is that even if they attempt to account for a structural dimension of systemic risk, they will not enable identifying systemically important financial institutions. It follows that, if based solely on the "risk board" indicators, the process of systemic risk management may be hampered. Thus, systemic risk indicators should be considered as input elements for risk analysis process, whereas systemic risk measurements methods should be considered the outcome (Jajuga et al., 2017).

6.6 Network Theory in Systemic Risk Analyses

As economic entities and financial institutions do not work in isolation, but they forge relations with other entities, the empirical literature has endeavoured to analyse the ensuing risk. Such an approach referred to as network analysis defines the scale of connections among financial institutions and it measures the potential contagion effect being a vital element of the systemic risk concept. In line with the main objective of the analysis, the properties and behaviours of given entities are sequentially affected by the behaviours of entities connected with them directly and indirectly (Eisenberg and Noe, 2001). Thus, this method complements other systemic risk measures to include a cause-and-effect approach which is of high importance in the analysis of the process of risk spreading. So, with respect to the financial sector, the network theory allows to capture its structure, measurement and identification of contagion effect into a model as well as to define the entities most vulnerable to the said effect. These factors are identified by analysing the features of the existing network, so its density, concentration, identification of more tightly interconnected sub-groups, division into centres and peripheries or identification of the character of the relation (Caccioli et al., 2018). Hence, in this context, systemic risk level is largely determined by the structure of the entire financial system's network (Acemoglu et al., 2015).

Systemic risk analysis viewed through network theory is focused on the analysis of the size and dynamics of a specified scheme of interconnections, and the forming of the scheme itself among financial institutions is attributable to two effects. On the one hand, financial entities' willingness to expand their scale of connections is nurtured by the advantages of diversification effect (Frey and Hledik, 2018). On the other hand, though, a more complex structure of interconnections across the entire system propels a faster spread of contagion effect. For minor shocks, an interconnected system effectively absorbs losses, however, a sufficiently large shock may trigger a domino effect and loss amplification. Consequently, the literature which analyses network theory identifies a critical point of advantages of interconnectedness past which the diversification effect fades, and the degree of external shock amplification rises (Chan-Lau, 2013). In other words, while close connections among institutions may reduce the likelihood of the contagion effect, at the same time they start spreading on a larger scale once the effect occurs (Gai and Kapania, 2010; Allen and Carletti, 2012). Accordingly, what the network analysis with respect to systemic risk relies on is a statement saying that even the most robust system may in fact prove fragile (robust-yet-fragile approach; e.g., Haldane, 2013; Glasserman, 2015; Karkowska, 2015).

As pointed out before, an important part of the size network analysis is its structure, which determines the transmission dynamics of the primary shock across the financial system (see, e.g., Allen and Gale, 2000b; Freixas et al., 2000; Drehmann and Tarashev, 2011). In other words, it should be pointed out that the less cascade-like the structure of a financial system, the earlier the risk impulse expires. In such an environment, a rising number of entities in a system (or a network) may inspire a rise of systemic risk, however, only moderately and in a linear fashion (Figure 6.4). In some cases, however, the structure identifies a reinforcing loop effect which consequently gives rise to a most robust growth of systemic risk, even in a non-linear fashion (e.g., Freixas et al., 2015). Accordingly, network structure and its complexity determine how important a given entity is for the system. The structure of a majority of networks also proves to include many large entities concentrating their connection in the centre (so-called "core") and having relatively fewer connections with smaller entities on the system's peripheries (core-periphery structure). Such a network structure is essentially resilient

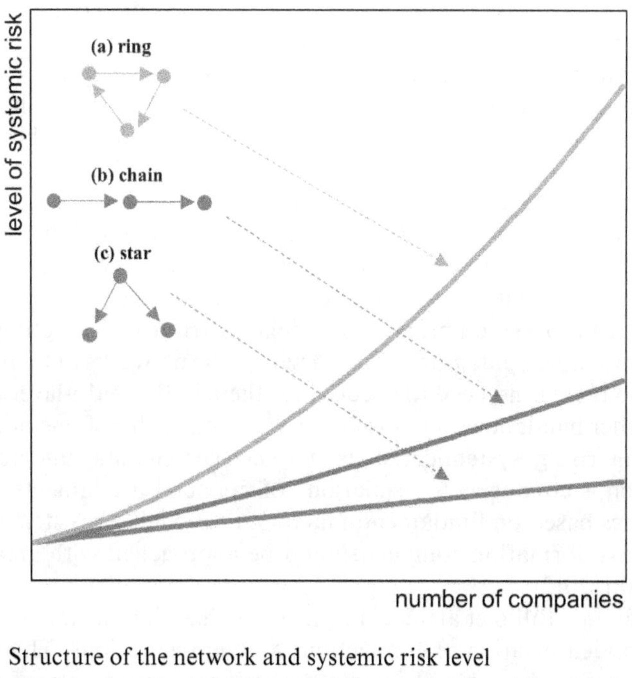

Figure 6.4 Structure of the network and systemic risk level
Source: Own work.

to shocks which affect peripheral entities and simultaneously vulnerable to those affecting (or deriving from) centrally situated entities (Albert et al., 2000; Boss et al., 2004; Fricke and Lux, 2012). Empirical literature also provides evidence for a separate character of the entities identified as too big to fail (TBTF) from too interconnected to fail (TITF; see, e.g., Iyer and Peydro, 2011; Covi et al., 2019). It is because the latter may be relatively small, albeit having such numerous, relatively complex connections that they significantly increase the structural dimension of systemic risk.

In accordance with the above approach to network analysis, an existing network allows to comprehensively conclude on the structural phenomena taking place. In practice, however, the network scheme may be constructed for many risk layers which may intertwine, which is of tremendous importance for a full analysis of systemic risk. Montagna and Kok (2016) come up with a good illustration for this approach. They identify three important layers for which a network of interconnections may be empirically constructed: (i) lending-borrowing network which takes account of long-term mutual relations in the financial system; (ii) liquidity network which takes account of short-term mutual exposures; and (iii) overlapping portfolios which take account of connections among portfolio exposures to respective categories of financial assets. Each of these networks constructed for the banking system may have a different structure, which means in turn that it will also have different dynamics of transmitting disturbances across the system. In addition, these categories are not disjoint, so, for such a complex issue as systemic risk, the analysis should, next to connection among entities, address also network interconnection (see Figure 6.5). Consequently, analytical approach focused solely on one risk layer may be conducive to underestimation of the level of systemic risk. At the same time, however, for an analysis to be comprehensive, highly complicated analytical tools should be employed at the cost of a rising model risk.

Alternatively to the said methodological complication, the literature proposes to employ tools making up a financial system network with the use of market data rather than balance sheet data on entities' mutual exposures. Starting with information effectiveness of financial markets, such an approach is based on prices of financial instruments reflecting an entire range of potential contagion channels within the networks of financial institutions, so there is no need to account for them in the multi-layer approach. On the other hand, however, it is vital to remember that if one of the causes underlying rising systemic risk is market participants' underestimating risk, which is conducive to "isolation" of financial instruments' valuation from values based on fundamental factors, the conclusions stemming from the prices' information contents should be approached with great caution (Głogowski, 2012).

Accordingly, Billio et al. (2012) came up with an important empirical approach to identification of connections among institutions. This approach aimed to define the scale of interconnectedness among various sectors of

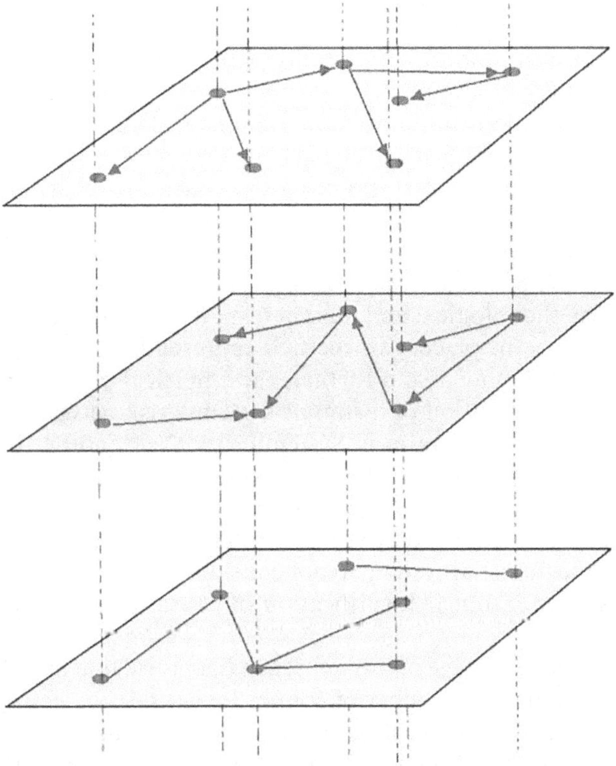

Figure 6.5 Network multidimensionality problem in the context of the systemic risk analysis

Source: Montagna and Kok (2016).

financial institutions (banks, insurance companies, investment companies and hedge funds) based on market data. In order to analyse the strength and the directions of connections among the entities, this concept drew independently from two methods – principal component analysis (PCA) and Granger's causality. Owing to the first method, PCA, it is possible to identify common factors which explain the variability of a data set examined. If entities' financial situation (manifested by changes in stock prices and investment results) largely relies on a small number of common factors, it shows similarity in investment strategies applied. Hence, it may also represent some of the signals that testify to aggravated systemic risk. Namely, under such circumstances, even a relatively minor disturbance confined to an economy sector which weighs much in investment portfolios may trigger disturbances all across the financial sector. Yet, another method originally put forward also by Billio et al. (2012) and gaining in popularity is a method of constructing a network of interconnected institutions in a financial system, based on the identification of statistical cause-and-effect relations (Granger's causality).[6] In line with this approach, it is identified whether a given feature of a specific institution (such as profitability, change in market valuation, risk appraisal) may potentially affect a similar feature of another institution. In its original approach, the identification of causality network was applied for changes in stock prices of financial institutions. However, it is worth pointing out that in case financial market information proves fully effective, such an approach should identify no causality whatsoever among financial institutions and it should prevent the construction of the analysed financial sector network. Still, amid the regulatory, methodological and market (e.g., transaction and information costs) restrictions in place, this method represents desired properties in risk assessment. Going a step further, the empirical part of this study is based on the construction of a similar systemic risk network, albeit only with respect to unit measures of systemic risk. Yet, another weakness of this method is its linear character which does not allow for, central to the risk phenomenon, non-linear relations. Notwithstanding, the outcome of empirical analyses shows that the networks of connections constructed thus within the financial system do not considerably vary from those made with the use of non-linear identification of causal relations (Billio et al., 2010).[7]

An important advantage of this approach is, in turn, that it enables (based on the strength and the number of connections inside the network) a two-way view of the transmission of risk factors, i.e., the analysis of a given entity impacting the risk of other entities, and the other way round, risk transmission from other entities. Consequently, such an analysis identifies two types of institutions which are important given the spread of risk – entities which represent a source of risk (so-called "net exporters of risk factors", i.e., those with numerous entities they affect) and vulnerable entities (so-called "net risk importers" characterized by a high number of channels of impact from third parties). Such an approach shows it is possible to differentiate between systemic and simple credit events with respect to a relatively important entity. It is because the first event pertains to shock transmission by the two specified categories of entities, while the other is normally only analysed with respect to the first category named.

6.7 Selected Systemic Risk Measurement Methods

Systemic risk measurement methods,[8] also referred to as systemic risk models (Rosati, 2014) or advanced measurement methods (Jajuga et al., 2017), are a tool to enable a comprehensive approach to the analysis of systemic risk allowing for its particular character. Typically, the methods take account of interconnections among entities and with respect to what the connections carry along on the level of financial system, often being asymmetric and/or non-linear. Consequently, they follow advanced statistical and econometric approaches, taking account of statistical multivariate distributions and stochastic processes (Jurkowska, 2018). An important feature of advanced models of systemic risk measurement is that their information value is much higher. Next to the assessment of the magnitude of risk, they primarily address the identification of its sources (Benoit et al., 2015). It follows that the models quantify systemic risk itself. They consider it to be a source rather than one of manifestations of financial instability.

As no clear systemic risk measure has been developed yet and as its history is relatively short, the literature attempts at devising (still an ongoing process) a widely accepted classification of a broad set of systemic risk measurement methods. In this context, it is the three-layered approach proposed by Di Cesare and Picco (2018) that approximates the treatment presented in this study the most and is also the most comprehensive. Its starting point is a definition of the objective for which systemic risk would be measured. Once the objective has been named, it further determines the later criteria for classifying individual measures. Thus, the classification shows three approaches to the measurement of systemic risk (Figure 6.6):

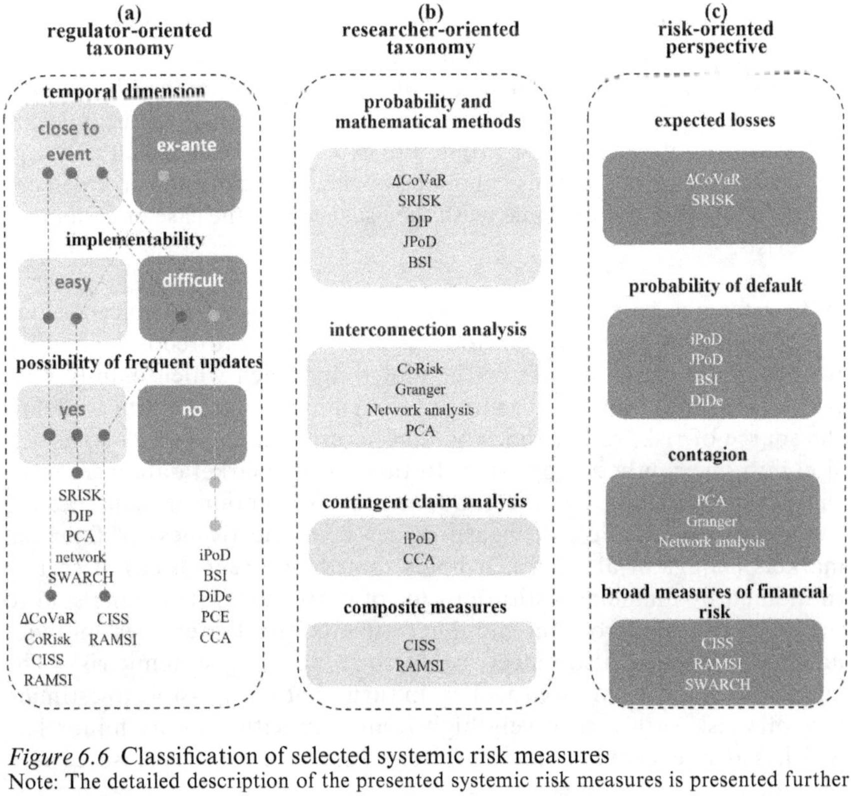

Figure 6.6 Classification of selected systemic risk measures

Note: The detailed description of the presented systemic risk measures is presented further in the chapter.

Source: own work based on Di Cesare and Picco (2018).

- Supervisory orientation, that is, defining the importance of a given measure by defining the usefulness in regulatory processes. Namely, the features of systemic risk measures that supervisory authorities value the most are those which can be incorporated into macroprudential policies, i.e., indicators' leading properties which enable the identification of a systemic risk rising or a regular revision of estimates. In addition, as regulatory bodies seek to use transparent and understandable approaches to their policy, an important feature of risk measure in this context is also how much a given measure is complicated and whether it is easy to interpret.
- Research orientation, that is, a given measure's contribution to identifying the theoretical backgrounds for systemic risk and its consequences. An approach which directly relates to this treatment and is widely used in the literature is one proposed by Benoit et al. (2015). They came up with a classification based on methods addressing systemic risk sources (source-specific approach) and the global approach venturing to determine the scale rather than the sources of systemic risk.
- Risk orientation, that is, defining the dimension of systemic risk, i.e., expressing it as a parameter that lends itself to being interpreted in comparison with other measures. For instance, systemic risk indicators alone are interpretable measures, albeit their comparability from interdisciplinary perspective is limited. In contrast, some relevant measures of systemic risk attempt to express the level of that risk, e.g., in terms of a cost to the economic system, the magnitude of which can be compared, for example, with the fiscal cost in the case of a financial crisis.

With reference to the above classifications, the most advanced group of systemic risk measurement tools (which will also directly be applied in this study) arose as part of the global approach which mainly rests on market data. Global measures of systemic risk do not aim to define the source of risk, rather they combine several channels of its transmission into one synthetic approach. In turn, if the market data were to be the basis, it means that the fundamental assumption in constructing a number of systemic risk measures lies with effectiveness of financial markets (Jajuga et al., 2017). It holds that the current prices of securities issued by financial institutions (or of derivative instruments sold to them), next to macroeconomic determinants and the entities' individual characteristics, also reflect risk factors, including systemic risk. The main advantage of this approach is, in turn, that it is possible to estimate systemic risk with a relatively high frequency with an only minor lag, which is also reflected in the supervisory orientation of the measures used (Figure 6.6).

6.7.1 Expected Shortfall – Measures of Expected Capital Shortfall

The concept of marginal capital shortfall has in recent years become one of the most important foundations for systemic risk estimates. What may have largely propelled the elaboration and expansion of the methods belonging to this family of models was the recommendation of the Basel Committee on Banking Supervision itself that proposed to base the market risk regulation on the capital shortfall concept, thus reducing the role of value-at-risk concept (VaR, BCBS, 2013, 2014). During financial crises, the losses of financial institutions have a tendency to grow above average, thus generating costs and jeopardizing the security of the entire financial system. What such a situation immediately entails is capital shortfall over the entire system as a total of individual components. Originally, this measure was proposed by Acharya et al. (2010, 2017) and then significantly expanded to a conditional version by Brownlees and Engle (2017). The starting point for this method is measuring financial risk at bank level, i.e., value-at-risk. It follows that from this perspective, the systemic risk measure is the value of capital by which the bank's equity should grow in order to redress the equity-to-assets ratio to a safe level which secures a further unimpeded operations of the bank. In line with this approach, MES (marginal expected shortfall) stands precisely for a marginal expected capital shortfall in the banking system caused by capital shortfall in a single bank (or, in a wider sense, a financial institution) during a crisis. It means that the higher the indicator, the higher the systemic risk and the broader the scale of additional capital a bank requires in a crisis.

In the model approach, this measure starts off with the expected capital shortfall (ES_i^q), i.e., such a shortfall which is necessary to cover the bank's loss (L_i) in excess of that estimated by the level of value at risk (VaR) with a given probability (q). It is when capital shortfall expands this concept to include a situation whereby the entire sector, rather than a single bank, is undercapitalized (by value L) and it measures by how much the undercapitalization will rise if the importance of a given entity grows ($w_{i,t}$). Thus, the vulnerability of risk level within the sector to the risk level of a given entity is defined, identifying the entity's systemic importance. The above idea for i-bank may simply be presented as follows:

$$ES_i^q = E\left(L_i \middle| L_i \rangle VaR_i^q\right) \tag{6.1}$$

$$MES_i^q = \frac{\partial ES_i^q}{\partial w_{i,t}} = E\left(L_i \middle| L \rangle VaR^q\right) \tag{6.2}$$

In reality, the above-mentioned conceptual view, also in the original approach proposed by the authors, comes down to changes in market stock valuation of analysed entities in a specified time unit. Thus, the above-named bank losses (L_i) are replaced in the implementation procedure by losses brought on by capitalization changes ($R_{i,t}$), just like the marginal value is defined in the values of material change in a company market valuation (C). More precisely speaking, MES is presented as follows:

$$MES_{i,t}(C) \equiv E\left(R_{i,t} \middle| R_{m,t} > C\right) \tag{6.3}$$

A certain expansion of the concept which became to be employed directly in other measures of systemic risk is long-run marginal expected shortfall, LMRES, put forward by Acharya et al. (2012).[9] This measure stands for an expected decline in the valuation of a given entity if its equity falls below the threshold value over a specified medium-term period (in market categories, usually six months) and it is estimated as follows:

$$LMES_{i,t}(C) \equiv 1 + exp\left(\gamma \cdot MES_{i,t}(C)\right) \tag{6.4}$$

Departing from the category of vulnerability and referring directly to the concept of systemic risk, the measure of systemic expected shortfall (SES) should be pointed out which is in fact estimated by the quantities. This measure shows by how much the equity of a given entity ($W_{i,t}$) will fall below the threshold value (defined as a percentage k of assets $A_{i,t}$) in case a systemic crisis arises. It is expressed as a linear combination of measure MES and of financial leverage of a given institution as follows:

$$SES_{i,t} = kA_{i,t} - W_{i,t}\left(1 + E_{t-1}\left(R_{i,t} \mid W_{M,t} < kA_{M,t}\right)\right) \tag{6.5}$$

In other words, this measure shows that if a given institution experiences capital shortfall in the wake of a systemic crisis, this institution will generate a strong adverse externality for the real economy as the other institutions in the sector will not be able, in a short-term perspective, replace liquidity shortfall and, in the case of a bank, of credit supply to the private sector (Freixas et al., 2015).

6.7.2 SRISK – Systemic Risk Model

What considerably expands the concept of MES and SES which became popular in the literature and in practice is SRISK model put forward by Brownlees and Engle (2017). This measure is yet another microeconomic view of the systemic importance of individual institutions sharing a similar interpretative character, i.e., as in the previous cases, it defines the expected equity shortfall of an institution whenever an entire system plunges into a crisis. The higher the shortfall, the higher the systemic risk generated by a given entity. However, this model, next to market variables which underlie the measures referred to earlier, also incorporates balance sheet variables of individual institutions such as the level of assets or of financial leverage. Moreover, the SRISK method is considered an *ex-ante* systemic risk measure of relatively good prediction properties (see, e.g., Grinderslev and Kristiansen, 2016). In spite of interpretative convergences, it is the prediction properties that distinguish model SRISK from measure SES defined earlier. Estimating the latter, next to structural assumptions, requires, however, that the input data allow for a financial crisis, which in numerous cases will mean this measure cannot be used.

Formally speaking, SRISK is equal to the size of a given institution's capital shortfall (CS_i), expected at moment t, to be reached in the future ($t+h$), provided a crisis event defined as a fall of market value of assets below the threshold level ($R_{m,t:t+h} < C$) occurs:

$$SRISK_{i,t} = \max\left\{0,\ E_{t-1}\left(CS_{i,t+h} \mid R_{m,t:t+h} < C\right)\right\} \tag{6.6}$$

$$E_{t-1}\left(CS_{i,t} \mid R_{m,t:t+h} < C\right) = E_{t-1}\left(\left(k\left(D_{it} + W_{it}\right) - W_{it}\right) \mid R_{m,t:t+h} < C\right) \tag{6.7}$$

where k is the macroprudential capital adequacy ratio,[10] D_{it} stands for the value of liabilities and W_{it} stands for a bank's equity based on the current market value (company capitalization).

Assuming further that, in the case systemic event occurs, the size of debt must not be renegotiable, that is ($E_{t-1}(D_{i,t} \mid R_{m,t:t+h} < C) = D_{i,t}$) the said measure takes on another interpretative meaning which can be presented as follows:

$$SRISK_{it} = max\left[0; \overbrace{k\left(D_{it} + \left(1 - LMRES_t\right)W_{it}\right)}^{\text{required capital}} - \overbrace{\left(1 - LMRES_t\right)W_{it}}^{\text{available capital}}\right] \tag{6.8}$$

Accordingly, the proposed measure conditions the systemic risk level directly on the features of the entity examined (Benoit et al., 2013), i.e., with a given coefficient k, the lower the bank's equity or the higher the liabilities, the higher the systemic risk generated by this entity.[11] The said theoretical considerations with respect to a given entity also hold for the overall macroeconomic perspective. Namely, on aggregate level, the systemic risk of the entire banking sector equals the total of individual values of coefficient SRISK for banks.[12]

As noted above, SRISK, next to market parameters, also employs the features of individual institutions, such as: size, probability of a credit event (e.g., default) or the scale of interconnections inside of a financial system. In an endeavour to define a relative importance of these features for the assessment of systemic importance of a given entity, a simulation may be attempted whereby only one feature is changed, with the other factors remaining intact. Such a stylized simulation shows that the most important feature in the context of its impact on systemic risk is entity size (see Figure 6.7). Of a slightly lesser importance is the scale of interconnections, and what matters the least is the probability of default.[13] What is vital is that the impact of none of the features is linear. Much as the first two were largely overproportionate, the scale of credit event's importance seems to be, at least at the low level, non-proportionate. Such an analysis is indicative of a high importance of TBTF paradigm for the measurement of systemic risk with the use of SRISK, which concomitantly differentiates this measure from, e.g., ΔCoVaR measure presented later on in this study.

The described measure allows also to analyse precisely the sources of the systemic risk since it can be easily decomposed into tree factors – debt, equity and risk – as follows:

$$\Delta SRISK = \overbrace{k \cdot \Delta D}^{\text{debt contribution}} - \overbrace{(1-k)(1-LRMES)\cdot \Delta W}^{\text{equity contribution}} + \overbrace{(1-k)\cdot W \cdot \Delta LRMES}^{\text{risk contribution}} \tag{6.9}$$

Such a decomposition carried out for two major financial sectors from a global perspective – namely the US and euro area – allows for the identification of sources of a build-up process in systemic risk that can be observed during the GFC (see Figure 6.8). In that background, systemic risk estimates

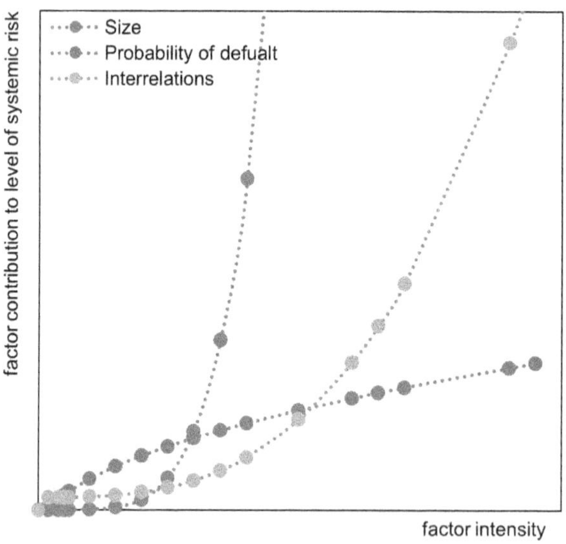

Figure 6.7 The stylized effect of bank's characteristics on the level of systemic risk
Source: own work based on Huang et al. (2012).

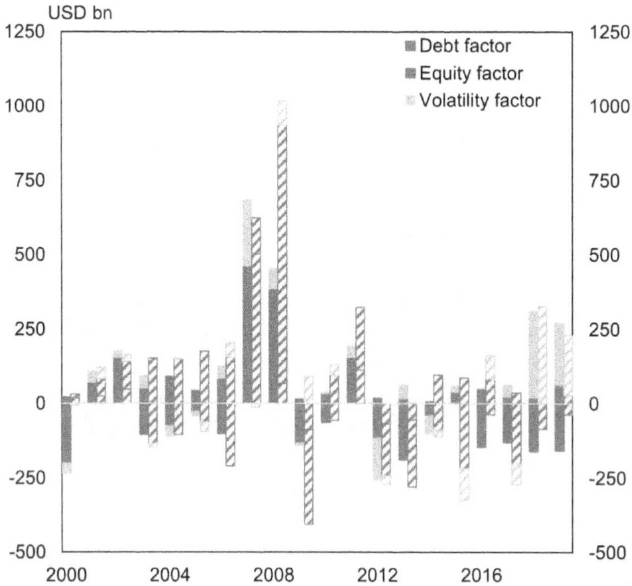

Figure 6.8 Decomposition of the annual change in SRISK measure in the USA and the euro area

Note: Estimates for 100 financial institutions from the United States and the euro area with the greatest level of systemic risk measured by SIRK; estimates for monthly data, aggregated to a country level; the United States – filled columns, euro area – dashed columns.

Source: Own work based on Bloomerg and Eikon data.

were firstly driven by the overproportional rise in debt (debt factor contribution) in both economies, which secondly converts into a significant contribution of capital shortfall (equity factor contribution). The most recent experience seems to be characterized by significantly different drivers since the systemic risk arises primarily from the contribution of the risk factor. In that context, this observation may suggest that the vulnerability of the financial sector to systemically important risk episodes is gradually increasing. Moreover, the time coherence of these factors for both economies – thus their co-occurrence – suggests that the tendency may imply a significant role of international or even global factors in shaping systemic risk over the recent years (Figure 6.8).

Next to numerous advantages, including interpretative ones, the main defect of the named approaches is that a crisis in the banking sector captured in a model does not reflect the entire systemic risk. It shows in fact that the risk is viewed as an exogenous factor. It is because the measures assume that capital shortfall in the economy triggered by, for instance, bankruptcy of one of the banks, will be refilled by other entities. In fact, however, the bankruptcy of one bank, especially a large one, may disrupt the process of transacting, including on the interbank market, given information asymmetry and shortage on this market, rise in counterparty risk and, consequently, amid worsened liquidity conditions of the entities remaining in the system, constraints on the supply of financial products on the market (Rosati, 2014). It means that a crisis may hit not only when the capital of the entire sector falls below a defined threshold (as implied by the measures analysed) but also whenever aggregate capital exceeds the threshold, however, also in a situation whereby the mechanism of liquidity flow to banks is critically impeded. Thus, these models do not adequately take account of all the externalities.

The above-mentioned considerations have focused on estimating SRISK on the domestic level; however, if computed internationally, it required a more complex procedure. Such an expansion seems to be necessary, however, for a broader look at the systemic risk because of a large impact of international factors, such as global business activity, economic policy (including monetary) or the regulatory environment, which may clearly vary systemic risk level versus the measures estimated domestically. In the context of SRISK, this problem was first addressed by Engle et al. (2012) who wanted to expand the original methodology to include the domestically diverse European banking sector. Consequently, they defined a three-layered approach to estimating a given bank's ($r_{i,t}$) individual rate of return identifying the global ($r_{W,t}$), regional ($r_{E,t}$) and domestic ($r_{C,t}$),[14] factor which affect, in a cascade-like fashion, the individual values (with force β) in accordance with the following:

$$
\begin{aligned}
r_{i,t} &= \beta_{i,t}^{C}\ r_{C,t} + \beta_{i,t}^{E}\ r_{E,t} + \beta_{i,t}^{W}\ r_{W,t} + \beta_{i,t}^{L}\ r_{W,t-1} + \varepsilon_{i,t} \\
r_{C,t} &= \beta_{C,t}^{E}\ r_{E,t} + \beta_{C,t}^{W}\ r_{W,t} + \beta_{C,t}^{L}\ r_{W,t-1} + \varepsilon_{C,t} \\
r_{E,t} &= \beta_{E,t}^{E}\ r_{E,t} + \beta_{E,t}^{W}\ r_{W,t} + \beta_{E,t}^{L}\ r_{W,t-1} + \varepsilon_{E,t} \\
r_{W,t} &= \beta_{W,t}^{L}\ r_{W,t-1} + \varepsilon_{W,t}
\end{aligned}
\tag{6.10}
$$

Owing to such an approach, the market or the financial system defined earlier has somewhat a broader scope than originally viewed: $R_{M,t} = \{r_{C,t}, r_{E,t}, r_{W,t}, r_{W,t-1}\}$. Such an approach in a relatively technically simple manner enables an international comparability of two measures of systemic risk, SRISK and LMES, and whose added value in analytical terms is to be observed, e.g., in the European economies. With this approach, it is also possible to identify Western European countries as relatively less susceptible to a systemic event (Figure 6.9, right panel); notwithstanding, the scale of this vulnerability is clearly less diversified than that of the systemic risk alone measured with the use of SRISK (Figure 6.9, left panel).

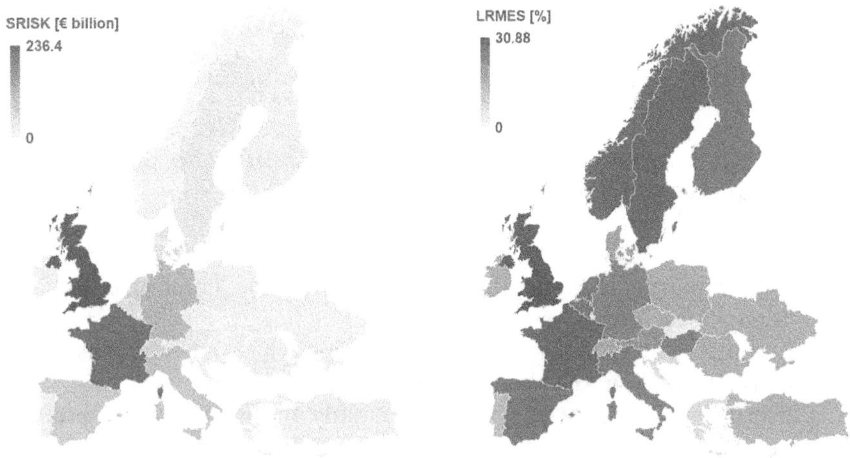

Figure 6.9. Systemic risk country map for Europe – SRISK (left panel) and LMES (right panel)

Note: The picture as of the end of 2019.

Source: Own work based on Engle et al. (2012) estimates.

6.7.3 ΔCoVaR – Conditional Value at Risk

Yet another and equally often applied systemic risk measure, also VaR-based, is the model of conditional value-at-risk (CoVaR)[15] put forward by Adrian and Brunnermeier (2016). It starts off with the ideas proposed in turn by Engle and Manganelli (2004). This measure pertains to VaR estimated for the entire financial system, and not just on standalone basis, in isolation from other entities. This measurement allows for connections among individual institutions which are vital for systemic risk concept.[16] In such an event, CoVaR stands for a conditional parameter VaR for the entire financial system (S) (or any other institution j) providing another institution i under the influence of a credit event so strong that it has driven down the return on its assets (X_i) so much that the institution is in a crisis ($C(L^i)$). Therefore:

$$P\left(X_j \leq CoVaR^q_{j|C(X_i)} \mid C(X_i)\right) = q \tag{6.11}$$

$$P\left(X_S \leq CoVaR^q_{S|C(X_i)} \mid C(X_i)\right) = q \tag{6.12}$$

Consequently, the difference between the outcome of CoVaR for the entire sector whenever institution i is in crisis and a corresponding measure for normal (i.e., historically average) conditions is what defines the institution's contribution to the overall systemic risk level:

$$\Delta CoVaR_{i,S}^{q} = CoVaR_{S|C(X_i)}^{q} - CoVaR_{S|\ X_i=median\ (X_i)}^{q} \tag{6.13}$$

Owing to its endogenous approach to systemic risk structure, the said methodology allows to identify several vital connections:

- quantifying the side effects of volatility contagion, which is particularly important for institutions which are "too connected to fail" (Karkowska, 2015);
- estimating the indirect effects of contagion which may arise as assets are rapidly sold in the absence of market liquidity;
- identifying entities which have potentially the highest adverse effect on the entire system's stability, i.e., systemically important financial institutions;
- given institution's vulnerability examined from the perspective of systemic event load.

Another feature of this measure, as in the case of the earlier defined SRISK, is that it allows to specify how individual features of institutions (e.g., financial leverage, the scale of assets' mismatch) affect the level of systemic risk, which may provide grounds for mitigating risk in those domains by macroprudential policy (Kapadia et al., 2013). Simultaneously, however, the method's serious defect is that it is impossible to tell causal relationships between the impact one institution has on another from those brought on by a factor common for the entire system (Kemp, 2017). In addition, such a systemic risk measure requires that a large volume of market data of relatively high frequency is available, for example, regarding stock market capitalization, market value of liabilities, market quotations of credit risk (CDS contracts).[17] It means that the measure cannot be estimated for all the entities in the banking sector, i.e., it will not apply primarily for relatively small economies in the case of which market data are scarce. What is more, it will not apply for all the world's economies given a different level of financial markets' development.

Summing up, the global measures of systemic risk, depending on the input marginal measure and the conditioning event, may be represented in terms of a simple matrix (Table 6.2). From this perspective, measures MES and CoVaR may be, in a way, considered as their own mirror reflections. The first one defines the level of systemic risk triggered by an external impulse, i.e., market environment, while the other shows that the initial impulse is on the level of a given entity and only then is it transmitted into the system.[18] Consequently, in this study, the first three of the concepts discussed (MES, SES, SRISK) are considered as a top-down approach, whereas concept CoVaR,

Table 6.2 Classification of selected systemic risk measure in a space of marginal measure and conditionality

		Conditional event	
		at the system level	*at the entity level*
Referred marginal measure	VaR	MVaR	CoVaR
	ES	MES	CoES

Source: Own elaboration.

as bottom-up for systemic risk measurement. It is because, a juxtaposition of both categories of measures, under an aggregate approach, provides a full picture of systemic risk's structural dimension at a given moment.

6.8 Comparison of Selected Systemic Risk Measures

The above-presented measures represent but a small set of applicable systemic risk measures. Next to the classification and characteristics of individual measures provided, it is reasonable to compare them from theoretical, empirical and implementation perspective.

6.8.1 Theoretical Comparison of Systemic Risk Measures

Table 6.3 complements the above classification of systemic risk measures. It includes characteristics of selected systemic risk measures as well as the assessment of their potential advantages and defects. This table primarily shows that there is no single universal systemic risk measurement method. It is because the measures simultaneously draw from highly diverse approaches – from standalone data to aggregate measures, from one risk category only (e.g., the spread of contagion impulse across the financial system) to attempts of devising a synthetic risk indicator. It should also be pointed out that none of these theoretical proposals is free from defects, to start off with ignoring the contagion effect important for the systemic risk concept, through implementation constraints for large entities which are due to data accessibility, to only linear relations in financial systems being taken into account (see Table 6.3).

The constructions of individual measures compared show that in the absence of one universal systemic risk measure, it is reasonable to use complementary methods. It should also be remembered that systemic risk measurement naturally carries a great deal of uncertainty arising not only from imperfections of data underlying a given method (e.g., popular market parameters) but also uncertainty which concerns the future development of a given financial system's stability (or instability).

What testifies the importance of individual measures is also how commonly they are used, both in the literature and in practice by institutions

Table 6.3 An overview of systemic risk measures

Measure	*Author*	*Brief characteristic*	*Institutional usage*	*Major advantages*	*Major disadvantages*	*Type of input data*
ΔCoVaR	Adrian and Brunnermeier (2016)	Impact of a selected institution being in distress on the entire sector	ECB, ESRB, IMF	High frequency of estimates; Captures spillover effect	Sensitive to extreme event identification; Bivariate only	Market data
SES **SRISK**	Acharya et al. (2010, 2017); Brownlees and Engle (2017)	Expected capital shortfall of an instruction given the whole financial system is undercapitalized	ECB, IMF	*Ex-ante* measure; Theoretical justification	Measures only the average, linear, bivariate dependence	Market and balance sheet data
DIP	Huang et al. (2009)	Theoretical premium to a risk-based deposit insurance scheme that guarantees against most severe losses for the banking system	ECB	*Ex-ante* measure; Economically intuitive	Incorporates liquidity appetite in addition to systemic risk	Market data
CCA	Gray and Jobst (2013)	Measuring systemic solvency risk by incorporating mutual liability exposures of institutions	IMF	Integrates market-implied expected losses in a multivariate specification of joint default risk	Requires difficult-to-acquire data; difficult to implement	Balance sheet and market data
iPoD	Capuano (2008)	Market-based measure of the probability of default	IMF	Default barrier determined endogenously	No information about time of possible default; Applicable only to the largest institutions	Market data
Joint-PoD **BSI**	Segoviano and Goodhart (2009)	The probability of default of the entire system, i.e., the tail risk of the system the expected number of banks becoming distressed given that at least one bank has become distressed	ECB, IMF	Embeds linear and non-linear time-varying dependence; Measures banks' interdependence structure	Not a measure of pure systemic risk; may also incorporate liquidity risk and risk aversion into the financial system	Market data

DiDe		distress-specific contagion effect				
PCE		identification of a cascade of distress				
Principal Component Analysis (PCA)	Billio et al. (2012)	Identification of common components among different sectors of the financial markets	ECB	*Ex-ante*, forward-looking; Easy to calculate	Vulnerable to common factors that may not be of systemic importance	Market data
Granger causality	Billio et al. (2012)	Detection of the level and the direction of causality between institutions in the financial sectors	ECB	*Ex-ante*, forward-looking; Allows for identification of causality chains (domino effect); Relatively easy to implement	Vulnerable to individual characteristics of inputs	Market data
Network analysis	Esponosa-Vega and Sole (2011)	Identification of financial interlinkages among institutions, tracking the reverberation of events throughout the system	IMF, ECB	Easy to calculate; Allows most systemic and vulnerable institutions to be identified	Static measure; Requires non-public supervisory data	Balance sheet data, mutual exposures
CISS	Holló et al. (2012)	Indicator of the current state of instability, i.e., the current level of frictions, stresses and strains (or the absence thereof) in the financial system	ECB, ESRB	Calculated with high frequency, in real time; Robust to the arrival of new information	An overall macroeconomic perspective only; Not based on a structural model	Market and balance sheet data
RAMSI	Aikman et al. (2011)	Measure of institution-specific and system-wide vulnerabilities	IMF, ECB	Comprehensive measure	Univariate measure only	Balance sheet and market data
SWARCH	Gonzalez-Hermosillo and Hesse (2011)	Assessing financial volatility and the likelihood of a crisis with a state space model	IMF	Easy to update; High frequency of estimates	Macroeconomic perspective only	High-frequency market data

Source: Own elaboration based on the literature review and Di Cesare and Picco (2018).

responsible for macroprudential policy. The analysis of how the measures were employed shows that, as is the case of the theoretical platform, there is no single widely used systemic risk measure (Figure 6.11). Numerous financial institutions and regulators draw from a wide range of systemic risk measures, not conditioning their conclusions on what only one of them indicates. At the same time, the methods which enable a measurement of how much a single institution has contributed to the overall systemic risk are the most often used in practice and in the literature alike. Among them, the most popular are SRISK and ΔCoVaR (Figure 6.10), which is highly attributable to their capacity of being easily implemented into other analytical models, including macroeconomic ones. It should also be reminded that the methods have only been developed recently, based first and foremost on global financial crisis experience, which demonstrates quite a high pace of their growing popularity. In turn, indicators are still in use, including the relatively most popular, particularly with respect to the European financial system, CISS. The scale of their use is less extensive, albeit still relevant. It may also be observed that the more methodologically complicated and also more difficult to interpret a systemic risk measure is, the less of an interest it becomes for regulatory bodies and the academics.

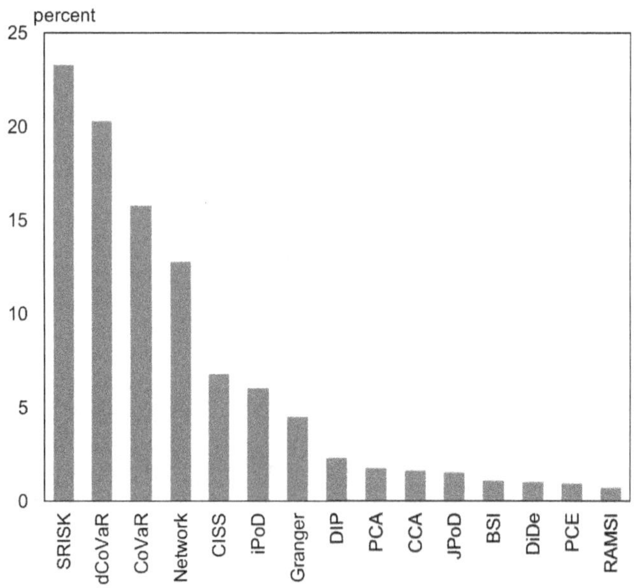

Figure 6.10 Frequency of usage of selected systemic risk measures in research studies

Note: Calculations for 250 research articles published in JCR journals that refer to systemic risk.

Source: Own work based on Novickytė and Dičpinigaitienė (2018).

6.8.2 Empirical Comparison of Selected Systemic Risk Measures

Owing to empirical comparison of systemic risk measures, it is possible to make a comprehensive specification of their main characteristics. Four perspectives have been applied here: (i) identification of differences in estimating systemic risk level, (ii) distribution of this risk across the financial system, (iii) connections among individual risk measures and (iv) coherence of signals in defining a systemic institution. The aforementioned comparative analysis will be carried out for relevant measures of systemic risk, with respect to their implementation value, both for the purposes of this study and for the practical usefulness.

All of the measures analysed show that the level of systemic risk is not constant over time, thus corroborating the empirical assumptions pertaining to their methodological construction (Figure 6.11). The measures at hand have also shown high implementation flexibility since they may be presented as applicable internationally, domestically and individually for respective units analysed. What is of critical importance for this issue, however, is that all the measures identify a rise in systemic risk during the GFC. Still, what draws attention is a glaring similarity in how the three measures, i.e., MES, CoVaR and ΔCoVaR, behave as well as a different reaction of their SRISK counterparts. The difference stands out with respect to two properties. First, the last of the measures mentioned indicated a higher systemic risk at the relatively earliest stage, and, second, it showed that higher risk persisted for longer (even several years) after the original impulse was triggered (Figure 6.11). Namely, such observations are attributable to the very construction of indicators, i.e., relying to a greater extent on a given entity's features in case of SRISK and estimates based on a contingent measure which depends on whether the event alone occurs in the case of other measures. In addition, long-term risk measures – such as the estimated LMRES – to a lesser extent reflect pro-cyclical properties of systemic risk than, e.g., financial leverage incorporated into SRISK (Kalemli-Ozcan et al., 2011). Consequently, it may be noted that SRISK can be considered a better leading indicator with respect to the occurrence of a systemic event. The above considerations trigger a question about the universal character of systemic risk measures. On the one hand, Brownlees et al. (2015) confirmed that the indicated systemic risk measures, i.e., both SRISK and ΔCoVaR, have enabled identifying all the banking crises that have taken place in the United States over the last two centuries. On the other hand, though, the measures tend to show varied results on microeconomic level as regards identification of SIFIs. For instance, CoVaR usually overestimates the contribution to systemic risk from banks which are not systemic at the cost of underestimating a contribution generated by those of systemic importance (Liu, 2017).[19]

The above analysis may be further expanded to include the connections among systemic risk and financial risk measures, whereby the latter are represented by VaR indicators and beta coefficient for stock valuation.[20]

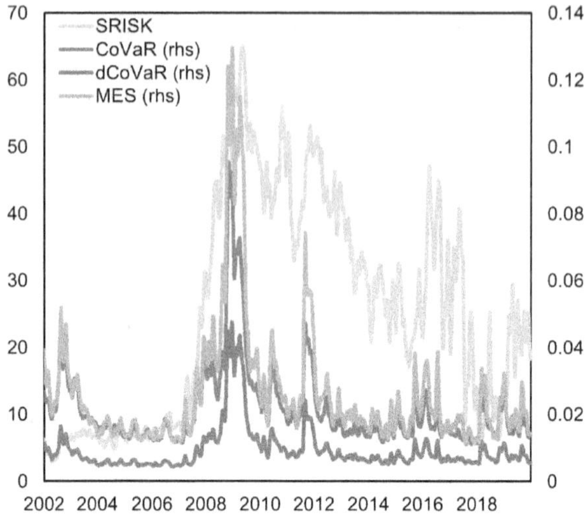

Figure 6.11 Comparison of selected systemic risk measures

Note: Estimates for 428 banks from 12 economies, e.g., for the research sample from the empirical chapter of this book (Chapter 7).

Source: Own work based on Bloomberg, Eikon and banks' financial statement data.

The conclusions of such an analysis further show that the largest amount of information on systemic risk is contributed by the value-at-risk (see, e.g., Danielsson et al., 2013) – mostly to measures such as ΔCoVaR and MES and, to a lesser extent, to CoVaR (Figure 6.10). It means that these measures being used simultaneously to assess risk level or incorporated into a synthetic indicator replicate the information value. It is largely because these measures may be, technically and under certain conditions, presented as linear combinations of themselves (Benoit et al., 2013). Accordingly, what may prove to be an important value added is that the conclusions also take account of SRISK as it does not manifest any linear correlation with any other measure with respect to neither systemic nor market risks (Figure 6.10). Such an approach implies that what may provide the broadest and the most informative look at systemic risk is a simultaneous application of SRISK and ΔCoVaR.[21] This conclusion may also be one of the reasons for the aforementioned greater popularity of exactly these two systemic risk measures (Figure 6.10). The analysis at hand proves that it is reasonable to differentiate between the concepts of systemic and systematic risks also empirically. Namely, all of the systemic risk measures examined show a low or non-existent degree of correlation with beta coefficient which manifests systemic risk in this analysis (Figure 6.12).

The issue of systemic risk, as has been emphasized in this study, is highly complex. Hence, the approach to the analysis of only the values of systemic risk measures estimated for the entire financial system may not be sufficient.

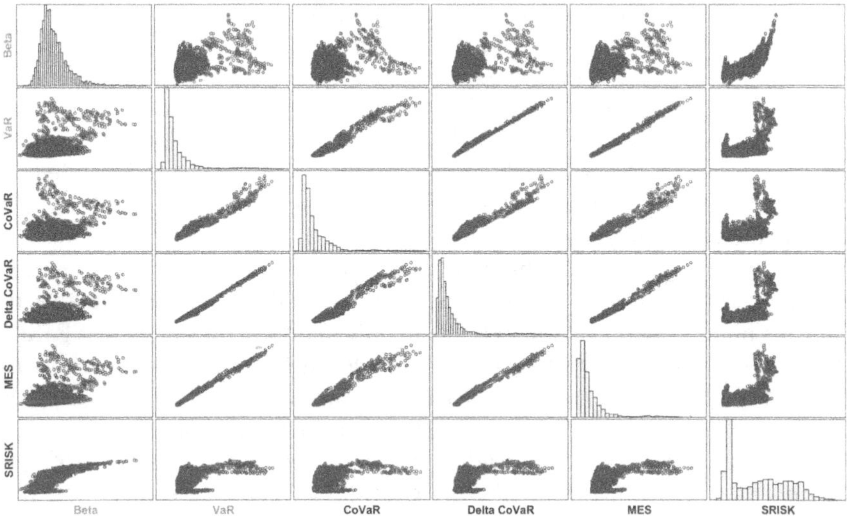

Figure 6.12 Correlation matrix of individual risk measures

Note: Estimates for 428 banks from 12 economies, e.g., for the research sample from the empirical chapter of this book (Chapter 7).

Source: Own work based on Bloomberg, Eikon and banks' financial statement data.

In this context, using the flexibility of the analysed measures suggested earlier and the possibility to analyse them also individually, it may be useful to assess the risk level based on the distribution of these individual measures across the entire financial system (Figure 6.14). Such an approach additionally brings out the differences among the analysed measurement methods and produces several new important conclusions. First, not only the value of systemic risk measures on aggregate level but also its distribution across the financial system vary over time, albeit to a lesser extent. Second, the analysis shows a diverse character of the distribution of risk measures with respect to individual financial institutions estimated for given methods. Third, in near-crisis situations, the distributions of systemic risk measures clearly flatten. It has been identified for both the analysed models, i.e., ΔCoVaR and SRISK. This means a phenomenon of a gradual spread of risk impulse across the system has been identified, whatever the method adopted for estimating systemic risk alone. This observation is quite important, much as it may seem to defy intuition. It is because, intuitively, the breadth of the distribution of systemic risk measures could remain relatively intact even in crisis situations or the entire distribution should shift towards higher values of systemic risk. Meanwhile, for both the systemic risk models, a diversification between the measures has clearly developed. The development is precisely reflected in the breadth of the distribution and it shows that the importance of extremely risky entities is rising in the system. It also demonstrates that there remain entities which, in spite of an event hitting the entire system, are only moderately vulnerable. Fourth, while risk distribution implied by SRISK is highly asymmetrical and approximating low values over a long (non-crisis) time period, the systemic risk defined with the use of CoVaR displays both higher asymmetry and a tendency to build medium-term "equilibrium points" whereby the entire distribution of measures remains at a relatively similar level all over the group. It follows that, while in the case of SRISK it is individual measures that change independently, for ΔCoVaR the measures may be determined by parameters for the whole group, hence the presumed change of entire distribution over time. This feature may yet again be attributable to a higher importance of market variables in estimating the latter measure (the variables being vulnerable to similar factors) with no such effect recorded for the estimates of SRISK. Fifth, risk measures lingering on very low levels for a rising number of entities may not suggest (as it might seem) a low level of systemic risk, rather underestimation of such a measure by market variables (Figure 6.13).

One of the tasks of macroprudential policy is to curb the impact of systemic risk materialization and the likelihood of systemic institutions' default, while the tools being important elements in their identification are systemic risk measures. As already shown, however, the measures may change dynamically and identify various levels of this risk (Figure 6.11). Consequently, it may suggest that the rankings of systemic institutions based on these measures may also evolve over time (see, e.g., Benoit et al., 2013). It is because institutions which are systemically negligible during high economic activity may prove systemically highly important during a severe economic downturn. It may be attributable to varying degrees of how individual entities embrace a volatile macroeconomic environment, both in

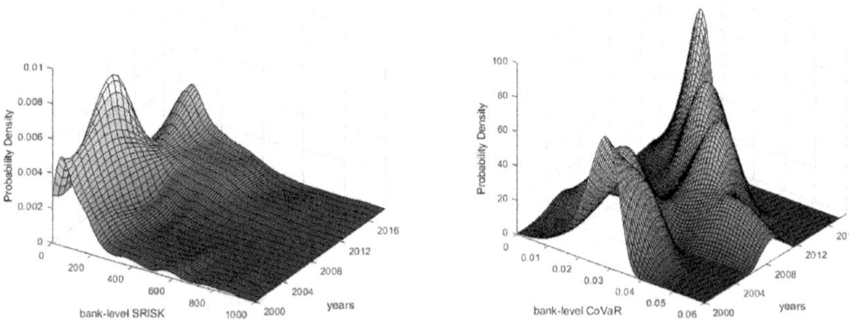

Figure 6.13 Time evolution of distributions of selected individual systemic risk measures (left panel – SRISK, right panel – CoVaR)

Note: Estimates for 428 banks from 12 economies, e.g., for the research sample from the empirical chapter of this book (Chapter 7); densities proxied with kernel density estimator, range of measures limited due to outliers.

Source: Own work based on Bloomberg, Eikon and banks' financial statement data.

terms of individual features (such as the size and debt level), but primarily the scale of inter-institutional connections.

Owing to all of the above-mentioned methods, it is possible to rank financial institutions with respect to the risk they generate. Consequently, it is natural (particularly in the context of regulatory policy) to ask about the convergence and comparability of such classifications. In other words, it is a question of whether the conclusions based on various methods of classifying systemic institutions are similar from financial safety net institutions. To try to answer this question, a ranking of systemically important institutions (i.e., those carrying the highest risk) based on earlier estimates at a given moment can be made, followed by an estimated similarity coefficient among the rankings (see Figure 6.14).[22]

Rankings of systemically important institutions are highly varied depending on the risk measure applied. In particular, no combinations out of the analysed systemic risk measures, in any of the examined period have yielded an identical ranking. At the same time, the most similar rankings

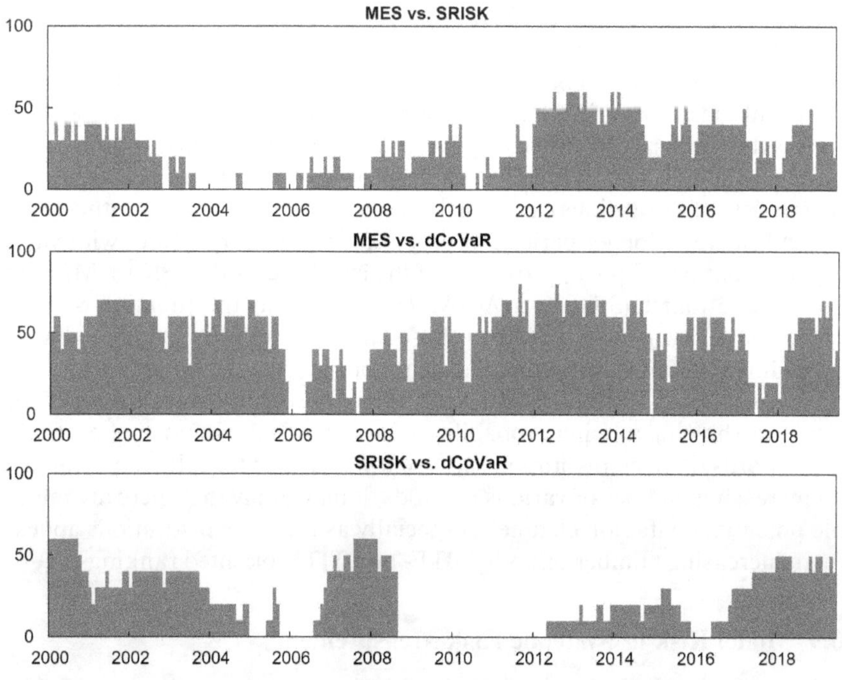

Figure 6.14 Similarity index for rankings of systemically important financial institutions identified by different measures

Note: Similarity index presents fraction of 10-element rankings of institutions with highest level of individual systemic risk measure estimated with different models; estimates for 428 banks from 12 economies, e.g., for the research sample from the empirical chapter of this book (Chapter 6).

Source: Own work based on Bloomberg, Eikon and banks' financial statement data, Benoit et al. (2013) methodology.

are those generated with the use of MES and ΔCoVaR (Figure 6.14), whereby every other institution has been included in both of them on average over the last 20 years. On the other hand, SRISK-based rankings are markedly less similar, both as compared to MES and ΔCoVaR. They show on average that only every fourth institution hit both the lists in a given period. This divergence may be methodologically motivated. Ranking is created based on SRISK. In a sharp contrast to such measures as MES or ΔCoVaR, they primarily favour institutions which are large from the perspective of their balance sheet total. In addition, the information content SRISK provides is relatively broader than others as it includes information on a given entity's shareholding structure. One of the reasons why the measures concerned fail to fully identify the same entities as systemically important may also arise from financial markets' information not being adequately effective. As a result of quoting various financial assets, measures which rely both on balance sheet and market data reflect various scopes of risk factors, not only systemically important risks. Consequently, financial institution rankings based on SRISK should be identified as viewing the institutions from too big to fail (TBTF) perspective, whereas those MES- and ΔCoVaR-based, more in terms of being too interconnected to fail (TITF).

Some more valuable conclusions also come from an analysis of the pertinent rankings' similarity changing over time. Namely, the most stable over time is the similarity in identifying systemically important institutions based on MES and ΔCoVaR. It is only for a short period that they implied virtually diverse sets of institutions carrying the highest systemic risk. The other cases are indicative of longer periods of providing supervisory bodies with varying information – from approx. 15% of the last 20 years (SRISK vs. MES) to around one-fourth (SRISK vs. ΔCoVaR). What draws the attention is also a rising similarity in the structure of those rankings in the period immediately preceding the GFC, especially in the case of the most methodologically different systemic risk measures. Hence, such an observation may be one of the elements showing a rising probability of a systemically important event. In other words, if given institutions are identified as systemically important by an increasing number of various methods, it may imply that there are multiple potential contagion channels, especially as the same institutions appear in an increasing number of both TBTF- and TITF-oriented rankings.

6.9 Model Risk in Systemic Risk Measurement

One conclusion from the above analyses is that the information provided by various measures of systemic risk can be quite heterogeneous. Therefore, they should be treated with due caution, especially when attempting to devise a comprehensive risk assessment based on the results of single models. Consequently, in the literature, there has been an increasing focus on the risks directly related to the models used to analyse systemic risk, that is, model risk.[23] Among multiple sources of this risk, there are several worth particular attention in terms of systemic risk measurement:

- uncertainty concerning the choice of a relevant measurement method (e.g., Hull and Suo, 2002). Such a problem arises at the stage of systemic risk indicator construction, whereby some authors take account of a broad range of measures, thus exposing themselves (in case there is no attempt to isolate a common factor) to a risk of replicating information value. In extreme cases, it may strengthen a signal from one only market segment to the systemic level.[24]
- assuming that the disturbance driving up financial sector risk is endogenous, while an intrinsic feature of the rise in systemic risk is its endogenous character (Danielsson and Shin, 2003; Brunnermeir and Sannikov, 2014).
- building a model with good prognostic values for a crisis event requires that such an event is allowed for in the research sample. Meanwhile, the literature shows that in OECD countries, a banking crisis hits on average every 35 years (Danielsson et al., 2018). As a consequence, multiple estimates of its probability are based on periods free of crisis. It requires to estimate the probability with the use of stochastic process assumptions (including the behaviour of financial instrument price changes), with a reservation that the process may run totally differently.
- accumulation of model risk as part of "technical cascading" of systemic risk structural measures. The majority of systemic risk measures are directly (CoVaR) or indirectly (MES, SRISK) based on value at risk (VaR). Thus, model estimates (carrying a specified error) are a basis for further estimates, which means that systemic risk models naturally inherit a portion of model risk already generated by source models.

Danielsson et al. (2016) endeavoured to quantify model risk with respect to systemic risk measurement methods. They showed that normally the risk level is relatively low during periods of economic calm, however, it markedly rises in crisis, i.e., whenever the interest in finding the actual systemic risk level is the greatest. What is vital, this feature was shown as being mostly attributable to the above-mentioned cascade character of the measures analysed (MES, CoVaR, SRISK). Concomitantly, in the medium term, the risk of model CoVaR is, on average, higher during calm periods, and notably higher during crisis, than that identified for models MES. It should be noted, however, that the results do not imply a sharp decline in systemic risk model quality during a crisis. What they demonstrate is that such a period favours more varied indications among models with respect to the actual scale of risk; still, it does not impede the very tendencies indicative of the risk growth or, largely, its entity-based structure.

Summary

This chapter endeavoured to outline the theoretical basis for the second pillar of the main research topic in our study, i.e., systemic risk. It was demonstrated that, although the definitions of systemic risk clearly vary, most of them focus on two aspects. First, this risk is present in the financial system and, when materialized, it primarily causes disturbances to the way the system works, by impairing certain system functions and, finally, adversely impacting the real economy. Second, what appears to be the key element is the likelihood of transmitting the disruptions among entities interconnected in the financial system. It is a contagion effect whose role is vital not only theoretically but also in the empirical research on the measurement of systemic risk. These indications underpin empirical studies which were largely devoted to the role of contagion effect in the transmission of shocks evoked by monetary policy measures.

The literature has so far failed to develop one universal measure of systemic risk or how to comprehensively address the measurement of this phenomenon. It is partly due to a multi-layered aspect of systemic risk itself. Namely, an appropriate measurement method is primarily determined by systemic risk dimension. The issue of systemic risk measurement should be understood comprehensively with respect to three layers: as systemic risk estimate in the financial system, definition of the scale of distress transmission across the financial system (i.e., risk transmission mechanism) and identification of channels and the extent of systemic risk impact on the real economy.

Indicators may be identified to measure only selected aspects or the dimensions of systemic risk. It implies a need to use numerous complementary measures of this phenomenon in practice. At the same time, however, it exposes decision makers to an additional type of risk, i.e., overinterpretation of signals which appear with respect to one type of information which is, on the other hand, replicated by several measurement methods being used simultaneously. Thus, it should be emphasized out that given uncertainty brought on by what the systemic risk actually is and by little practice in using methods to measure it, expert judgement remains one of the key elements in assessing risks to financial stability.

Notes

1 Financial system is an important element for macroeconomic models, constructed also by central banks (see, e.g., Mishkin, 2011).

2 It should be noted that systemic risk can also be generated by the market infrastructure institutions (responsible for clearing and settlement of payments, securities and derivatives). The systemic risk models usually do not account for this fact, yet it may be a significant source of risk. Such a modelling approach arises from great difficulties to properly quantify this specific source of risk.

3 The list of presented sources of systemic risk is not exclusive and complete. There are a range of theories that try to identify origins of systemic risk – e.g., the behavioural approach to procyclicality in the banking sector. According to

that, financial institutions are not able to properly identify and measure the risk as the institutional memory of risk factors weakens over time (e.g., Berger and Udell, 2003).

4 The mentioned relations are non-linear (see Nier et al., 2008). It means that for low levels of systemic risk, a small increase of diversification (thus the interrelations within sector) translates into a significant contribution of a potential contagion effect. After exceeding a threshold, however, further rise in interrelations results in proportionally weaker risk for the system (as within the rule of decreasing marginal effects).

5 It turns out that market-based measures (which rely on, e.g., credit default swaps) may provide a reliable systemic risk assessment for the overall financial system as well as for particular institutions. These measures are also employed in studies on risk-taking channel of monetary policy. It should be pointed, however, that they include a range of factors that may not be associated with systemic risk exclusively (e.g., market liquidity risk).

6 This group of methods includes also a spillover index, which analyses the impact of one institution (or financial asset) on the other. It was originally proposed for the financial market contagion effect (Diebold and Yilmaz, 2009) and then expanded to include relations across financial institutions (Diebold and Yilmaz, 2014).

7 One approach to implementing nonlinearity into causality relations is calculating Granger causality but for different regimes identified with the use of Markov-switching models (see, e.g., Billio et al., 2010).

8 In this chapter, systemic risk measures are presented from conceptual and analytical perspectives, while their implementation is presented in the empirical chapters.

9 Brownlees and Engle (2017) proposed that LRMES be estimated based on a simple extrapolation. For instance, based on a daily quantity MES (at a threshold of 2%), they propose the following estimate: $LRMES_{i,t} \simeq 1 - \exp\left(18 \times MES_{i,t}\right)$, which defines the average expected loss over a half-year horizon. Such a methodological approach has also been applied for this study.

10 Empirical studies usually rely on the Brownlees and Engle's (2015) proposition to assume k=8% and C=20%. The empirical sections of this book follow this practice.

11 Such a presentation allows to identify a channel of macroprudential policy transmission to systemic risk (through capital requirements). Still, the overall effect should include also indirect effects (arising from transmission via LMRES).

12 SRISK calculations at the international level may need some adjustments, which arise, e.g., from differences in accounting standards between Europe and the USA.

13 It should be noted that a relatively modest impact of probability of insolvency on systemic risk may be, at least to some extent, determined by lack of changes in other factors. These findings can be interpreted as follows: the effect of further increase in the size of institution (given its constant probability of default) has a greater effect on systemic risk than rise in the latter but with no changes in the size and interconnectedness. In such a case, the room for a strong contagion effect is limited.

14 In many cases, this measure is calculated on the basis of daily market data, for which differences in time zone may be of high importance. This problem was also raised by Engle et al. (2012), who claim that European markets at t+1 point in time are pricing in information from Asian markets that originated in day t+1

and from American markets from day t. This time shift of information spillover should be incorporated into the measurement approach.

15 In some studies, the meaning of prefix 'Co-' is assigned not only to 'conditional' but also to 'commovement' and 'contagion'.

16 From the formal perspective, CoVaR is estimated with employment a quantile regression technique.

17 For example, Adrian and Brunnermeier (2016) estimate the ΔCoVaR with an implementation of quantile regression technique employed towards weekly market valuation of financial institutions' assets.

18 Interestingly, this classification allows for estimation of other measures, like MVaR or CoES. They can be used to complement the most popular systemic risk measure but remain more popular in the academic literature than in practical implementations.

19 At this point, it should be noted that none of the MES-related measure did identify any of financial institutions that were relevant for Global Financial Crises of 2007–2008 (Lehman Brothers, Fannie Mae, Freddie Mac, Countrywide) to be a source of systemic risk.

20 In finance, the beta coefficient is a measure vulnerability of how an individual asset reacts (on average) to the changes of the overall stock market.

21 This finding has been directly implemented in the empirical part of the book, in which we rely on two systemic risk measures.

22 This ratio of similarity will take values from 0 to 1, which describes the fraction of rankings that contain same institutions.

23 In general, model risk might be described as a risk that arises from incorporating an incorrect model towards real problems.

24 To a great extent, it might also arise from incorrect assumptions that translate into unrealistic findings, which in turn lead to inappropriate action of policymakers.

Bibliography

Acemoglu, D., Ozdaglar, A., Tahbaz-Salehi, A., (2015). Systemic Risk and Stability in Financial Networks, *American Economic Review*, vol. 105, no. 2, pp. 564–608.

Acharya, V.V., (2009). A Theory of Systemic Risk and Design of Prudential Bank Regulation, *Journal of Financial Stability*, vol. 5, no. 3, pp. 224–255.

Acharya, V.V., Engle, R.F., Richardson, M., (2012). Capital Shortfall: A New Approach to Ranking and Regulating Systemic Risk, *American Economic Review*, vol. 102, no. 3, pp. 59–64.

Acharya, V.V., Pedersen, L.H., Philippe, T., Richardson, M., (2010). *Measuring Systemic Risk*, Federal Reserve Bank of Cleveland.

Acharya, V.V., Pedersen, L., Philippe, T., Richardson, M., (2017). Measuring Systemic Risk, *The Review of Financial Studies*, vol. 30, no. 1, pp. 2–47.

Adrian, T., Brunnermeier, M.K., (2016). COVAR, *American Economic Review*, vol. 106, no. 7, pp. 1705–1741.

Adrian, T., Shin, H.S., (2008). Liquidity and Financial Contagion, *Financial Stability Review. Special Issue: Liquidity,* Banque de France, no. 11, pp. 1–7.

Agresti, A.M., Baudino, P., Poloni, P., (2008). *The ESB and IMF Indicators for the Macro-Prudential Analysis of the Banking Sector. A Comparison of the Two Approaches*, European Central Bank, Occasional Paper Series, no. 99/November 2008.

Aikman, D., Alessandri, P., Eklund, B., Gai, P., Kapadia, S., Martin, E., Mora, N., Sterne, G., Willison, M., (2011). Funding Liquidity Risk in a Quantitative Model of Systemic Stability. Central Banking, Analysis, and Economic Policies Book Series, [in:] Rodrigo Alfaro (ed.), *Financial Stability, Monetary Policy, and Central Banking*, Central Bank of Chile, vol. 15, ch. 12, pp. 371–410.

Albert, R., Jeong, H., Barabási, A.L., (2000). Error and Attack Tolerance of Complex Networks, *Nature*, vol. 406, pp. 378–382.

Alexander, K., Dhumale, R., Eatwell, J., (2010). *Managing Systemic Risk. The Rationale for International Financial Regulations*, Oxford Scholarship Online.

Allen, F., Carletti, E., (2012), Systemic Risk and Macroprudential Regulation, [in:] Allen, F., Aoki, M., Fitoussi, J.F., Kiyotaki, N., Gordon, R., Stiglitz, J. (eds.), *The Global Macro Economy and Finance*, Palgrave Macmillan, London.

Allen, F., Gale, D., (2000a). Bubbles and Crises, *The Economic Journal*, vol. 110 (460), pp. 236–255.

Allen, F., Gale, D., (2000b). Financial Contagion. *Journal of Political Economy*, vol. 108, pp. 1–33.

BCBS, (2013). *Fundamental Review of the Trading Book: A Revised Market Risk Framework. Technical Report*, Basel Committee on Banking Supervision.

BCBS, (2014). *Fundamental Review of the Trading Book: Outstanding Issues. Technical Report*, Basel Committee on Banking Supervision.

Benoit, S., Colletaz, G., Hurlin, C., Perignon, C., (2013). A Theoretical and Empirical Comparison of Systemic Risk Measures, *SSRN Electronic Journal*.

Benoit, S., Colliard, J.-E., Hurlin, C., Perignon, C., (2015). *Where the Risks Lie: A Survey on Systemic Risk*, HEC Paris Research Paper, FIN-2015-1088.

Berger, A., Udell G., (2003). *The Institutional Memory Hypothesis and the Procyclicality of the Bank Lending Behaviour*, BIS Working Paper, no. 125, Bank for International Settlements.

Bernaciak, A., (2012). *Zmiana stabilności a wzrost gospodarczy regionów Polski*, Wydział Zarządzania, Uniwerstytet Ekonomiczny w Poznaniu. [available only in Polish]

Bertalanffy, L., (1984). *General Systems Theory*, World Scientific Publishing Co Pte Ltd.

BIS, (2013). *Global Systemically Important Banks: Updated Assessment Methodology and the Higher Loss Absorbency Requirement*, BCBS, July 2013.

BIS, (2018). *Global Systemically Important Banks: Revised Assessment Methodology and the Higher Loss Absorbency Requirement*, BCBS, July 2018.

Billio, M., Getmansky, M., Lo, A.W., Pelizzon, L., (2010). *Measuring Systemic Risk in the Finance and Insurance Sectors*, MIT Sloan School Working Paper, no. 4774/10.

Billio, M., Getmansky, M., Lo, W.L., Pelizzon, L., (2012). Econometric Measures of Connectedness and Systemic Risk in the Finance and Insurance Sectors, *Journal of Financial Economics, Market Institutions, Financial Market Risks and Financial Crisis*, vol. 104, no. 3, pp. 535–559.

Blundell-Wignall, A., Roulet, C., (2013). Macro-prudential Policy, Bank Systemic Risk and Capital Controls, *Organizacja Współpracy Gospodarczej i Rozwoju, OECD Journal: Financial Market Trends*, 2013/2.

Borio, C., Lowe, P., (2002). Assessing the Risk of Banking Crises, *BIS Quarterly Review*, December, pp. 43–54.

Borio, C., Lowe, P., (2004). *Securing Sustainable Price Stability the Wilderness?* BIS Working Papers, no. 157.

Boss, M., Elsinger, H., Summer, M., Thurner, S., (2004). Network Topology of the Interbank Market, *Quantitative Finance*, vol. 4, pp. 677–684.

Bradsen, G., Linquist, K., Tsomocos, D., (2006). *Evaluation of Macroeconomic Models for Financial Stability Analysis*, Working Paper of Financial Market Department, Norges Bank.

Brownlees, Ch., Chabot, B., Ghysels, E, Kurz, Ch., (2015). *Backtesting Systemic Risk Measures during Historical Bank Runs*, Federal Reserve Bank of Chicago, Working Paper, 2015/09.

Brownlees, Ch., Engle, R.F., (2017). SRISK: A Conditional Capital Shortfall Measure of Systemic Risk, *The Review of Financial Studies*, vol. 30, no. 1, pp. 48–79.

Brunnermeier, M.K., Oehmke, M., (2013). Bubbles, Financial Crises, and Systemic Risk, [in:] Constantinides, G., Harris, M., Stulz, R. (eds.) *Handbook of the Economics of Finance*, Elsevier, pp. 1221–1288.

Brunnermeier, M.K., Sannikov, Y., (2014). A Macroeconomic Model with a Financial Sector, *American Economic Review*, vol. 104, pp. 379–421.

Bullard, J., Neely, Ch.J., Wheelock, D.C., (2009). Systemic Risk and the Financial Crisis: A Premier, *Federal Reserve of St. Louis Review*, pp. 403–417.

Caccioli, F., Barucca, P., Kobayashi, T., (2018). Network Models of Financial Systemic Risk: A Review, *Journal of Computational Social Science*, vol. 1, no. 1, pp. 81–114.

Capuano, C., (2008). *The Option-iPoD. The Probability of Default Implied by Option Prices Based on Entropy*, IMF Working Paper, no. 08/194, International Monetary Fund.

Chan-Lau, J.A., (2013). *Systemic Risk Assessment and Oversight*, Risk Books.

Claessens, S., Dornbush, R., Park, Y.C., (2001). Contagion: Why Crises Spread and How This Can Be Stopped, [in:] Claessens, S., Forbes, K.J. (eds.), *International Financial Contagion*, Springer, Boston, MA.

Claessens, S., Kose, M.A., Terrones, M.E., (2012). How Do Business and Financial Cycles Interact? vol. 87, no. 1, pp. 178–190.

Constancio, V., (2012). Contagion and the European Debt Crisis, *Financial Stability Review*, no. 16, Banque de France.

Covi, G., Gorpe, M.Z., Kok, C., (2019). *CoMap: Contagion Mapping the EA Banking Sector. A Granular Investigation of the Euro Area Banks' Large Exposures and their Systemic Risks Implications*, ECB Working Paper, no. 2224.

Danielsson, J., James, K.R., Valenzuela, M., Zer, I., (2016). Model Risk of Risk Models, *Journal of Financial Stability*, vol. 23, pp. 79–91.

Danielsson, J., Shin, H-S., (2003). *Endogenous Risk, Modern Risk Management – A History,* Risk Books.

Danielsson, J., Shin, H-S., Zigrand, J-P., (2013). *Endogenous and Systemic Risk*, University of Chicago Press by NBER, Chicago.

Danielsson, J., Valenzuela, M., Zer, I., (2018). Learning from History: Volatility and Financial Crises, *The Review of Financial Studies*, vol. 31, no. 7, pp. 2774–2805.

Di Cesare, A., Picco, A.R., (2018). *A Survey of Systemic Risk Indicators*, Bank of Italy Occasional Paper, no. 458.

Diebold, F.X., Yilmaz, K., (2009), Measuring Financial Asset Return and Volatility Spillovers, With Application to Global Equity Markets, *Economic Journal*, vol. 119, pp. 158–171.

Diebold, F.X., Yilmaz, K. (2014), On the Network Topology of Variance Decompositions: Measuring the Connectedness of Financial Firms, *Journal of Econometrics*, vol. 182, no. 1, pp. 119–134.

Drehmann, M., Tarashev, N., (2011). *Measuring the Systemic Importance of Interconnected Banks*, Technical Report, Bank for International Settlements.

Duffie, D., Zhu, H., (2011). Does a Central Clearing Counterparty Reduce Counterparty Risk?, *Review of Asset Pricing Studies*, vol. 1, no. 1, pp. 74–95.

ECB, (2009). *The Concept of Systemic Risk, Financial Stability Review*, European Central Bank, December 2009, pp. 134–142.

ECB, (2010). *Financial Stability Review*, European Central Bank, June 2010.

ECB, (2017). *Financial Stability Review*. European Central Bank, November 2017.

ECB, (2018). *Financial Stability Review*, European Central Bank, May 2018.

Eisenberg, T., Noe, H., (2001). Systemic Risk in Financial Systems, *Management Science*, vol. 47, no. 2, pp. 236–249.

Engle, R.F., Jondeau, E., Rockinger, M., (2012). *Conditional Beta and Systemic Risk in Europe*, HEC Lausanne Working Paper.

Engle, R.F., Manganelli, S., (2004). CAVaR: Conditional Autoregressive Value at Risk by Regression Quantiles, *Journal of Business and Economic Statistics*, vol. 23, no. 4, pp. 367–381.

Esponosa-Vega, M., Sole, J., (2011). Cross-Border Financial Surveillance: A Network Perspective, *Journal of Financial and Economic Policy*, vol. 3, no. 3, pp. 182–205.

ESRB, (2016). *Macroprudential Policy Issues Arising from Low Interest Rates and Structural Changes in the EU Financial System*, Joint Task Force of ESRB Advisory Technical Committee (ATC), ESRB Advisory Scientific Committee (ASC), and ECB Financial Stability Committee (FSC), November 2016.

Flejterski, S., (2006). *Nowa strategia i polityka bezpieczeństwa na rynkach finansowych Unii Europejskiej*, Prace Naukowe Akademii Ekonomicznej we Wrocławiu. [available only in Polish]

Freixas, X., Laeven, L., Peydro, J-L., (2015). *Systemic Risk, Crises, and Macroprudential Regulation*, The MIT Press, Cambridge.

Freixas, X., Parigi, B., Rochet, J-C., (2000). Systemic Risk, Interbank Relations and Liquidity Provision by the Central Bank, *Journal of Money, Credit and Banking*, vol. 32, no. 2, pp. 611–638.

Frey, R., Hledik, J., (2018). Diversification and Systemic Risk: A Financial Network Perspective, *Risks*, vol. 6, no. 2.

Fricke, D., Lux, T., (2012). Core-periphery Structure in the Overnight Money Market: Evidence from the e-mid Trading Platform, *Computational Economics*, vol. 45, pp. 359–395.

FSB, (2010). *Reducing the Moral Hazard Posed by Systemically Important Financial Institutions*, 20 October 2010.

Gadanecz, B., Jayaram, K., (2009). Measures of Financial Stability – A Review, *IFC Bulletin*, no. 31.

Gai, P., Kapania, S., (2010). *Contagion in Financial Networks*, Bank of England Working Paper, no. 383.

Glasserman, H.P., (2015). How Likely is Contagion in Financial Networks? Journal of Banking and Finance, vol. 50, pp. 383–399.

Głogowski, A., (2012). *Ryzyko systemowe – aspekty sieciowe*. Bezpieczny Bank, vol. 3, no. 48, pp. 74–95. [available only in Polish]

Gonzalez-Hermosillo, B., Hesse, H., (2011). Global Market Conditions and Systemic Risk, *Journal of Emerging Market Finance*, vol. 10, no. 2, p. 227–252.

Gray, D., Jobst, A., (2013). *Systemic Contingent Claim Analysis – Estimating Market-Implied Systemic Risk*, IMF Working Paper, no. 13/54, International Monetary Fund.

Grinderslev, O.J., Kristiansen, K.L., (2016). *Systemic Risk in Danish Banks: Implementing SRISK in a Danish Context*, Danmarks Nationalbank Working Papers, no. 105.

Haldane, A.G., (2013). Rethinking the Financial Network, [in:] S.A. Jansen, E. Schröter, N. Stehr (eds.), *Fragile stabilität-stabile fragilität*, Springer, Wiesbaden, pp. 243–278.

Hansen, L.P., (2013). *Challenges in Identifying and Measuring Systemic Risk*, CEMFI Working Paper, no. 1305.

Harrington, S.E., (2009). The Financial Crisis, Systemic Risk and the Future of Financial Regulation, *The Journal of Risk and Insurance*, vol. 76(4), pp. 785–819.

Hartmann, P., Straetmans, S., de Vries C.G., (2004), Asset Market Linkages in Crisis Periods, *Review of Economics and Statistics*, vol. 86, pp. 313–326.

Helwege, J., (2009). Financial Firm Bankruptcy and Systemic Risk, Regulation, *Regulation*, vol. 32, pp. 24–29.

Holló, D., Kremer, M., Duca L., (2012). *CISS – A Composite Indicator of Systemic Stress in the Financial System*, Working Paper Series no.1426, European Central Bank.

Huang, X., Zhou, H., Zhu, H., (2009). A Framework for Assessing the Systemic Risk of Major Financial Institutions, *Journal of Banking and Finance*, vol. 33, pp. 2036–2049.

Huang, X., Zhou, H., Zhu, H., (2012). Systemic Risk Contributions, *Journal of Financial Services Research*, vol. 42, no. 1, pp. 55–83.

Hull, J., Suo, W., (2002). A Methodology for Assessing Model Risk and its Application to the Implied Volatility Function Model, *The Journal of Financial and Quantitative Analysis*, vol. 37, no. 2, pp. 297–318.

Illing, M., Liu, Y., (2003). *An Index of Financial Stress for Canada*, Bank of Canada Working Paper, no. 14.

IMF, (2006). *Financial Soundness Indicators. Compilation Guide*, International Monetary Fund.

IMF, (2009). *Global Financial Stability Report*, International Monetary Fund.

IMF, (2014). *How Big is the Implicit Subsidy for Banks Considered Too Important to Fail?*, Global Financial Stability Report, April 2014.

IMF, (2016). *Global Financial Stability Report*, International Monetary Fund.

Iyer, R., Peydro, J-L., (2011). Interbank Contagion at Work: Evidence from a Natural Experiment, *Review of Financial Studies*, vol. 24, pp. 1337–1377.

Jajuga, K., (2008). *Zarządzanie ryzykiem*, Wydawnictwo Naukowe PWN, Warszawa. [available only in Polish].

Jajuga, K., Karaś, M., Kuziak, K., Szczepaniak, W., (2017). *Ryzyko systemowe. Metody oceny i ich weryfikacja w wybranych krajach*, Materiały i Studia, nr 329, Narodowy Bank Polski. [available only in Polish]

Jurkowska, A., (2018). *Polski sektor bankowy wobec ryzyka systemowego. Analiza banków giełdowych*, Wydawnitwo Uniwersytetu Ekonomicznego w Krakowie. [available only in Polish]

Kalemli-Ozcan, S., Sorensen, B., Yesiltas, S., (2011). *Leverage Across Firms, Banks and Countries*, Working Paper, University of Houston.

Kapadia, S., Drehmann, M., Elliott, J., Sterne, G., (2013). Liquidity Risk, Cash Flow Constraints, and Systemic Feedbacks, [in:] *Quantifying Systemic Risk*, National Bureau of Economic Research.

Karkowska, R., (2015). *Ryzyko systemowe. Charakter i źródła indywidualizacji w sektorze bankowym*, Wydawnictwo Wolters Kluwer. [available only in Polish]

Kemp, M.H.D, (2017). *Systemic Risk. A Practitioner's Guide to Measurement, Management and Analysis*, Macmillan.

Kiyotaki, N., Moore, J., (1997). Credit Cycles, *Journal of Political Economy*, vol. 105, no. 2, pp. 211–248.

Knight, F.H., (1921). *Risk, Uncertainty and Profit*, University of Boston Press, Boston.

Kollintzas, T., Konstantakopoulou, L., Tsionas, M., (2011). Stylized Facts of Money and Credit over the Business Cycles, *Applied Financial Economics*, vol. 21, no. 23, pp. 1735–1755.

Liu, X., (2017). Measuring Systemic Risk with Regime Switching in Tails, *Economic Modelling*, vol. 67, pp.55–72.

Masciantonio, S., Zaghini, A., (2017). Systemic Risk and Systemic Importance Measures during the Crisis, *Temi di Discussione*, no. 1153, Bank of Italy.

Mishkin, F.S., (2011). *Monetary Policy Strategy: Lessons From The Crisis*, NBER Working Paper Series, no. 16755, Cambridge.

Montagna, M., Kok, Ch., (2016). *Multi-layered Interbank Model for Assessing Systemic Risk*, ECB Working Paper Series, no. 1944.

Nelson, W.R., Perli, R., (2007). Selected Indicators of Financial Stability, [in:] *Risk Measurement and Systemic Risk*, ECB, Frankfurt am Main, pp. 343–372.

Nier, E.W., (2009). *Financial Stability Frameworks and the Role of Central Banks: Lessons from the Crisis*, IMF Working Paper no. WP/09/70, Międzynarodowy Fundusz Walutowy.

Nier, E.W., Yang, J., Yorulmazer, T., Alentorn, A., (2008). Network Models and Financial Stability, *Journal of Economic Dynamics and Control*, vol. 31, no. 6, pp. 2033–2060.

Novickytė, L., Dičpinigaitienė, V., (2018). Application of Systemic Risk Measurement Methods: A Systematic Review and Meta-analysis using a Network Approach, *Quantitative Finance and Economics*, vol. 2, no. 4, pp. 798–820.

Olszak, M., (2015). Zjawisko nadmiernej procykliczności sektora finansowego z perspektywy polityki makroostrożnościowej – źródła, metody ograniczania i ich rudymentarne słabości, *Problemy Zarządzania*, vol. 55, no. 2, pp.72–96. [available only in Polish]

Ostalecka, A., (2009). *Kryzysy bankowe i metody ich przezwyciężania*, Difin, Warszawa. [available only in Polish]

Ostalecka, A., (2012). Ryzyko systemowe i jego ograniczanie. Rola nadzoru makroostrożnościowego, [in:] I. Pyka, J. Cichorska (eds.), *Finanse w niestabilnym otoczeniu – dylematy i wyzwania. Bankowość*, Studia Ekonomiczne. Zeszyty Naukowe Wydziałowe, Uniwersytet Ekonomiczny w Katowicach, Katowice. [available only in Polish]

Pietrzak, B., Polański, Z., Woźniak, B., (2004). *System finansowy w Polsce*, praca zbiorowa, PWN, Warszawa. [available only in Polish]

Pipień, M., Wdowiński, P., Kaszowska, J., (2018). *Identyfikacja cech cyklu finansowego i analiza jego synchronizacji z cyklem koniunkturalnym*, Materiały i Studia, no. 332, Narodowy Bank Polski. [available only in Polish]

Pyka, I., (2010). *Bank centralny na współczesnym rynku pieniężnym*, C.H. Beck, Warszawa. [available only in Polish]

Rodríguez-Moreno, M., Peña, J.I., (2013). Systemic Risk Measures: The Simpler the Better? *Journal of Banking and Finance*, vol. 37, no. 6, pp. 1817–1831.

Rosati, D.K., (2014). Regulacje makroostrożnościowe a stabilność sektora bankowego, *Bank i Kredyt*, vol. 45, no. 4, pp. 373–406. [available only in Polish]

Santos, J.A.C., (2014). *Evidence from the Bond Market on Banks' "Too-Big-to-Fail" Subsidy*, Economic Policy Review, Federal Reserve Bank of New York, pp. 29–39.

Scott, H.S, (2010). The Reduction of Systemic Risk in the United States Financial System, *Harvard Journal of Law and Public Policy*, vol. 33, no. 2, pp. 671–735.

Segoviano, M., Goodhart, C., (2009). *Banking Stability Measures*, IMF Working Paper, no. 09/04.

Smaga, P., (2014a). Istota ryzyka systemowego, *Studia ekonomiczne, Polska Akademia Nauk*, nr 1(80), pp. 36–63. [available only in Polish]

Smaga, P., (2014b). *Rola banku centralnego w zapewnianiu stabilności finansowej*, CeDeWu, Warszawa 2014. [available only in Polish]

Smaga, P., (2015). Procykliczność – przyczyny i sposoby zapobiegania, [in:] Ostaszewski, J., (ed.), *O nowy ład finansowy w Polsce. Rekomendacje dla animatorów życia gospodarczego*, Szkoła Główna Handlowa w Warszawie, Warszawa. [available only in Polish]

Smaga, P., (2020). *Polityka makroostrożnościowa w sektorze bankowym. Teoria i praktyka*, Oficyna Wydawnicza SGH, Warszawa 2020. [available only in Polish]

Szczepańska, O., (2008). *Stabilność finansowa jako cel banku centralnego. Studium teoretyczno-porównawcze*, Wydawnictwo Naukowe Scholar, Warszawa. [available only in Polish]

Szpunar, P., (2012). *Rola polityki makroostrożnościowej w zapobieganiu kryzysom finansowym*, Materiały i Studia, vol. 278, Narodowy Bank Polski. [available only in Polish]

7 Negative Interest Rate Policy versus Systemic Risk

7.1 Analysis of NIRP Impact on Systemic Risk Concept

This sub-chapter provides our research approach along with the rationale behind the empirical methods in use. The research method employed in this study embraces seven stages (please see also Iwanicz-Drozdowska and Rogowicz, 2022):

1. Estimation of systemic risk measures;
2. Construction of a network of connections among systemic risks of individual units over the banking sector;
3. Specification of hypothetical impulse transmission across the systemic network;
4. Measurement of the direct effect of monetary policy impulse;
5. Measurement of the contagion effect in systemic risk network directly on the effect of interest rate primary impulse;
6. Measurement of the impact of the aggregate indirect effect of intra-system monetary policy impulse transmission;
7. Varied impact of monetary policy on systemic risk depending on the monetary policy tool used.

All this shows that the method in place is a novelty approach to the analysis of monetary policy and systemic risk interaction, much as it uses accessible and widely used tools. This novelty character must be seen from two perspectives. First, two complementary empirical tools are used, i.e., a concept of time-series modelling (to take account of the time dimension of systemic risk) paired with a network view (reflecting the structural dimension of the risk). Second, they are employed to compute the measures of systemic risk for individual institutions, which has been relatively uncommon in the literature to-date, in particular, in the analysis of such a broad research sample. Such an approach is required by an unprecedented character of the analysed NIRP phenomenon which was never so popular under the current circumstances of monetary policy. Thus, if the methods known to-date were used in a traditional way (e.g., methods of time-series analysis), the importance of this phenomenon may have not been reflected properly.

DOI: 10.4324/9781003312116-7

The above research perspective aims to enable a verification of three auxiliary research hypotheses which hold as follows:

- Monetary policy which employs interest rates as the main monetary policy tool impacts systemic risk;
- The impact of central bank's interest rates on systemic risk is non-linear;
- The contagion effect is of vital importance for the effect of both negative and positive interest rates on systemic risk.

The conceptual view of individual research stages will be presented later on in this sub-chapter starting from individual research stages featured in Figure 7.1, whereas empirical findings and a discussion will be given in subsequent sub-chapters.

First, the systemic risk level must be quantified, which will proceed with respect to individual financial institutions. As a consequence, this research stage is based on relevant measurement tools for this risk, namely, SRISK and ΔCoVaR. In the literature, these measures are the most common methods to measure systemic risk for a specified institution and they are based on the balance sheet and market data for individual banks. Further, these measures being used at the same time ensure a higher outcome quality than

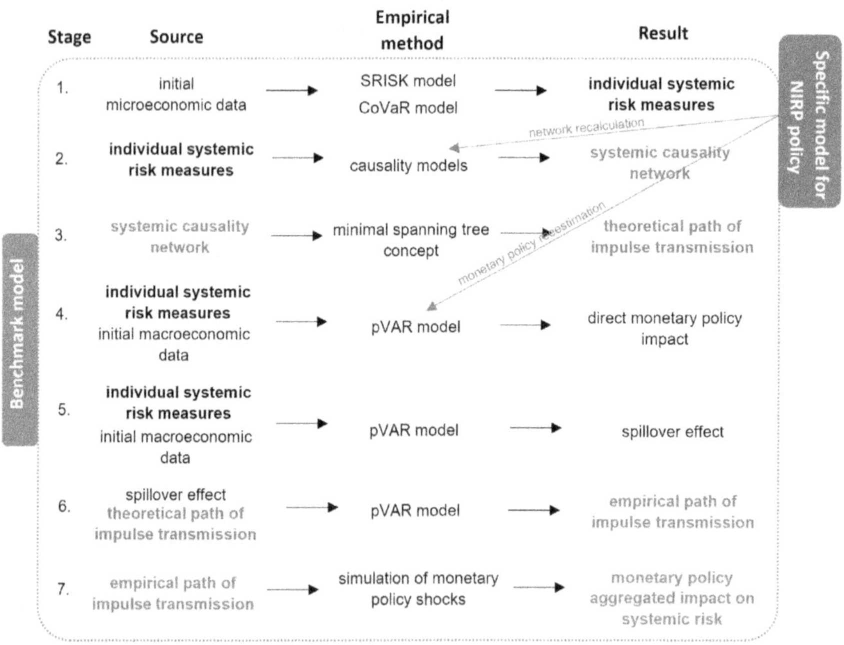

Figure 7.1 Approach to measuring the impact of NIRP policy on systemic risk – research methodology concept

Source: Own work.

if only one of them were used. It is because of important differences in the way the results are interpreted. To this aim, for each entity analysed, two complementary measures will be estimated. The first one represents a top-down perspective and it allows to analyse a relative exposure of a given institution to systemic risk in case the entire system is in an aggravated risk phase. In contrast, the other measure provides yet another approach, i.e., bottom-up, which is about the entire sector being relatively exposed to risk, providing that a given institution is in a crisis phase.

As the research aims to analyse the transmission of monetary policy impulses, at the second stage, a network of connections was constructed among banks in terms of the contagion effect potentially spreading, thus allowing for a structural dimension of systemic risk. A methodology proposed by Billio et al. (2012) and based on Granger's causality was used to manifest the scale of sectoral connections among the analysed entities. In the original approach, the assumption was that if the effect of a bank's change of stock price causing (in the medium term) a change in another bank's stock value can be identified, then, in the case the former defaults, adverse consequences will also be reflected in the latter. In this way, it is possible to build a causal sequence, and the number of such relations defines the scales of sectoral connections.

An approach employed in this study expands the original concept of constructing networks in two respects – the measures underlying the identification of connections and the incorporation of a relevant extent of causality among them. This methodological view aims not only to estimate the systemic risk in the strict sense but first and foremost to identify connections among individual entities. It means that, at the very onset, it will not be market valuations of the analysed entities (stock prices in particular, as in the original approach), but rather systemic risk measures estimated beforehand that will be taken into account to define the connections. Application of such a concept entails the following advantages:

- It enables incorporation of information value carried not only by the market data but also balance sheet items of individual entities.
- Only systemic events are included in the network structure. Consequently, this type of network is less responsive (than if it was only market data-based) to such events which impact the entire banking sector (i.e., bank market valuations), but they simultaneously do not affect systemic risk (such as, for instance, information shock on the financial market). Such a perspective is of particular importance in terms of this study's objective, i.e., precise identification of negative interest rates' impact. It is because the measures taken by central banks affect financial instruments' market valuations. It means that constructing a network based on this type of data may allow for an excessive effect of this policy. On the other hand, if systemic risk measures are employed directly in a network's foundations, it can be taken explicitly that the effect of

monetary policy will be analysed in terms of systemic risk rather than other market aspects, such as valuation.

- It ensures increased stability over time of the network of connections under construction. A network of connections devised for market parameters is relatively highly volatile by nature. On the contrary, relations among entities based on the latter's individual systemic risk measures should reflect structural relations that are stable at least in the medium term.

With the use of times series for systemic risk of two entities (s_t^i and s_t^j), the following linear model will present their mutual relations:[1]

$$\begin{aligned} s_{t+1}^i &= a^i s_t^i + b^{ij} s_t^j + e_{t+1}^i \\ s_{t+1}^j &= a^j s_t^j + b^{ji} s_t^i + e_{t+1}^j \end{aligned} \tag{7.1}$$

whereby e_{t+1}^i and e_{t+1}^j stand for two non-correlated processes bearing white noise characteristics, whereas a^i, a^j, b^{ij} and b^{ji} stand for model parameters. Accordingly, entity j is identified as the cause in Granger's causality i, whereby parameter b^{ij} is statistically different from zero, and conversely, i is the cause as construed by Granger's causality j when b^{ji} is different from zero.

The above approach to the construction of a network of connections is, however, expanded to include a general concept of systemic risk accrual. In this context, measures of causality should be defined per a specified time unit. To account for such an approach, the methodology was expanded to include long-term causality with a long period in terms of high data frequency and consistency with other measurement methods will stand for causality estimated on a quarterly basis.[2] Such an approach is used in the literature primarily in terms of identifying the channel of risk-taking by commercial banks (e.g., Colletaz et al., 2018).[3]

Methodology used in this study follows an approach proposed by Dufour and Renault (1998) and expanded by Dufour and Taamouti (2010) in line with which variable i is the cause of variable j over a previously defined horizon h only when the past values of variable i improve the predictive values of variable j over horizon $t+h$. In this context, an overall approach presented earlier may, however, be understood as short-term causality as it only focused on defining relationships in the upcoming period $(t+1)$.[4] At the same time, an approach aimed at identifying long-term relationships may be a sort of a filter which allows – particularly concerning this study – to identify only systemic relationships while ignoring, *inter alia*, responses to information shock.

With the above concept in mind, for each pair of potential entity-based relations, a model is estimated. It is an empirical model of the vector autoregression approach (VAR) for a system of three variables. Two of them, as in the approach referred to in equation (7.1), are systemic risk measures at a standalone level (s_i, s_j), whereas the third parameter is an auxiliary variable (z) which may identify indirect effect among individual entities.[5] Consequently, if $W = \left(s^{i'}, s^{j'}, z'\right)$, notation for the construction of estimating causality looks as follows:

$$W_t = \sum_{i=1}^{p} \Phi_i W_{t-i} + e_t \tag{7.2}$$

where Φ_i denotes a matrix of model coefficients, whereas e_t such a random expression that $\mathrm{E}(e_t) = 0$, $\mathrm{E}(e_t, e_t') = \Sigma_e$ is non-singular matrix and $\mathrm{E}(e_t, e_s') = 0$ for all $t \neq s$.

Accordingly, in line with the approach proposed by Colletaz et al. (2018), causality measures rely on a comparing covariance matrix for a prediction error over horizon W_{t+h} derived for two model versions – restricted and unrestricted. Accordingly, prediction error over horizon h is expressed in equation (7.3), whereas the aforementioned covariance matrix of prediction error for an unrestricted model (much as a similar approach applies for a restricted model), is described by equation (7.4).

$$W_{t+h} - \mathrm{E}_t\left(W_{t+h}\right) = \sum_{i=0}^{h-1} A^i e_{t+h-i} \tag{7.3}$$

$$\Sigma(h) = \sum_{i=0}^{h-1} A^i \Sigma_e A^{i'} \tag{7.4}$$

whereby A is matrix of parameters resulting from a comparison of form W, so that $\tilde{W} = A\tilde{W}_{t-1} + \tilde{\varepsilon}_t$, whereas $\tilde{W} = \left(W_t, W_{t-1}, \ldots, W_{t-p+1}\right)$ and $\tilde{\varepsilon}_t$ is a vector denoted as follows: $(\varepsilon_t, 0, \ldots, 0)'$.

What results is a specification of causality relationship from j to i over horizon h as follows:

$$C\left(j \xrightarrow{h} i \mid F\right) = ln\left[\frac{det\left(J_0 \Sigma_0(h) J_0'\right)}{det\left(J_1 \Sigma(h) J_1'\right)}\right] \tag{7.5}$$

whereby $\Sigma(h)$ is covariance matrix of a random element for unrestricted model over horizon h, whereas $\Sigma_0(h)$ for a restricted model and leaving out variable j. $J_0 = [1\ 0]$, whereas $J_1 = [1\ 0\ 0]$ are used to identify a portion of covariance matrix referring to variable i. The determinant of the covariance matrix for the prediction error of the restricted model (numerator) should be higher than the corresponding measure for the unrestricted model (denominator) when j is the cause of i over horizon h.

What the above stages are expected to yield, i.e., estimated systemic risk measures on standalone level and identified relations among them, should be the construction of a systemic risk network (Figure 7.1). Formalized notation of such a network is normally manifested by an adjacency matrix which specifies all the relations in the system and can simply be denoted as follows:

$$[A]_{ji} = (j \rightarrow i) \tag{7.6}$$

A network thus estimated and denoted allows to define the direction of systemic impulse transmission. An approach to this type of analysis may be twofold – with respect to analysing an overall network structure or individual transmission paths. Later on, in this chapter, the latter approach is primarily addressed.

Next to analysing its characteristics, the network of connections among individual entities constructed at this stage first aims to analyse the impact of a primary impulse (in the form of, e.g., rise or fall of interest rates) on systemic risk all over the sector. It brings out that it is necessary to assess the network in more detail rather than generally. The assessment may be based on an analysis of individual transmission paths. An examination of how two parameters (i.e., direct and indirect impact measures) develop will be foundation for an analysis of impulse impact. A direct impact defines the scale of the effect central bank actions have on systemic risk of a given entity which is identified in isolation from responses of corresponding measures of other entities. In turn, an indirect impact additionally allows for adjustment responses of individual banks (to embrace the first shock) which can spur on spillover impact on subsequent entities in the network of connections. In other words, the issue of direct impact allows for an exogenous character of monetary policy effect on systemic risk and it refers to an impact as part of the classical monetary policy transmission, whereas indirect impact may be equated with the relationship's endogenous element.[6] Accordingly, an indirect impact additionally takes account of interactions between individual entities in the network and it structurally depends on the three features:

- strength of direct impact of an external primary shock on a given entity which consequently becomes an impulse of an indirect effect;
- strength of interactions among entities understood here as contagion effect or spillover effect;
- length of a hypothetical transmission path among banks, that is, of a series of mutual relations among entities which is viewed through mutual connections among systemic risk measures, whatever the type of shock fed into the system.

All of the above components brought together are conducive to defining how long a monetary policy primary impulse will hold once fed into the network until it expires altogether. It is, in turn, an empirical path of impulse transmission that is a measure which manifests transmission of a specific shock inside of a network of interconnections. In other words, out of possible relations among entities as regards impact on systemic risk (illustrated by a hypothetical path), this measure concentrates on a specific type of disturbance, which is, monetary policy impact in this case.

The fundamental assumption for a way of impulse transmission in a network of connections is the strength of the primary impulse fed into the system being identical for each entity in the system. This assumption is consistent with an empirical approach used in this chapter and fully intuitive for monetary policy analysis. A change in central bank's interest rates is defined on the macroeconomic level and therefore this level is identical for

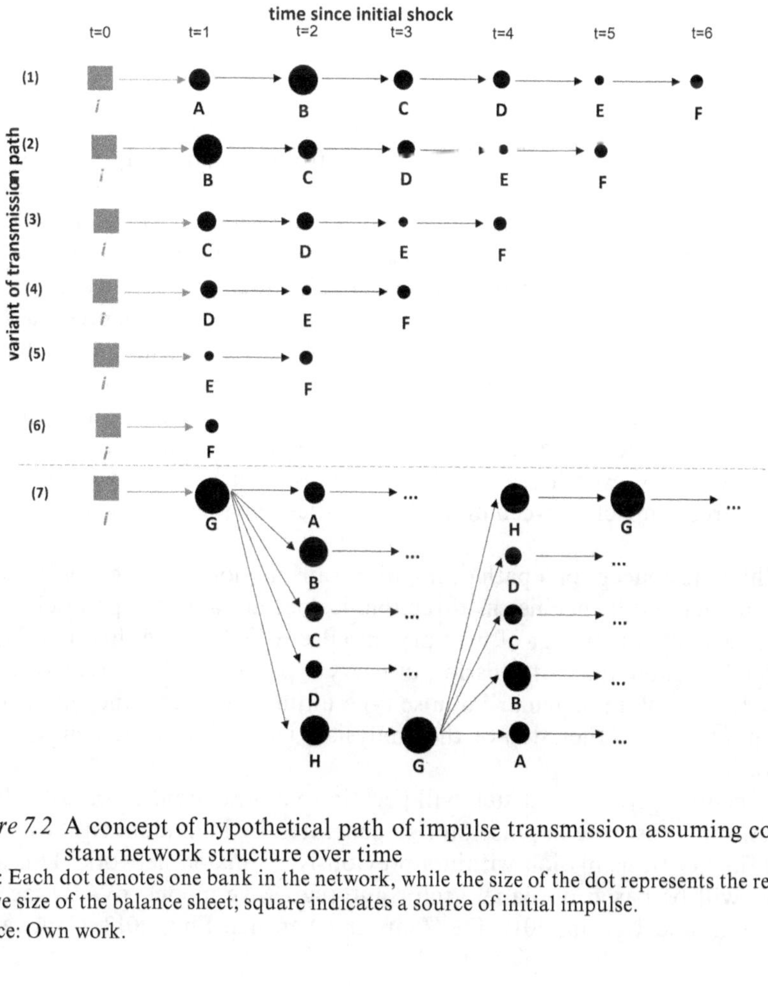

Figure 7.2 A concept of hypothetical path of impulse transmission assuming constant network structure over time

Note: Each dot denotes one bank in the network, while the size of the dot represents the relative size of the balance sheet; square indicates a source of initial impulse.

Source: Own work.

individual entities. Its final effect varies for various entities having specific economic traits; however, the variation does not concern the scale of primary shock.

Figure 7.2 presents an approach to measuring the indirect effect of monetary policy shock on systemic risk and it points to three fundamental assumptions which enable measuring a scale of the effect empirically:

- Impact of a given single impulse on a specified entity may be multiple, at various periods. For instance, entity *F* on the given example is under the influence of the primary impulse in each of the periods concerned – in the first one as direct effect and each successive as indirect effect.
- At its most extreme, the above conclusion may also refer to a looping effect of a given impulse on a specified entity. For instance, impact on entity *A*, next to being a direct impact (variant 1, Figure 7.2) is exerted on multiple occasions by another entity *G* (variant 7), and it occurs on a cyclical basis at even intervals of several periods and entails another series of direct responses transmitted by entity *A* to other entities connected in the sector.
- As the chain of impulse transmission extends, the effect of the impulse on an entity moving along the chain gradually wears off. It means that the indirect effect gradually expires over time, similarly like the direct effect. In the case of direct effect, it arises solely from its dynamics in the macroeconomic system, for indirect effect – what adds up here is attributable precisely to the effect of moving along successive stages of causality chain. For instance, although entity *F* is under the influence of a primary impulse in all of the transmission variants presented, it is highly probable the influence will be wearing off along with the progress from variant 6 to variant 1, with its bottom hit at variant 7. Such a knowledge of network structure and dynamics enable analysing the scale of indirect effect from the perspective of hypothetical transmission path, even if the particular type of disturbance or the strength of direct impact between individual entities remains unknown.

While the concept of a path of impulse transmission identifies the existence of impact and it specifies its direction, it does not allow to precisely define the scale of the impact of primary impulse. It is because this path is supposed to show the transmission of every type of impulse it receives. How the impact of a particular impulse type ultimately affects the entire sector requires yet another step of the analysis – i.e., the measurement of effect strength.

Accordingly, the next step will pertain to a measurement of both the effect of interest rate impulse on risk generated by individual entities and of its further transmission within a previously estimated network. This analysis will be based on panel vector autoregressive model (pVAR; see, e.g., Doytch and Uctum, 2011; De Haan and Van den End, 2013; Canova and

Ciccarelli, 2013). Such an approach combines the advantages of modelling time series and it introduces elements of system dynamic interdependencies while simultaneously allowing for a wide scope of information which panel modelling offers. This approach considers all system variables as endogenous and it concomitantly allows individual variables inside the system to be heterogeneous. As this model is dynamic, it also allows to analyse – in temporal and spatial terms – transmission of a shock fed from outside (ε_{it}). The basic equation may look as follows:

$$\begin{bmatrix} X_t \\ Y_{it} \end{bmatrix} = A_t + B(L) \begin{bmatrix} X_t \\ Y_{it} \end{bmatrix} + \varepsilon_{it} \tag{7.7}$$

whereby X_t is a vector encompassing time series of macroeconomic variables which describe both the economic environment and the monetary policy (money market interest rate), whereas vector Y_{it} takes account of individual features of individual banks. In particular, these vectors cover the following:

$$\begin{aligned} X_t &= \left[gdp_t,\ cpi_t,\ neer_t,\ r_t \right] \\ Y_{I,t} &= \left[roa_{it},\ leverage_{it},\ risk_{it} \right] \end{aligned} \tag{7.8}$$

whereby gdp_t denotes annual growth of the gross domestic product, cpi_t denotes yearly dynamics of consumer price index, $neer_t$ denotes a change of a nominal effective exchange rate and r_t stands for short-term interbank interest rate which manifests the monetary policy pursued, roa_{it} denotes return on the bank's assets, $leverage_{it}$ denotes financial leverage computed as a ratio of liabilities[7] to assets and $risk_{it}$ denotes a measure of systemic risk for various model versions – SRISK or ΔCoVaR. A_t is a matrix of fixed effects for individual banks which first and foremost takes account of asset market value, whereas $B(L)$ is a matrix of parameters for variables with their lags (selected as per Akaike's information criterion). Owing to such a perspective, it is possible to condition the effect of a factor examined (i.e., change of central bank's interest rates) on varying input features of individual entities, as well as the scale of their connections in the banking sector.

Once the vector model is applied for data panel structure, implications arise which add up to the methodology presented in the literature in the following way:

- With respect to time-series analysis with the use of panel data, the literature is usually only confined to macroeconomic data. It means that such an analysis particularly aims to identify differences among the economies. In turn, with respect to microeconomic perspective (i.e., analysis of standalone data of individual entities), the analysis is usually limited to the data from a single country. In order to estimate the particular type of monetary policy, this study requires that both approaches are combined. As it is attempted to quantify an impact of monetary policy on risk measures at a standalone level, limitation to a given economy only may not reflect the nature of the phenomenon studied adequately. In particular, due to such a limitation, the only reference point would be the historical experience in a given economy. In this context, NIRP – which was employed in a vast majority of the economies for the first time – is an important structural change. Thus, its analysis should be presented in comparison with the impact of conventional monetary policy in a given period and among countries.

- For the most part, the literature on the analysis of standalone panel data is limited to estimating standard regression models, defining the exogenous character of selected variables. For this reason, owing to the proposed vectoral autoregression on a temporal and spatial sample, it is possible to avoid a need to force the exogenous nature of variables as all of them in this approach are deemed endogenous in the equations.
- Owing to such an approach, it is possible to allow for a heterogeneous nature of individual items in a given sample under study. The approach proposed slightly complicates the above assumption saying that a process generating data is identical for all units in a data set. In applying the vectoral autoregression for standalone panel data, however, this assumption is just impossible to meet. Consequently, in the case of samples including entities broken down into countries, a fixed effect was adopted which is particular for individual entities and equally coherent for individual countries. It follows that such an approach takes account of NIRP being introduced by various economies in various periods, defining differences among them and among the economies which remain in negative interest rate environment.[8]

In order to specify the effect of an external impulse on the system thus structured, a standard procedure of analysis of impulseresponse function (IRF) with respect to a given variable responding to the impulse fed to the system will be used. The response function specifies a dynamic response of ith endogenous variable in the model to a shock jth variable, assuming all the other shocks remain constant. However, it is necessary to decompose model residuals to make them orthogonal. To this aim, Cholesky decomposition was used. The most frequent convention is accepting a specified sequence of exogenous variables, i.e., ordering scheme. In this case, the assumption is that individual variables must potentially respond. It means that those which respond earlier in the impulse ordering scheme are considered more exogenous, whereas late responders are more endogenous, respectively. For this model, a standard response chain scheme was adopted that assumed the most exogenous variable, i.e., the first responder, is interest rate which

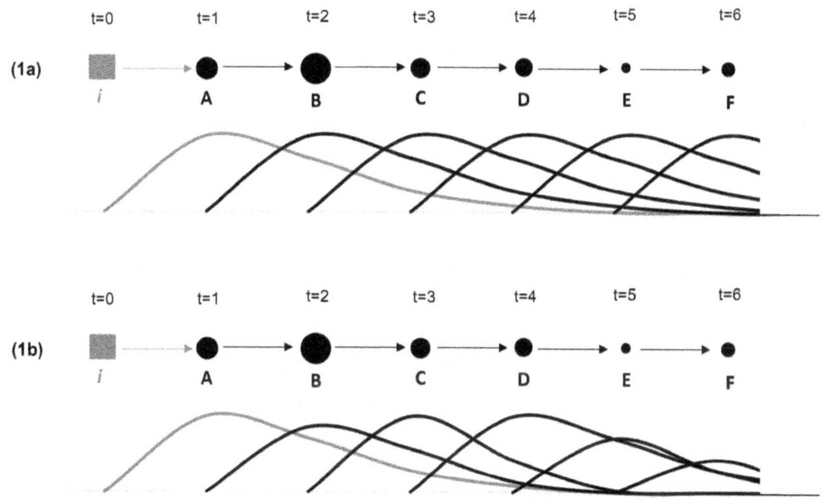

Figure 7.3 A concept of empirical measurement of direct and indirect effects with an implementation of impulse response functions

Note: Each dot denotes one bank in the network, while the size of the dot represents the relative size of the balance sheet; square indicates a source of initial impulse; waved lines imply impulse response functions and point out their different shapes.

Source: Own work.

then affects economic activity which, in turn, affects price processes in the economy. It is bank variables, i.e., financial leverage which consequently impacts entities' profitability, that were defined as more endogenous. Finally, the most endogenous variable analysed is systemic risk measure. For a panel approach, the contagion effect affecting an entity's systemic risk level after the entity's individual variables was also taken into account.[9]

A full exploitation of the impulse response function largely complements and also complicates the analytical approach previously presented by Figure 7.2. The approach the figure represents assumed that the effect of the impact materialized fully in the next period after the impulse occurs. Meanwhile, the effect of the impact may spread over time and although it did not materialize fully at the level of a given institution, its transmission to another entity may already begin. Figure 7.3 presents an example of such an approach for one of the above variants.

What should be noted is that the empirical path of connections is divided into stages, which stems from the above-explained concepts. The underlying reason is that an empirical model's function is to measure the relationships identified as part of the hypothetical path of transmitting a specific impulse, rather than to build an independent network of connections. In other words, the pertinent approach first defines a general structure of cause-and-effect relationships among commercial banks viewed through the connections among systemic risk measures. Second, only a monetary policy impulse is defined out of the range of potential external impulses, and its network transmission is measured (see Figure 7.1).

The above relationships imply that both paths of impulse transmission, hypothetical and empirical one, may differ from each other (Figure 7.4). Largely, such a difference may be attributable to the aforementioned concepts which use various methods to measure relationships among network elements. Such an empirical construction and the ensuing differences affect the way the model is analysed. First, the most sought-after solution is when an empirical model indicates a structure of connections corresponding to the hypothetical path (e.g., path 1, Figure 7.4). Second, it may be possible that the path indicated by empirical estimates overlaps with the hypothetical path only to some point, and then it moves on between other entities (e.g., path 2, Figure 7.4). Third, empirical estimates may show the theoretical path has been "interrupted", i.e., no statistically relevant impact has been found in the relations between two entities previously incorporated into the hypothetical path (e.g., path 3, Figure 7.4). In all of these situations, the prevailing approach in ultimately defining the empirical path is one which focuses on the common part, that is, taking into account only such relations among entities that have been corroborated by both the methods on both stages of constructing a network of connections[10].

The considerations to-date have mostly pertained to analysing monetary policy impulse fed into the system. Hence, our approach is a generalized concept which is restricted to isolating specific features of negative nominal interest rates. It follows that defining NIRP impact should be the final stage of the measures concerned. In order to achieve that, the pertinent scheme of model connections was estimated in sub-samples. In this way, a comparative analysis is possible for a given economy's NIRP by reference to a period of positive rates in the economy or versus a peer group. In particular, in order to define the particular character of NIRP effect on systemic risk, the comparative analysis is presented in two dimensions by:

- identifying changes in the direct effect based on re-estimation of transmission model and simultaneous maintenance of a network structure of relationships among financial institutions stable over time;
- identification of changes in the indirect effect based on a maintenance of transmission of monetary policy's direct impact and estimating a dynamic structure of relationships among institutions.

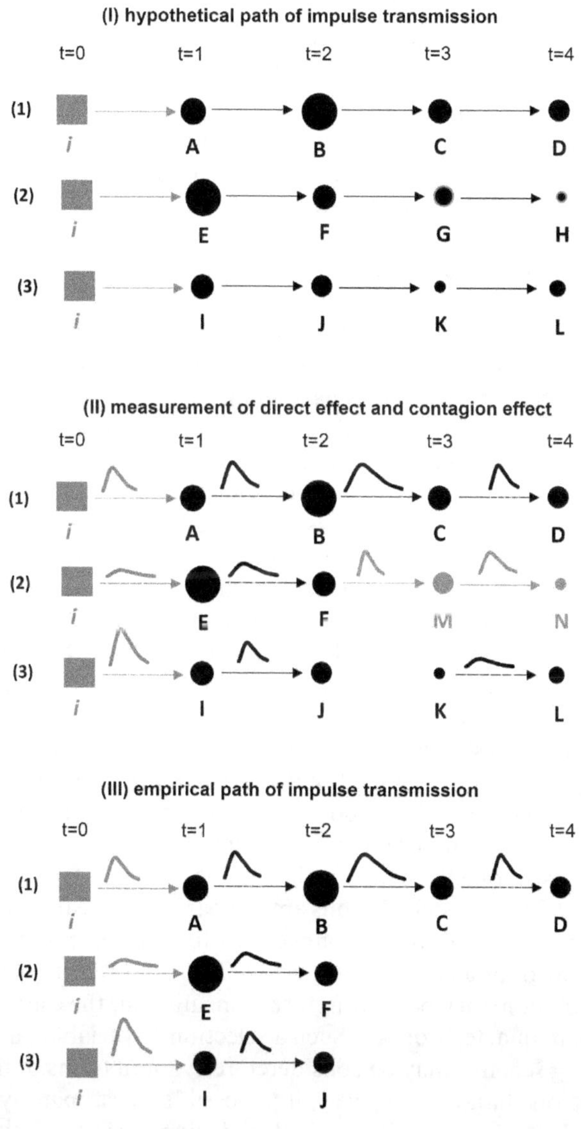

Figure 7.4 A concept of construction of empirical network of systemic relations

Note: Each dot denotes one bank in the network, while the size of the dot represents the relative size of the balance sheet; square indicates a source of initial impulse; waved lines above the arrows imply impulse response functions and point out their different shapes.

Source: Own work.

7.2 Research Sample Characteristics

The above-explained methodology has been used for standalone data of 428 commercial banks from 12 economies. The study encompasses both economies with negative nominal interest rates (eurozone, Switzerland, Sweden, Denmark, Japan) as well as those whereby conventional policy is pursued, that is, the peer group. Hence, the second group of economies covers both developed (United States, Canada, Australia, United Kingdom) and developing countries (Brazil, Russia, China). Such a geographical coverage means that it has been carried out for the economies whose total GDP accounts for approx. 80% of the global GDP with the total assets of entities covered by this study at approx. 60% of the global banking sector's assets. Thus, our findings will be indicative of general global regularities, but they may also be vulnerable to factors particular for individual economies. This study is only confined to entities listed on a regulated stock market because of data accessibility and comparability with respect to international accounting standards in place that affect assets valuation, including market valuation. The research sample was controlled with respect to events for individual banks, i.e., in the case of mergers and acquisitions, new banks were created for retrospective insight. In addition, extreme observations for given periods were swapped for relevant percentiles so as to contain the effect of outliers (i.e., winsorising). These measures aimed at constructing the most possibly balanced dataset[11] enabling correct and statistically unbiased conclusions on potential economic relationships.

The measures of systemic risk of each single entity are estimated on the basis of weekly data, as is the case of building networks of connections among the entities and defining the hypothetical path.[12] The concept of a model identifying network structure will be estimated for each possible combination of relations among the banks in the sample, which in fact translates into an analysis of 90,000 model relations among banks. Thereafter, the relations will determine the structure of connections for a given point in time and will be re-applied for a consecutive period. Then, in order to define the empirical path of monetary policy impulse transmission, the estimates will be aggregated into quarterly data.[13] Such a selection of variables, as in the case of the ordering scheme, may be considered relevant in terms of the research topic. On the one hand, in this way, it is possible to estimate systemic risk measures and the dynamic, in particular, during periods of disturbances, relations among banks developing relatively frequently. On the other hand, owing to high quarterly frequency variables being used, it is possible to allow for a relatively more staggered effect of monetary policy on systemic risk (than the effect on business operations and price processes).

The period of our analysis spans between the first quarter of 2000 and the fourth quarter of 2019 with a particular prominence given to the periods whereby NIRP was implemented in particular countries. The selection of the timeframe was based on the need for long time series, albeit limited by access to a relatively broad group of banks. The selected period takes into account a relatively long time of NIRP being pursued by selected central banks. It should also be mentioned that effective October 2019, the European Central Bank decided to change NIRP implementation principles. The change was crucial as it ended a period of clearly different use of this tool in comparison with similar tools used by other central banks. Thus, owing to such a selection of the timeframe, it is possible to cover the whole period whereby the differences between monetary policy instruments existed and to identify potential differences in systemic risk impact.

The discussion of results will follow in next sub-chapters. These findings, in spite of being estimated for unit level, are presented from macroeconomic perspective for their interpretation to account for economic relationships.

7.3 Analysis of the Scale of Connections among Individual Measures of Systemic Risk in the Banking Sector

According to our methodology, the analysis of monetary policy effect on systemic risk starts off with a construction of an impulse transmission path among entities which is attributable to transmission through standalone measures of systemic risk. To this end, a network of connections was built among individual entities which based on casual relationships and the ensuing results are presented below (please see also: Iwanicz-Drozdowska and Rogowicz, 2022).

The effects of how systemic risk network is constructed globally show that there is a clear geographical diversification of the structure of connections depending on systemic risk model used. For SRISK, the region which shows by far the higher interconnectedness of risk among individual entities is Japan, and then, albeit with a markedly lower interconnectedness, the United States (Figure 7.5). Conversely, CoVaR indicated an explicit predominance of concentration among eurozone and certain Asian economies (e.g., South Korea).

Given the structure of information allowed for in both risk measure types, at this stage of analysis, the eurozone was identified as an area vulnerable to an information shock with Japan and the United States being exposed to a balance sheet shock.[14] An example of information shock in this context includes a short-term impact of a monetary policy decision or potential political tensions, whereas a balance sheet shock may be manifested by, *inter alia*, higher default risk of borrowers, as well as a long-term impact of monetary policy reflected in economic slowdown. It means that, whatever the measure used (or, indirectly, a network structure), an impact of monetary policy on systemic risk should be observable. It should also be expected that in the network structure defined by CoVaR, this impact will be stronger in the short run, whereas for SRISK – in the medium term. In addition, these observations are consistent with the earlier discrepancies for individual risk measures in the procedure for identifying, *inter alia*, systemically important

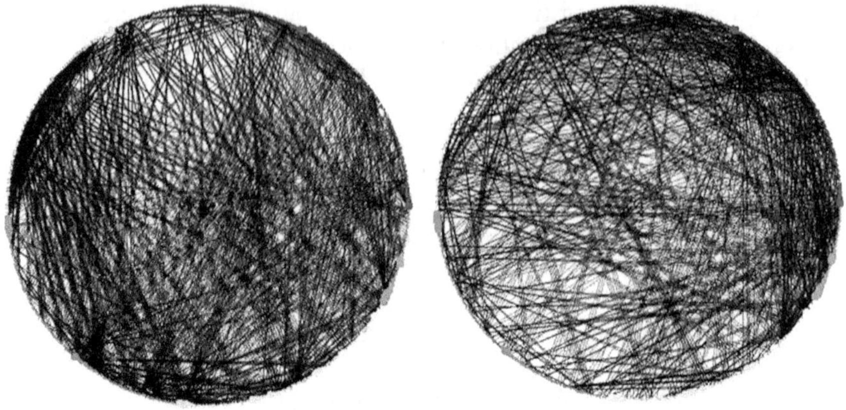

Figure 7.5 Global interconnection of systemic risk – evidence for the full period
Note: Lines indicate causality relations between two banks; banks are represented by dots located around the perimeter of the presented circles; the size of a dot denotes the relative size of an entity in terms of its assets.
Source: Iwanicz-Drozdowska and Rogowicz (2022).

financial institutions. Per analogy, as the number of interconnections rises, particularly in the periods immediately preceding a systemic disruption (e.g., a financial crisis), the geographical diversification will probably fade.

The theoretical approach of a hypothetical path of impulse transmission referred to in the previous sub-chapter is reflected in empirical terms as minimum spanning tree (MST), also referred to as the shortest dendrite. Analysis of such a construction allows to recognize and assess the concentration (or dispersion) of individual points across an identified network of connections, in this case, among commercial banks.[15] Assessment of a network's concentration degree is often the starting point to further characterize the spatial structure of a given system. In graph modelling of financial networks, minimum spanning trees are used primarily on account of their properties of filtrating and compressing highly complex systems having network-like structures (Ozimek, 2017).[16] MST concept is used in finance mainly to analyse financial market and the changes of its interconnections, including foreign exchange rates (Mizuno et al., 2006; Naylor et al., 2007) or stock market indices (Onnela et al., 2003a), as well as to identify if a given material disturbance (e.g., capital market crisis) does impact the structure of such interconnections (Onnela et al., 2003b). For simplicity, the presentation of this concept in this sub-chapter differs from its technical notation. MST should be viewed as a graph method that creates a layout in the space of the financial system that represents the shortest possible path for the transmission of a given external impulse through the entities in the network. Consequently, the structure is a direct reference to the feature of hierarchy in the concept of hypothetical path of impulse transmission mentioned earlier.

In line with our approach, the construction of a minimum spanning tree is a basis for how the empirical impulse transmission path is determined. In addition, however, graphical analysis of such structures may yield more conclusions regarding the features of the pertinent systemic risk network:

- MSTs constructed for various systemic risk measures have an entirely different structure, which is mainly attributable to the networks themselves varying;
- an advantage MST has over a presentation of a full network structure is that it is possible to identify "centres of disturbance", which is, areas whereby one institution clusters around itself other, smaller paths of the spreading effect;
- a tree devised with the use of SRISK highlights a clear division of a potential contagion effect into one large cluster (regional, probably) which describes the relations of several large and several dozen small banks (Figure 7.6, left panel, highlighted area) and the other, less formalized relations among medium and large banks that emerge internationally; in addition, transmission paths for SRISK are characterized by a higher concentration of entities, primarily among small banks, mostly in the eurozone;
- a tree based on CoVaR being the fundamental model of systemic risk is characterized by a higher number of clusters which are relatively alike with respect to a number of entities and the size pattern (i.e., from a large entity, through medium, to small); the clusters are more concentrated geographically and they are confined to large banks in the United States, Canada, United Kingdom, Australia and, partly, the eurozone (Figure 7.6, right panel);
- structure of connection concentration within MST differs from those previously identified for the entire systemic risk network. In particular, in the case of transmission path analysis, there is not a single systemic risk model for which such a clear geographical concentration has been identified as for network structure analysis. It means that the impulse fed into the networks is transmitted faster by international connections than those concentrated locally. At the same time, country connections play a vital role, although transmission of risk spread effect through such connections comes with a relative lag with respect to foreign impulses.

The last conclusion shown above particularly emphasizes that it is necessary to consider all relationships in the system, not just those implied by MST. Namely, it is the transmission of local impulses of monetary policy, prominence given to the eurozone, that is analysed in detail here. For instance, as part of the analysis of a full network of connections implied for SRISK, the Japanese banking sector was shown as highly regionally concentrated (Figure 7.5), whereas a corresponding connection was not found for MST (Figure 7.6). Consequently, if the MST-based aggregate effect of monetary policy impulse transmitted through the network had no important international implications, it could be clearly underestimated for regional banks. Admittedly, a corresponding connection is not observed for overall long-term relations in the eurozone's banking sector. However, it could still be shown in the estimates of short-term specific effects.

The path of impulse transmission may have a twofold definition – based on the shortest transmission path of a given impulse (the minimum spanning tree mentioned before; Figure 7.7, left panel) or incorporating all the possible impacts inside of the system (Figure 7.7, right panel). The first approach allows to track down the transmission of the primary impulse broken down into stages and to estimate, from the point of view of a given entity, a period following which the effect of indirect impact materializes. At the same time, on account of methodological constraints, this method may lose ample information on relations among individual entities, which explicitly arises from the visual comparison in Figure 7.7.[17] It is for this reason that this study has employed a path that allows for all the relations, with MST still as the starting point. A relation between MST-based impulse transmission and one which takes account of all the relations shows that most of monetary policy impulse by far is transmitted through MST.[18]

Figure 7.6 Theoretical transmission of a medium-term impulse within the worldwide risk network – MSTs for SRISK (left panel) and CoVaR (right panel) measures

Note: Lines indicate causality relations between two banks; the size of a dot denotes the relative size of an entity in terms of its assets.

Source: Iwanicz-Drozdowska and Rogowicz (2022).

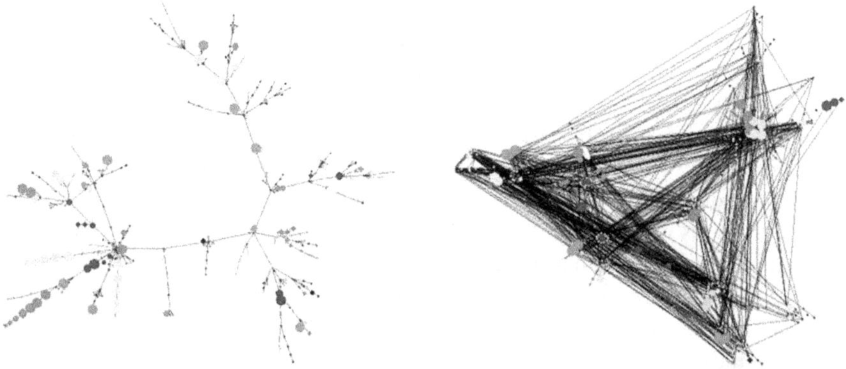

Figure 7.7 Theoretical transmission of a medium-term impulse within the worldwide risk network – MST (left panel) and all identified relations (right panel)

Note: Lines indicate causality relations between two banks; the size of a dot denotes the relative size of an entity in terms of its assets.

Source: Own estimates.

The above general relations were indicative of a medium-term static approach. In fact, however, such a structure of connections among institutions may gradually "evolve" over time as mutual relations among banks and factors determining their operations change. Finally, in order to capture all the changes that have taken place due to NIRP introduction, a dynamic approach is necessary for the estimated connections.

An example of such a dynamic view of a network structure for systemic risk estimated in line with CoVaR is presented by Figure 7.7. Once the dynamic approach was used for a network of connections, both the network structure[19] alone and the hypothetical impulse transmission path were shown to vary over time. It means that a significant portion of causal relationships is only short term and it only materialises in certain periods as relevant conditions arise. It is worth noting that amid an overall relations volatility, some kind of core interconnectedness may be identified, that is, connections persisting among entities for a relatively long period which may last more than ten years (Figure 7.7, upper panel). Such relations are not only formed for a single economy but also internationally. Given at least medium-term character of such relations, they may propel an international transmission of monetary policy impulses to systemic risk. What is more, owing to such connections, it is possible to identify some universal characteristics which defy short-term disturbances. For instance, in a network estimated for CoVaR model, such a structural feature of the system is higher concentration of causality among eurozone banks than other economies, whatever the period analysed.

In comparing the volatility of the very structure of a network of connections and the hypothetical impulse transmission path it should be noted that while the latter's structure fully relies on the former, the volatility of MST path is markedly higher. In other words, even a minor alteration in the network structure (e.g., Figure 7.6, right panel vs. Figure 7.8, panel c) may result in an entirely structurally different impulse transmission path.[20] With reference to the structural characteristics of the minimum spanning tree, a condensation of the connection structure, contrary to the common intuition, does not have to entail a higher indirect effect of the transmitted primary impulse. For instance, a higher condensation of network structure during the GFC (Figure 7.8, upper panel) did not bring about any significant rise in centralizing the structure of the minimum spanning tree. It means that the main part of the external shock was still transmitted along MST whose structure (changed with respect to the entities that made it up) was still indicative of the indirect effect being relatively extended over time. Such a conclusion, however, requires two assumptions – among entities, an expiring transmission effect is prevalent in the network and the transmitted impulse is relatively moderate, such as default of an institution other than of systemic importance or a minor change in the interest rate level. However, even if such assumptions are met, a more condensed network structure still means more successive rounds of indirect impact which were not allowed for in the very structure of MST (Figure 7.8). At the same time, an impulse

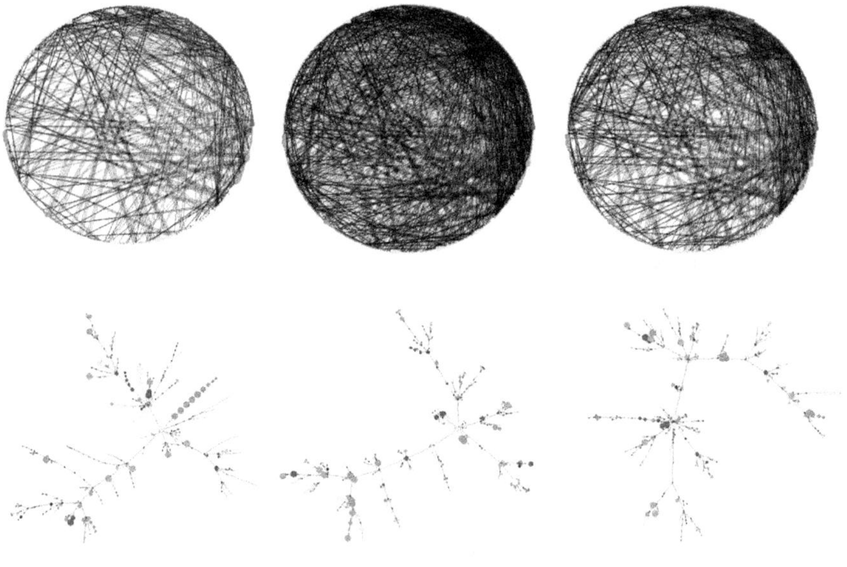

Figure 7.8 Evolution of the systemic risk causality network (top panel) and MST (bottom panel) over time for the CoVaR model

Note: All symbols are in line with the legend used for Figure 7.5.

Source: Iwanicz-Drozdowska and Rogowicz (2022).

in each of the rounds will have a decreasingly weaker effect on systemic risk and it will take place with a time lag which will allow the banks to adapt accordingly.

In addition, the hypothetical impulse transmission path, being a much more time-varying element, does not retain the core of the long-term observed universal relations that the connection network itself has. An ensuing implication for this study is that it is possible to forecast the very network's characteristics based on its recursive character (e.g., showing areas of larger clusters) and to infer accordingly on the potential systemic risk from aggregate perspective. Simultaneously, however, such an approach is markedly more difficult in case a specific impulse fed to the connection network is analysed, in particular, with respect to a higher volatility of such paths and their lesser tendency for recursivity.[21]

The network structure's dynamic character found at this stage is an important property which enables implementing this research method for further step of our analysis, especially an analysis of a particular character of NIRP's impact. It is because, owing to this result, it is possible to tell whether such a network will be different or constant in negative interest rate environment versus long-term tendencies. In the absence of such a property, the pertinent research method would be largely reduced to time-series empirical methods, which, in the case of such an unprecedented phenomenon NIRP is, could markedly distort the findings and conclusions.

7.4 A Direct Effect of Monetary Policy on Systemic Risk

This part of the research aims to assess the effect of monetary policy on systemic risk transmitted by the above-mentioned network structure for the banking sector. For such an impulse to be transmitted within a network, first, its direct effect (initiating effect) should be identified, the effect arising as the impulse is being fed into the system, that is, before it is "passed on". To this end, based on a panel model of vector autoregression, the effect of interest rate impulse[22] was estimated on systemic risk, as well as other banks' characteristics coherent with monetary policy transmission channel, such as financial leverage and profitability. Models estimated on a sample incorporating multi-directional monetary policy decisions show that money market rates fully or almost fully adjust to those of the central bank, and the adjustment is quick. Such conclusions hold for negative interest rates environment; hence, the above-mentioned disturbance was fed into the model through money market rate shock. Moreover, it was assumed that there are no other significant disturbances over the period under scrutiny, which means that the responses of selected macroeconomic variables only define the effect of interest rate change. Another impulse fed into the model and being a benchmark for interest rate effect is an impulse of term premium which manifests the impact of monetary policy through non-conventional instruments. As noted before, such an approach will be analysed by an assessment of response functions of selected variables (in particular, of systemic risk) on the impulses concerned.

The outcome of this stage of the analysis primarily demonstrated a statistically relevant impact of both the interest rate and the term premium on systemic risk. In particular, there is an inverse relation between a change in monetary policy parameters and a change in systemic risk on bank level (Figure 7.9). This relation exists irrespective of the systemic risk measure used. It means that monetary policy affects both individual banks' vulnerability to a systemic event and the entire system's vulnerability to a disturbance deriving from a specific institution. At the same time, whatever the systemic risk measure, the response of the other model variables to both monetary policy shocks remains relatively similar, which attests to the construction of a general model being resilient to a change of one variable.

What deserves special attention is, in turn, the very response of systemic risk measure. How response function behaves varies with respect to the measure used and it is reflected in two aspects: strength of the response and the period in which it takes on its maximum value.[23] In particular, in the case of interest rate increase by 1 p.p., the risk measure in SRISK falls by approx. 0.1% on average across the entire financial system following three quarters after the impulse emerged, whereas in CoVaR, by approx. 0.6% after four quarters, respectively (Figure 7.9). It follows that response strength in the first model is markedly lower than in the other. In the case of SRISK, the response rebounded strongly in fourth quarter, whereas for CoVaR, the rebound is more gradual with the maximum value after approx. two years following the primary impulse. Further, what stands out is how the behaviour of systemic risk function clearly varies over time. In response to an interest rate increase immediately following the shock, the aggregate systemic risk level rises in SRISK and falls in CoVaR. All in all, however, medium- and long-term response is consistent with the earlier mentioned intuition. What is more, risk response in SRISK seems more sustained (the median of response function is negative all over the response window) and less varied, whereas in CoVaR, some long-term responses are indicative of risk rising (Figure 7.9, upper bound of significance interval).[24] The above conclusions show that monetary policy affects more the vulnerability of the entire system to a credit event with respect to individual institutions than the institutions' vulnerability to a crisis. In other words, the impact of monetary policy is stronger on systemic risk from bottom-up perspective than the measure manifesting risk in the top-down approach.

The behaviour of systemic risk response varies more in the case of interest rate than term premium shock. In the latter case, the response varies only with respect to the scale, while its distribution over time is largely similar between the risk measures. In addition, systemic risk reaction to term premium shock comes with a bigger time lag than in the case of a response to an interest rate shock and it is clearly, around three or four times, stronger, just like the response of other macroeconomic variables (Figure 7.9). In

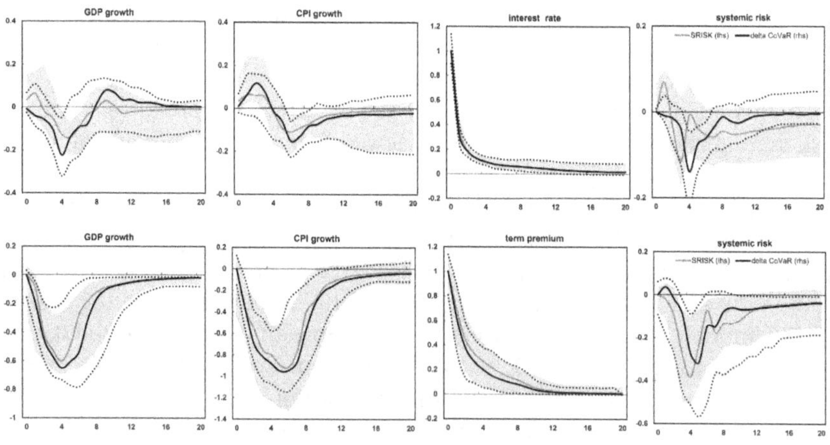

Figure 7.9 Impulse responses to a 1 p.p. interest rate shock (upper panel) or term premium shock (lower panel) differentiated by systemic risk measure

Note: The solid and dotted black lines represent the findings for delta CoVaR model (median response and confidence intervals, respectively), while light grey lines and shaded areas indicate similar information for SRISK model.

Source: Own estimates.

particular, an increase of term premium by 1 p.p. translates into systemic risk decline of around 0.3% cumulatively in the fifth quarter (for SRISK) or by around 1.1% in the fourth quarter (for CoVaR) after the impulse emerged.

Summing up this part of the analysis, the functions of systemic risk responses are symmetrical. It means that an expansionary shock of this policy is transmitted to the examined systemic risk measures in a similar order as the restrictive shock analysed above. It is because, due to an expansionary monetary policy shock, the measures banks take up may include a higher financial leverage to drive profitability (which was empirically corroborated at this stage, also with respect to the phenomenon's sequential character), thus impacting an individual systemic risk measure to go up.

7.5 Measurement of the Contagion Effect in the Banking Sector Triggered by a Monetary Policy Impulse

The analysis so far has measured the indirect effect of monetary policy on selected macroeconomic variables and the level of systemic risk. On the other hand, as the very concept shows, for a full effect to be examined, it is also necessary to analyse the impulse's later transmission around the system. In this context, it is necessary to account also for the indirect effect (i.e., the impact of a single bank on standalone risk measures of other entities) which is due to the influence of interest rates. To this end, at the next stage, the effect of systemic risk spread (which can also be referred to as a contagion effect) was estimated as well. In particular, we explore a response to systemic risk generated by individual banks with respect to this measure rising in another bank.

At this stage, primarily a relatively strong effect of spreading systemic risk among the banks was identified, viewed from the perspective of an international financial system. The strongest impact of this effect falls around the fourth or the fifth quarter after the primary impulse emerged. In turn, its scale (just like the direct reaction) varies with respect to systemic risk measure. At the same time, the varying degree is, however, markedly lower than in the case of the direct effect (Figure 7.10). In particular, in the case of SRISK model, the contagion effect at its extreme amounts to around 0.4 for the entire connection network, with around 0.6 in CoVaR. This value means that an increase of systemic risk for one institution by 1% will give rise, over a one-year horizon, to a change in a corresponding measure for another institution by 0.4% or 0.6%, respectively. At the same time, this change clearly varies for individual institutions from 0.04 up to as much as 1.4. The latter value confirms that in a part of the system, there are relatively strong relations among banks illustrated by multiplying shock fed to this part. It is because, in such a scenario, a 1% increase in risk of one institution results in a 1.4% risk increase for another. What is crucial is that this value is estimated for the entire sample period, i.e., a period whereby tension episodes are relatively rare. It suggests that this coefficient will most probably take on even higher values in stress periods.

We also estimated, for individual commercial banks, to what extent a specified feature (with respect to size or geographical location) was a

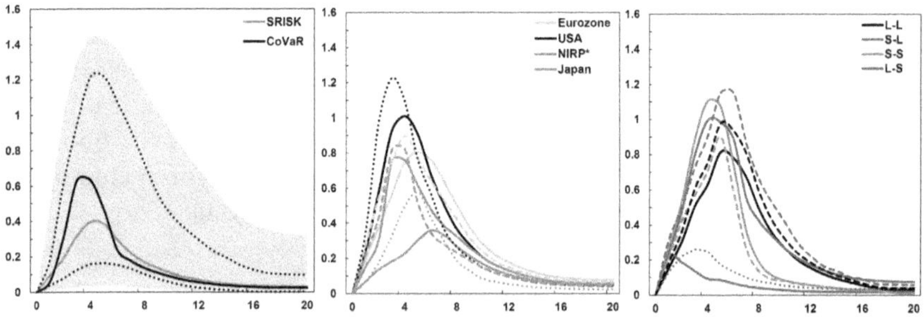

Figure 7.10 Contagion effect in the banking system and its differentiation given selected characteristics

Note: In the left panel solid lines denote the median contagion, effect while the dotted lines and grey area represent the interquartile range (for CoVaR and SRISK, respectively). In the remaining two panels solid lines represent indications for SRISK model while dashed lines for CoVaR model. L-S denotes the contagion effect from a large bank to a small one, with a large bank in this case being one with assets lying at or above the 66th percentile of the sample and with a small bank being one at or below the 33rd percentile. NIRP* denotes Denmark, Norway, Sweden and Switzerland. The graph represents the value of only those relations for which a causal effect has been statistically confirmed.

Source: Own estimates.

varying factor in the earlier identified averaged contagion effect in the financial system. This approach assumes that banks are active in similar market segments, and the entities on these markets (which are, *inter alia*, bank customers) similarly respond to ongoing economic processes, including the central bank policy. Consequently, a varying level of further primary impulse transmission in the system may be a reflection of a systematic variation in the behaviour of individual banks which have different characteristics (like, for instance, the size or capital structure). Such an approach is corroborated by a detailed analysis of contagion effect's structure (Figure 7.10).

In particular, a phenomenon of the risk spreading effect varying with respect to the institution size was corroborated. Notwithstanding, the contagion effect occurs among all the categories of entities, whatever their size (Figure 7.10, middle panel). It shows that the earlier identified average overall effect for the entire system does not arise from the predominance of entities of specified size. In particular, as expected, a relatively minor and short-term effect of a small entity spreading the contagion onto a bigger one was found.[25] An ability to diversify balance sheet and revenue structure allows big entities to relatively quickly absorb the contagion effect deriving from a small entity with non-significant economic impact. Still, the effect lingers on, which suggests that the size of assets does not secure a full immunity to an external shock. The strongest contagion effect was found for relations among small entities and not for a big entity affecting a small one. In particular, in the case of SRISK, the model may be described as multiplying. In other words, a 1% risk increase for a small bank translates into around 1.1% rise in this measure for another small bank following four to five quarters (Figure 7.10, middle panel). In turn, in the case of CoVaR, the risk impulse is partly extinguished for individual institutions and 90% of it is transmitted to other entities. The scale of this spreading effect, however, still goes beyond the scale of impact identified for the entire system without the size variation. Such a relation may partly be due to a tendency that a material rise in risk of one small bank may fuel concerns, including the customers', that other small banks may end up in a similar position soon. In addition, a small bank typically has a more limited access to diverse forms of funding and a lesser capacity of diversifying its balance sheet structure and revenue sources. Given the structure of SRISK, this feature is of vital importance precisely in assessing the transmission of the contagion effect calculated for this type of a measure. Consequently, a potential disturbance in the system is identified as affecting small entities more and as being more transmitted among them than in the case of big entities. Concomitantly, based on SRISK, impact of a big entity on a small one is relatively weaker as an external disturbance is partly absorbed by this entity before it is passed on. Quite to the contrary, in CoVaR, a model which relies less on balance sheet data, this type of relation between a big and a small entity is markedly stronger, consequently, the effect of spreading risk among smaller entities is weaker accordingly (Figure 7.10, middle panel).

It follows that it is among relatively small banks (based on SRISK) or in transmission from a big to a small one (CoVaR) that the impact of the central bank's monetary policy is the greatest. This conclusion confronted with the earlier identified scale of direct effect shows that the contagion effect among small entities will be constrained by a relatively minor scale of impact of direct monetary policy in SRISK, whereas for CoVaR, because of a stronger direct effect, this impact will be further strengthened in identified connection structures.

The effect of contagion among banks is also geographically diverse, much as its presence has been corroborated among entities of all the economies covered by the research sample (Figure 7.10, right panel). In this context, the strongest effect confirmed by both systemic risk models was estimated for the United States.[26] Such an outcome suggests that if there is a causal relationship among banks, it is relatively strong, and a 1% rise in systemic risk standalone measure in one bank denotes an identical (SRISK) or even a greater (1.2%, CoVaR) change in risk measure of another US bank, observable with a lag of three to four quarters.[27] Conversely, the contagion effect identified for the eurozone is relatively weaker than in the case of the United States. It materializes at a relatively later point, much as it holds for relatively longer. In particular, 1% rise in an individual measure of systemic risk in an eurozone bank translates into a 0.8–0.9 times change of this measure in another eurozone bank which falls on the fifth to the seventh quarter (whatever the systemic risk measure) after the primary impulse emerges. Notwithstanding, with reference to a relatively more condensed network structure in the eurozone (for CoVaR model in particular), a lesser, on average, scale of the effect of spreading among entities, than in the United States, does not have to stand for a weaker aggregate effect. What is vital is that the scale of the aforementioned contagion effect among entities is similar in the eurozone and in other economies pursuing NIRP, much as it occurs somewhat earlier in the latter case. Owing to such conditions, there is a higher likelihood of direct comparability between the eurozone and the other NIRP economies.

7.6 An Indirect and Comprehensive Effect of Monetary Policy on Systemic Risk

Once the direct effect of monetary policy impulse and its later transmission among individual banks are estimated, it is possible to determine a total aggregate effect of how monetary policy impacts systemic risk measured by CoVaR and SRISK.

To this end, a broad range of interest rate impulses has been simulated with varying magnitudes – from a change of 0.25 p.p. up to as much as 10 p.p. Such shocks were subsequently fed into an identified connection network in order to estimate an aggregate effect – both direct and indirect.

Aggregate effects are estimated by composing functions of individual entities' response to an impulse in line with the earlier presented approach. In order to estimate the indirect effect, additional two restrictions – a temporal and magnitude-based threshold – were established. In terms of the time limit, it was assumed that the duration of a full transmission path must not exceed the length of a full function of response to direct effect which, as identified in the previous sub-chapter, expires after 20 quarters (i.e., five years) since monetary policy impulse emerged. As for the other dimension, it was assumed that economically irrelevant elements of contagion effect will be ignored. To this end, it was planned that the impulse transmission along a given path will expire; then, its magnitude falls below 5 percentile of the distribution of all impulses at any stage of transmission at a given moment.

Additional conclusions are based on the analysis of monetary policy impulses affecting the systemic risk across the sector by splitting the effects into direct and indirect. In line with the indications to-date, the higher the interest rates, the lower the systemic risk, both for direct and indirect effect, and conversely, lower interest rates drive up systemic risk (Figure 7.8). At the same time, however, the relevance of direct and indirect effects for the entire system varies with respect to the scale of monetary policy primary shock. In other words, as the scale of changes in the central bank's interest rates grows, so do both effects that not only rise in absolute terms, but the indirect effect also starts to outweigh the direct one. In particular, for relatively minor alterations to interest rates, the direct effect is higher than indirect as the latter diminishes in the transmission network quite quickly. Such a conclusion shows that, much as monetary policy has a direct effect for standalone systemic risk measures, the system as a whole is not able, with non-significant scale of the primary impulse, to absorb this impact relatively quickly without giving rise to a major contagion effect. Still, what is interesting is that such a phenomenon at an aggregate level does take place although the range of individual measures of institutions' vulnerability in the connection network is relatively broad. That is to say, there are entities in the network which multiply the scale of a primary, even minor, monetary impulse fed into the system (Figure 7.11). However, as the strength of monetary policy primary impulse grows, not only does the indirect effect begin to prevail but it also becomes non-linear. At the same time, the direct effect remains linear, whatever the scale of the primary impulse. The identified non-linear character is mainly due to the contagion effect gradually growing across the connection network as the magnitude of shock goes up.[28] It means that, in contrast to a minor primary impulse, when this shock is sufficiently larger, it is absorbed to a far lesser degree at the level of a given entity while its larger portion is further transmitted. Consequently, as the monetary impulse becomes stronger, its transmission network expands to include entities new to this network, i.e.,

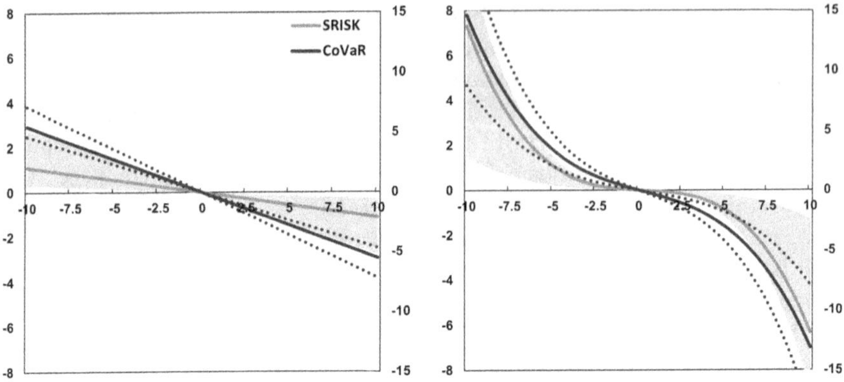

Figure 7.11 Direct (left panel) and indirect (right panel) impact of interest rate shocks on systemic risk in the banking sector

Note: The solid line denotes the median impact on the entire system based on the sum of individual responses. The sum comprises only those reactions that exceed the size threshold and take place within 20 steps of impulse initiation. One step is assumed to span one quarter, while the size threshold is set at the 5th percentile of the distribution of all banks' contagion effects in the system. The solid and dotted black lines represent the findings for delta CoVaR model (median response and 10- to 90-percentaile range, respectively) while light grey lines and shaded areas indicate similar information for SRISK model. Left axis corresponds to results for SRISK model, right axis – for CoVaR model.

Source: Iwanicz-Drozdowska and Rogowicz (2022).

which avoided the contagion effect when the scale of the shock was still non-significant. It follows that the contagion effect evoked by the monetary policy impact rises overproportionately versus the change in interest rates.

The conclusions presented so far are independent of the systemic risk model applied for this analysis. However, it is the very scale of the impact of monetary policy impulse that shows the variation caused by this feature. In particular, in case SRISK is applied as the reference measure of systemic risk, the pertinent estimates show that the quarterly change in the central bank's interest rates of 2.5 p.p. is where the relations between indirect and direct effects are balanced out (Figure 7.11). In other words, a rise in the central bank's interest rates by 2.5 p.p. means a fall in systemic risk across the entire financial system by approx. 0.25%, comparably for both effects. In turn, whenever interest rates rise by 5 p.p., a decline in systemic risk is implied by around 0.5% for the direct effect and around 1.1% for its direct counterpart. At the extreme point of a monetary shock, i.e., whereby interest rates rise by 10 p.p.,[29] the difference between these effects rises up to as much as 1.1% and 7.3%. On the other hand, with ΔCoVaR as the reference systemic risk model, a larger impact of monetary policy is implied (as shown before) to affect the systemic risk both in the form of direct and indirect effect. Nevertheless, an important thing is that the phenomenon of the direct and indirect effect balancing each other out is observed, with a corresponding scale of changes in the central bank's interest rates (i.e., by around 2.5 p.p.) – in such an event, the direct and indirect effect approximate each other by around 1.25% (in absolute terms). With interest rates rising by around 5 p.p., the direct effect indicates a decline in systemic risk by around 2.5% and the direct effect by 3.5%, whereas with a change in the rates of around 10 p.p., the effects propel a sharper rise in systemic risk by around 5% and 15%, respectively.

It should be noted here that even in the case of an extreme scale of changes in interest rates, their impact on systemic risk is still moderate. In particular, such a change does not imply at least a doubling of systemic risk level as for SRISK this impact reaches around 8.5% and for ΔCoVaR – around 20%. Such results suggest that the monetary policy itself is not a source of systemic risk, rather it only contributes to its change. Hence, the policy's impact on this risk will be notably lesser than, e.g., default of a systemically important financial institution.

What is more, with non-significant changes in interest rates, the non-linear effect of their impact is not observed. It means that the banking sector enters the domain of non-linear impact only when the changes in interest rates are significant and they occur over a relatively short period. For the estimates concerned, whatever the systemic risk model, the level of shock for interest rates which triggers a rise in moderately non-linear effect is around 2.5 p.p., whereas an explicitly non-linear effect starts to materialise with a shock reaching around 5 p.p. This conclusion implies that a change of a given magnitude affecting interest rates, albeit implemented over an extended period, allows the entire banking system to remain in the linear portion of monetary policy impact on systemic risk. In other words, a predictable monetary policy enhanced with adequate communication on the central bank's side enables flattening the path of changes in interest rates; thus, it translates into containing the scale of its impact on systemic level in the banking sector. This conclusion may be important first and foremost for a varying assessment of systemic risk in developed and developing economies. In particular, the level of nominal interest rates in developed economies is relatively lower than in developing ones; thus, the changes of rates are relatively milder. It means that the banking sector in developed countries may structurally operate more in the domain of linear effect of monetary policy on systemic risk. At the same time, in developing countries, a non-linear indirect effect may prevail, which adds up to the complexity of analyses pertaining to this phenomenon.

A summary of findings from our analysis follows in Table 7.1. These conclusions are presented in line with our conceptual framework (Figure 7.1).

Table 7.1 Summary of most important findings for the general systemic risk relations

Stage of analysis	*Most important findings*
Network structure of bank interrelations	• geographical differentiation of the structure of relations given the model of systemic risk • SRISK model: Japanese and US banking sectors are characterized with greatest scale of interrelations • CoVaR model: deepest concentration of interrelations identified for Euro area and some of Asian economies (e.g., South Korea) • network relations evolve over time – noticeable share of causality relations is short term and materializes only during stress episodes • the greatest deepening of network relations evidenced for period directly preceding and following the recent Global Financial Crisis • notwithstanding the model of systemic risk, there can be identified a so-called core of interrelations, e.g., the relations that are observed over the long term regardless of the market environment
Hypothetical path of impulse transmission	• the hypothetical paths of impulse transmission evolve to a greater extent and differ more significantly given the systemic risk model • paths allow the precise identification of banks that are sources of contagion • SRISK model: spillover effects concentrated within one significant cluster (which includes several sizeable banks and tens of smaller ones) as well as across many less formalized international relations • CoVaR model: highlights a much greater number of systemic risk clusters following a size pattern, more pronounced geographic pattern of those concentrations appears • time evolution of hypothetical path of impulse transmission is more prominent than time evolution of the full network • even a small change in the structure of network may be translated into a significant reformulation of the path structure
Direct impact of monetary policy	• regardless of the systemic risk model, both interest rate and term premium changes affect level of systemic risk in the economy (an inverse relation) • impulse response function to a monetary policy shock is differentiated by the implemented measure of systemic risk • interest rate shocks affect systemic risk to a significantly greater extent in CoVaR than in SRISK model; in both cases, extreme impact occurs after three to four quarters since the shock • the effect on systemic risk is more permanent since the impulse reaction function does not reverse to initial level even over the long term; the reaction function is also less differentiated across individual banks for the case of SRISK model

Contagion effect	• the systemic contagion effect between banks is confirmed to be relatively sizeable with its peak to fall around four to five quarters since the initial impulse • the strength of contagion effect is different for both systemic risk models, however, to a lesser extent than the direct effect • the median contagion effect between banks in the network amounts to an approximately 0.4× (SRISK model) or 0.6× (CoVaR model) of the size of the initial shock • the spillover effect is significantly differentiated by the size of institutions • SRISK model: the strongest contagion effect is identified for the impulse transmission between small banks, even surpassing that running from large to small ones • CoVaR model: the strongest contagion arises from large banks and is transmitted to small banks • geographic patterns confirm that the systemic risk impulse is most strongly transmitted within US banks; the effect identified for the Eurozone banking sector seems to be weaker and materializes with a slightly greater lag but remains longer in the system
Overall effect of monetary policy on systemic risk	• both direct and indirect transmissions of monetary policy are consistent with intuition since a policy rate increase translates into a risk reduction through both channels, while interest rate cuts add to the level of risk • the magnitudes of the direct and indirect effects differ with the size of the interest rate impulse, and most notably, the gap between these two effects gradually widens • for relatively small interest rate changes, the direct effect outweighs the indirect one, as the network transmission fades out relatively quickly – the banking system as a whole remains able to absorb the impulse at the very first stages of the contagion process • as the magnitude of interest rates rises, the indirect effect starts to prevail and becomes non-linear • regardless of the systemic risk measure, a change in central bank rates of approximately 2.5 p.p. imposes a kind of inflection point at which neither of the effects prevails and at which the mentioned non-linearity becomes noticeable • even in the case of a relatively extreme interest rate change, the reaction of systemic risk is clearly economically significant but not as severe as might be expected given the size of the shock • monetary policy actions are not intrinsically a source of systemic risk but rather affect its scale when the shock originates from other factors • the banking sector is pushed into the non-linear sphere of systemic risk when the monetary policy move is relatively rapid; when a sizeable change in interest rates is spread over time, the banking sector remains in the linear area of the impact on systemic risk • the banking sector in emerging economies may structurally operate within the non-linear region of systemic risk sensitivity to monetary policy

Source: Own work.

7.7 Diversification of Monetary Policy Impact on Systemic Risk Depending on the Tools Used by the Central Banks

The results presented so far have been estimated for a complete timeframe and a wide array of economies; hence, they identify medium-term economic relationships across the entire financial system. It should be noted, however, as is the case of the macroeconomic environment, that the monetary policy tools in place have evolved over time, particularly after the GFC. It follows that the results to-date reflect an assessment of relations between monetary policy and systemic risk in the long run. In this context, with a view to assessing such relationships for specific monetary policy instruments, a detailed analysis of NIRP will be carried out by identifying differences from the general relationships identified above, from entity-based and time perspective. The approach concerned is based on the assessment of international connections in the banking sector and on estimates of the direct impact of the monetary policy. They will be modified in NIRP analysis. In order to track down the changes taking place while NIRP was in place: (i) a network of connections has been estimated for sub-periods of this policy and (ii) the direct impact of monetary policy in corresponding sub-periods was estimated anew. Such a two-layer approach allows to identify the characteristics of the earlier mentioned general link between monetary policy and systemic risk which underwent a change in negative interest rate environment. In particular, the analysis will aim to determine if the monetary policy transmission mechanism has been reformulated so much that the direct effect of interest rate changes impacting systemic risk has changed or whether it is the processes taking place inside of the financial system and affecting the structure of connection network that matters more. Such an analysis was carried out similarly to the previous one, so it also simulated the effect of monetary policy impulses fed into a network of connections among entities, the impulses varying in magnitude. The results of this stage of the research are presented by comparatively analysing the impact of NIRP on systemic risk with respect to: (i) relationships from the overall model and (ii) corresponding specific models estimated for the periods and the economies operating in the environment of positive interest rates, the United States in particular. The results were presented for a simulation of a broad range of interest rate shocks (Figure 7.12) and were grouped for a cross-section of economies (Figure 7.13).

An initial expectation should be that it is primarily the network structure that has been modified in negative interest rate environment. Consequently, it was reflected in the strength of the risk impulse transmitted among entities and it led to modify the strength of indirect effect versus the overall model. Such expectations are due to an overall assessment of the network analysis whereby the network was identified as being more condensed during NIRP, in the eurozone in particular. It is because, in order to contain the negative effect of NIRP, the banks may get involved in other financial market investments, which boosts their interdependence reflected in systemic risk models.

At the same time, the pertinent higher density of interconnections is not as significant as in the years 2008–2009, whereby it was observed globally and not only regionally. In addition, higher concentration of connections may affect institutions which display a lesser effect of risk spreading. It means that, in spite of a higher concentration, the empirical risk transmission path in NIRP environment may in fact be shorter and the impulse itself may give rise to a lesser indirect effect. The analysis in this sub-chapter aims to examine which of these effects prevails.

An analysis of particular characteristics of negative interest rates impacting systemic risk primarily pointed out to a number of common characteristics with respect to the previously identified long-term relations. Whatever the interest rate environment, i.e., positive or negative, there is an inverse relationship between their change and the systemic risk response. In turn, as the interest rate shock goes up, so does the strength of the impact grow until it starts displaying non-linear relationships at some point (Figure 7.12). At the same time, whatever the interest rate environment, the rates' effect on systemic risk remains moderate even amid an extreme shock. Consequently, none of interest rate policies, and NIRP, in particular, is perceived as a systemic event which gives rise to a surge in systemic risk, rather as a contributing factor.

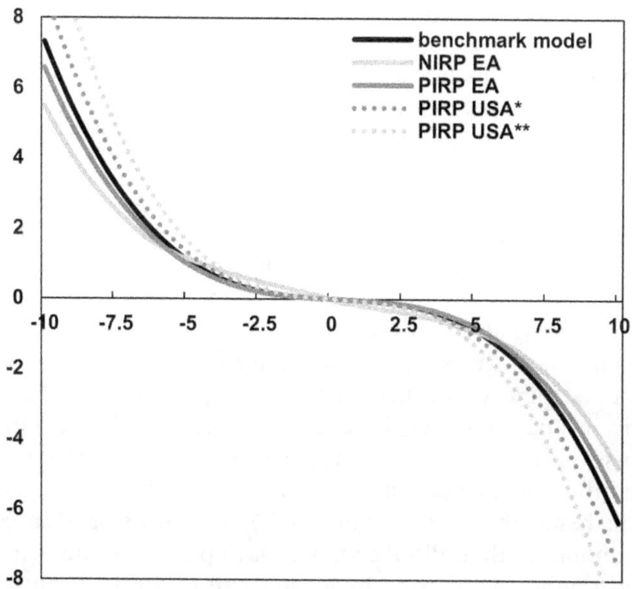

Figure 7.12 Time and geographical differentiation of indirect monetary policy effect on systemic risk

Note: The direct effect of monetary policy is assumed to be constant; all denotations as in case of Figures 7.11 and 7.13.

Source: Own work.

This stage of the research primarily points to certain parts of overall relationship differentiation, which is particular for NIRP. Especially in the eurozone case, the response of systemic risk (under the circumstances of negative interest rate environment) to a relatively minor interest rate shock exceeds the response observed for the overall model, and, what is crucial, also that for specific variants, *inter alia*, in the United States and for a period comparable with NIRP presence in the eurozone (Figure 7.12).[30] In the case of the eurozone, the effect is markedly stronger than for the United States, although the overall relationship identified for a full period of the analysis implied a higher contagion effect in the US banking sector than in the eurozone. This result confirms that a more condensed network of systemic risk causality in the eurozone observed during NIRP is at the same time marked for a similar effect of risk spreading that the one found for the whole timeframe (in particular, also in other economies analysed in a comparable period). It means that although NIRP has not been identified as a systemic event, its contribution to a rising vulnerability of the whole system to a systemic event (e.g., default of a SIFI), as well as the vulnerability of individual entities in the financial sector to a crisis, is higher than that of other interest rate policies.

We found that the transmission of monetary policy impulse among NIRP banks gives rise to a higher tendency (in comparison to positive interest rates) for this impulse to amplify. It means that even a minor change in the level of interest rates is relatively stronger transmitted at the initial stages of risk transmission path among entities (Figure 7.12), which translates into a higher aggregate indirect effect, and finally the total effect. Concomitantly, however, later on the transmission path, the effect clearly loses its momentum as opposed to other economies and the general relation. It follows that, during NIRP, owing to the magnitude of the transmission of risk spreading impulse being shifted to initial stages, the entire network became more vulnerable to a systemically important disturbance. For the overall relation and for other specific models, this impulse's transmission is more staggered and its capacity of being absorbed by individual institutions of the transmission chain is higher. It suggests that the above-mentioned rise in entities' vulnerability to a systemic event is primarily concentrated in short-term perspective, that is, in a period largely beyond the control of individual institutions.

Transmission of a large interest rate shock, on the other hand, develops somewhat differently. Under such circumstances, the systemic risk network of eurozone banks in the environment of NIRP shows on average a higher degree of immunity than PIRP economies. In particular, an extreme shock of monetary policy manifested by a rates rise by 10 p.p. translates into a rise in systemic risk by around 6% in eurozone's NIRP and by around 9% in the United States in a corresponding period, i.e., in the environment of positive rates. It should also be pointed out that specific models have shown that the entire curves of systemic risk responses to varying interest rate shocks (illustrated by Figure 7.12) have shifted. Such a shift means that the total effect of monetary policy influencing systemic risk has modified (versus the overall model), but only for a given interval of the magnitude of interest rate shock.[31] For a comparable period of the analysis (i.e., NIRP in the eurozone), these responses' curves shifted in multiple directions. It is particularly for the United States that the curve shifted upwards, i.e., it indicated a stronger (than in the overall model) response of systemic risk to a big interest rate shock, whereas it went downwards for the eurozone.[32] The change may suggest that a broader group of banks operating for a certain time in an environment of slightly negative interest rates adapt to absorbing a significantly expansionary monetary policy impulse, particularly if they were affected by its final intra-network transmission stages. Conversely, in PIRP environment, similar entities (i.e., being a part of the final transmission stages, too) grow "accustomed" to another type of conditions, i.e., to monetary policy indirect impulse expiring before it reaches them through other interconnected entities in the network. Thus, whenever the impulse is strong enough, the entities are as if "taken aback" by it and that is why its impact on systemic risk of a given institution is relatively more pronounced. Consequently, the scale of responses of systemic risk measures to a big interest rate shock is narrower in NIRP (identified as relatively more difficult to operate in) than in PIRP environment.[33] Namely, stronger direct impulses occurring relatively frequently in NIRP environment may develop, in the long run, a more effective mechanism for absorbing impulses deriving from within the system than directly from the central bank.

Notwithstanding, conclusions similar to those devised for the eurozone do not apply for the other NIRP economies, i.e., Switzerland, Sweden, Denmark and Norway (Figure 7.13). That is to say, these conclusions do not pertain to the entire NIRP area, but they are particular for NIRP pursued by ECB. Such particular characteristics of this policy were indicated at its implementation and transmission to other interest rates, including interest on loans and deposits. These characteristics distinguished ECB monetary policy from those pursued by other NIRP central banks and they suggested, *inter alia*, a higher burden on the banking sector, particularly with respect to the direct cost of deposit with the central bank. Accordingly, the particular characteristics of NIRP itself may translate into a particular behaviour of systemic risk measures in the eurozone showing a clearly higher vulnerability of the banking sector to a negative disturbance than is the case of other NIRP economies.

It should be pointed out in the light of the above-mentioned characteristics which distinguish the results of the eurozone versus the overall sample, both models share an important common feature. Namely, the direct effect of monetary policy on systemic risk remains markedly more pronounced than the indirect effect with minor interest rate alterations. At the same time, as the earlier conclusions showed, the difference in the impact between direct and indirect effect grows stronger in favour of the direct effect in NIRP environment as opposed to the whole sample model. It simultaneously implies

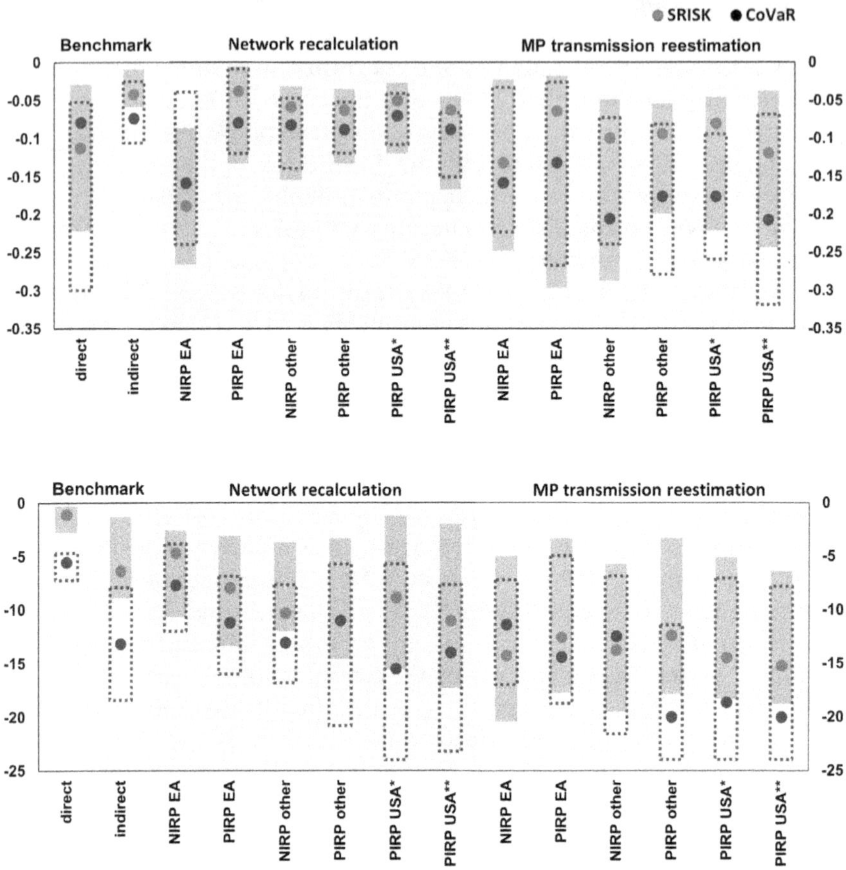

Figure 7.13 Direct and indirect impacts of 1 p.p. (upper panel) and 10 p.p. (lower panel) interest rate shocks on systemic risk for selected economies

Note: PIRP USA* denotes the model calculated for the United States for the time span comparable to PIRP EZ, that is, up to June 2014, while PIRP USA** denotes the model estimated for the period when NIRP was in force in the euro area. Dots denote median responses, while grey or dotted areas represent the interquartile range – in black for delta CoVaR model, in grey for SRISK model. Network recalculation stands for re-estimation of network structure while keeping the direct effect from benchmark model unchanged; monetary policy transmission re-estimation assumes unchanged structure of network and aims to re-estimate the direct effect of monetary policy on systemic risk.

Source: Iwanicz-Drozdowska and Rogowicz (2022).

that an effect of a non-linear impact of monetary policy on systemic risk in NIRP environment emerges with a relatively greater interest rate shock than in positive rate territory and the overall model. In addition, given historical experience with respect to interest rates, i.e., central banks focusing on rather small alterations, the banking sector in NIRP environment should remain within the domain of linear impact in medium-term perspective.

The above conclusions are coherent whatever the systemic risk model used. Both in the case of SRISK and CoVaR, the effect of connection network recalibration with the monetary policy direct effect remaining intact allows to conclude that the impact of NIRP on systemic risk is relatively stronger for minor changes in interest rates. At the same time, however, another feature particular for the eurozone in NIRP environment occurs due to various systemic risk measures being employed. In the overall model and the environment of positive interest rates, the effect of monetary policy impacting systemic risk was stronger in CoVaR-based specifications. In turn, when it comes to NIRP in the eurozone, the effect was stronger for SRISK (Figure 7.13). It follows that the NIRP environment increases banks' vulnerability to all-sector disturbances more than other interest rate environments. The impact is greater than the banks' effect on the system in the case of, for instance, a credit risk event.

Additionally, estimates of direct effects were added. They do not pertain to the whole research period, but rather to varying sub-periods attributable to a particular character of the interest rate policy pursued. As shown before, in the overall model, systemic risk response to a relatively minor interest rate shock was dominated by this very effect type. Such a relationship remained unchanged for all the economies under scrutiny, also in the option assuming re-estimation of such an effect. Further, as in the case of restructuring the network, the direct effect in the eurozone was identified as stronger for NIRP than the positive interest rate environment. Simultaneously, however, a change in direct effect owing to monetary policy impact model being re-estimated is markedly lesser than in the case connection network was recalibrated (i.e., risk transmission model) and it does not largely differ from other economies. It is particularly for a corresponding period that the direct effect was identified as intensified in the United States as well, albeit to a lesser degree. For the other NIRP economies, in turn, no significant change was recorded. It may suggest that a stronger direct monetary policy transmission to systemic risk in the eurozone during NIRP is not particular for this type of interest rate policy, rather it may be more attributable to, *inter alia*, structural changes in the global economy.

Our findings indicate that a negative interest rate policy clearly increases the importance of the indirect effect of its impact on systemic risk, i.e., the transfer of risk across institutions. At the same time, the identified rise in direct effect in NIRP environment, providing network structure has remained intact, does not play a vital role than in the case of overall long-term relations. Notwithstanding, a comprehensive assessment is necessary in order to fully account for the particular nature of NIRP. Accordingly, it should be noted that the rise in direct effect of NIRP impact on systemic risk in negative interest rate environment was modest, as opposed to a significant rise in its indirect counterpart. It follows that a comprehensive assessment hints at a significant structural change. Namely, even though the change in direct effect is not substantial, a multiplicative character of a markedly stronger indirect effect compounds the relevance of this phenomenon. In particular, such a structure of these effects' change implies a markedly stronger total effect of monetary policy impact on systemic risk than in the case the structure of changes went into the opposite direction (i.e., a clear rise in direct effect versus an only negligible rise in indirect effect).

Summing up, the conclusions presented in this sub-chapter may be structured with respect to common characteristics and the principles of generalizability of findings for positive and negative interest rates. Such a specification is given in Table 7.2.

Table 7.2 Summary of the most important findings for the NIRP-specific analysis

Characteristics that are common for NIRP and other monetary policy environments, including positive interest rates

- regardless of the interest rate environment, the opposite relationship with systemic risk remains
- the interest rate effect rises with the strength of the shock and reaches the non-linear area when the threshold is exceeded
- the impact of NIRP on systemic risk – as in the case of PIRP – remains relatively moderate even for extreme sizes of the initial shock
- neither of the rate environments themselves may be perceived as a systemic risk event, so they cannot translate into a rapid materialization of systemic risk; nevertheless, both categories of rate policies are identified as amplifiers of systemic risk

Characteristics that differ the NIRP from other monetary policy environments, including positive interest rates

- the reaction of systemic risk to a relatively small shock to interest rates in NIRP environment seems to outweigh that in the benchmark model and for other sub-samples
- in the face of the NIRP, banks' systemic risk network became tighter; the greater concentration of systemic risk translates into a quicker transmission of shock and, consequently, means that a relatively minor initial impulse may add significantly to the overall level of risk
- as the size of the shock increases, the relative difference from the benchmark model seems to diminish; positive interest rates have a stronger impact than negative rates as the size of the shock becomes extreme
- NIRP environment adds to systemic risk strongly when shock is small, but when the shock is relatively strong the effect of PIRP dominates
- NIRP triggers more significant consequences than PIRP since the banking sector remains in the space of a stronger central bank's impact on systemic risk in general
- interest rate impact on systemic risk in NIRP environment is significantly stronger in models that incorporate SRISK systemic risk measure; thus, NIRP more disproportionally adds to a bank's vulnerability to a systemic event than a bank's likelihood of being a source of systemic risk for others

Source: Own work.

Summary

NIRP impacts systemic risk more than a monetary policy pursued in positive interest rate environment. This impact, however, works mainly through a change of structure of interconnections in the banking sector than a change of monetary policy transmission mechanism. In other words, a prevalent effect on systemic risk is not caused in particular by a markedly lower profitability of banks attributable to, as found in the preceding chapters, incomplete transmission of interest rates to the interest on banking products. NIRP affects systemic risk in the way that commercial banks have a higher (versus positive interest rate policy) tendency to increase the scale of connections with other entities (indirectly, as a result of a strive to retain profitability intact amid a negative interest rates environment). Simultaneously, these tendencies bolster the institutions' vulnerability to the number and a varying character of disturbances deriving from other, connected entities. In other words, it was shown that in NIRP environment, the systemic risk level generated by a given entity rises largely due to the institution's increasing vulnerability to adverse disturbances generated by other entities in the sector, rather than, *inter alia*, directly due to a lower profitability.

Therefore, this chapter provides support for our main research hypothesis, stating that monetary policy which employs negative nominal interest rates affects the banking sector's interest rates more than monetary policy reliant on positive interest rates.

Notes

1 This concept assumes that for a given time series, the result is preceded by the cause. Thus, it is believed that one variable impacts the other if information it contains allows for an improvement in predictive ability of the latter (see, e.g., Syczewska, 2014).

2 It should also be pointed that the authors of this approach (see Billio et al., 2012) pay attention to a kind of medium-term relations since they try to identify interrelations for a volatility (by employing, e.g., GARCH models). Such an approach is useful for information extracted directly from financial markets, but its application towards systemic risk measures might not be appropriate.

3 An extension that allows for capturing longer-term causality relations was also employed for consistency reasons. In other words, if the market data were used for network construction, the proper measure of causality would be the short-term one. However, since the constructed network relies on systemic risk instead, the medium-term relations should be captured. Such an approach relates to the medium-term characteristics of systemic risk itself.

4 The main advantage of this approach can be characterized as follows: variable i might not cause directly the changes in variable j, but an indirect relation between them may still exist. This indirect relation might be transmitted through an additional variable z: over the medium term, variable i causes changes in variable z which are then transmitted to variable j. Therefore, a lack of identification of causality in the short term and with respect to direct relations does not necessary mean that such a relation does not exist.

5 The role of an auxiliary variable might be played by a range of market risk indicators, such as implied volatility measures, spreads of risk in the banking sector (e.g., LIBOR-OIS spread) or in the whole economy (e.g., TED spread) as well as by indicators that show the liquidity squeezes (e.g., cross currency basis swaps). In that context, also some artificial statistical indicators – like principal components from PCA analysis – can be employed.

6 It should be noted that the concept of direct and indirect effects presented in this chapter is different from the direct and indirect impact of NIRP on the financial system, which was described in Chapter 4. The difference between these two approaches comes down to the concept itself. The one presented previously is broader since it describes a NIRP impact on many categories in the financial system while the one presented in this chapter focuses only on the category of systemic risk. The NIRP impact on the financial system was presented from the perspective of factors that cannot be changed by commercial banks (direct effect) and those that lie within banks' decision-making processes (indirect effect). The NIRP impact on the systemic risk, in turn, is identified by taking into account interrelations between banks (indirect effect) and without this transmission channel (direct effect).

7 Bank's liabilities are calculated as a difference between total assets and equities.

8 These differences are then employed in order to identify the differences in real economy processes under different monetary policy regimes. A similar approach is then implemented for systemic risk measure as well.

9 An assessment and interpretation of impulse response function cannot be reliably performed without selecting the confidence intervals. These intervals in the presented approach derive from Monte Carlo simulations in a way originally proposed by Love and Zicchino (2006). The sample of the model coefficient was randomly selected and then the impulse response function was drawn. This procedure was repeated 15000 times in order to reliably generate 5th and 95th distributions percentiles, which then were used to select confidence intervals.

10 This approach omitted some relations that were identified as causal ones. However, the scale of this reduction is relatively small – it accounts to 1% on average and 6% in extreme (the GFC).

11 Balanced panel dataset is the one which for each object (each bank in this case), there is equal number of observations across time dimension. In this book, we allowed some level of imbalance, based on two criteria – specific and general. The specific one allows to include into the dataset those banks for which the data do not exceed 5% of the studied period. The general one assumes that lack of all possible datapoints for all banks in the sample must not exceed 1% of all possible observations in dataset.

12 Market quotations which are available through Bloomberg are the source of stock prices data used in this study.

13 Balance sheet data used in the estimations are collected via Bloomberg and Eikon services. In case of lack of some indicators, they are directly extracted from financial statements. Macroeconomic data, in turn, are collected from World Bank and IMF's databases.

14 Moreover, Japanese banking sector – as a relatively fragmented one – is characterized by a relatively weak impact of one institution on the whole sector. Therefore, the presented approach based on CoVaR model showed relatively poor concentration of causality relations. This characteristic, on the other hand, may indicate a relatively stronger capital relations across small entities; therefore, the SRISK model provided much greater concentration.

15 This technique aims to connect all possible entities in such a way that the distance between them is minimized (or the strength of aggregate interrelations

is the strongest). An analysis of such a tree allows, e.g., to identify and assess concentration of risk within some geographical or size patterns.

16 Aside from the formal details, there are three most popular techniques that are used for construction of minimal spanning tree – Borůvka's algorithm, Prim's algorithm and Kruskal's algorithm (Kruskal, 1956). For the purposes of this research, the latter one has been implemented (for details, see, e.g., Mróz, 2013).

17 For a N-element network, MST technique will find a path that has N-1 corners. It means that in extreme theoretical example, the MST identified for highly interrelated network might look exactly the same as for network with small numbers of relations. Precisely speaking, for a network of 100 banks, there is possibly 4950 relations to identify and in extreme case, all of them might be found relevant. Still, MST for such a deep network might look similar to those identified for the one that has only 99 relations across 100 banks.

18 On average, through the MST paths, as much as 80% of all impulses are transmitted within the system. During the stress periods, this number amounts to around 60%.

19 This observation is not compatible also with time evolution of the overall distribution of individual systemic risk measures, which was discussed earlier in this book.

20 It should also be mentioned that the empirical path of impulse transmission is a specific version of MST in which weights of relations are precisely identified by the possibility to transmit monetary policy through systemic risk measures.

21 In this context, a simple analysis of pattern repeatability over time showed that as much as 15% of network structures have tendency to be always, or very often, formulated (thus, it repeats in time). A similar analysis conducted towards MST showed than only 3% of the structure repeats.

22 Although this study targets at negative (and ultra-low interest rates), the interest rate shock that is introduced into the models is proxied by an increase (not a decrease further into negative territory) of interest rates.

23 The shape of the impulse response function confirms also that application of a dynamic approach to the analysis of risk transmission within the network was the right decision. If such an impulse response were to cumulate a great majority of the overall reaction exclusively in the first quarter, the static approach would be preferable instead.

24 Regardless of the pointed differences, the impulse response of systemic risk to a monetary policy shock in different risk models is of greater similarity than the network of systemic risk itself.

25 Size differentiation is conducted with respect to total assets of each institution. In that light, a large bank is the one with assets lying at or above the 66th percentile of the sample and a small bank is the one at or below the 33rd percentile.

26 Interestingly, the presented estimates showed a relatively weak contagion effect identified for emerging economies – with its peak to amount to around 0.2 after 4–5 quarters since the initial shock. This effect might arise from the structure of shock that affects emerging economies. In particular, the external shocks (e.g., monetary policy of the United States) are of greater importance for the emerging countries than its local monetary policy, as evaluated from the risk spillover perspective.

27 The results presented here are comparable with findings of other studies. For example, Pino and Sharma (2019) did not identify any relations across US banks at the country level, but they confirm strong relations at the state level, particularly for banks with similar size.

28 Interestingly, this non-linear effect can be identified even though the contagion impulses come from linear estimates.

29 It should be pointed that the interest rate shocks presented in the study do not mean a one-time change, but rather a cumulation over a horizon of one quarter. Since our study focuses on a medium-term perspective (to adequately address the systemic risk category) applied to a lower frequency of data (to remain comparable with macroeconomic models), the implemented interest rate shocks are not unlikely in reality; nevertheless, they should be perceived as extreme cases.

30 In that specific context, although the United States has never introduced negative interest rates, we extracted this specific period for comparability aspects with NIRP economies.

31 An upward shift in the whole spectrum of responses implies a significantly stronger effect for substantial interest rate shocks and a relatively comparable effect for small shocks.

32 Interestingly, the mentioned multi-directionality in the response curve for negative and positive interest rate environments might partially arise from the stance of monetary policies itself.

33 This finding indicates that although the network is relatively dense in the NIRP environment, it is also more flat at the further stages of transmission. It also implies that the network in the NIRP environment is characterized by a smaller number of cyclical relations than the one identified for the PIRP environment, both in the United States and eurozone.

Bibliography

Billio, M., Getmansky, M., Lo, W.L., Pelizzon, L., (2012). Econometric Measures of Connectedness and Systemic Risk in the Finance and Insurance Sectors, *Journal of Financial Economics, Market Institutions, Financial Market Risks and Financial Crisis*, vol. 104, no. 3, pp. 535–559.

Canova, F., Ciccarelli, M., (2013). *Panel Vector Autoregressive Models: A Survey*, Working Paper Series no. 1507, European Central Bank.

Colletaz, G., Levieuge, G., Popescu, A., (2018). Monetary Policy and Long-run Systemic Risk-taking, *Journal of Economic Dynamics and Control*, vol. 86, pp. 165–184.

De Haan, L., van den End, J.W., (2013). Banks' Response to Funding Liquidity Shocks: Lending Adjustment, Liquidity Hoarding and Fire Sales, *Journal of International Financial Markets, Institutions & Money*, vol. 26, pp. 152–174.

Doytch, N., Uctum, M., (2011). Does the Worldwide Shift of FDI from Manufacturing to Services Accelerate Economic Growth? A GMM Estimation Study, *Journal of International Money and Finance*, vol. 30, pp. 410–427.

Dufour, J.-M., Renault, E., (1998). Short Run and Long Run Causality in Time Series: Theory, *Econometrica*, vol. 66, no. 5, pp. 1099–1125.

Dufour, J.-M., Taamouti, A., (2010). Short and Long Run Causality Measures: Theory and Inference, *Journal of Econometrics*, vol. 154, no. 1, pp. 42–58.

Iwanicz-Drozdowska, M., Rogowicz, K. (2022), Does the choice of monetary policy tool matter for systemic risk? The curious case of negative interest rates, *Journal of International Financial Markets, Institutions & Money*, vol. 79, 101608

Kruskal, J.B., (1956). On the Shortest Spanning Subtree of a Graph and the Traveling Salesman Problem, Proceedings of the *American Mathematical Society*, vol. 7, pp. 48–50.

Love, I., Zicchino, L., (2006). Financial Development and Dynamic Investment Behavior: Evidence from Panel VAR, *The Quarterly Review of Economics and Finance*, vol. 46, no. 2, pp. 190–210.

Mizuno T., Takayasu H., Takayasu M. (2006), Correlation Networks among Currencies, *Physica A: Statistical Mechanics and its Applications*, vol. 364, pp. 336–342.

Mróz, A., (2013). *Minimalne drzewo rozpinające*, Uniwersytet Mikołaja Kopernika w Toruniu [available in Polish only].

Naylor, M.J., Rose, L., Moyle, B.J. (2007), Topology of Foreign Exchange Markets using Hierarchical Structure Methods, *Physica A: Statistical Mechanics and its Applications*, vol. 382, no. 1, pp. 199–208.

Onnela, J.-P., Chakraborti, A., Kaski, K., Kertész, J. (2003a), Dynamic Asset Trees and Black Monday, *Physica A: Statistical Mechanics and Its Applications*, vol. 324, no. 1, pp. 247–252.

Onnela, J.-P., Chakraborti, A., Kaski, K., Kertész, J., Kanto, A. (2003b), Asset Trees and Asset Graphs in Financial Markets, *Physica Scripta*, vol. T106, pp. 48–54.

Ozimek, K., (2017). *Badanie reakcji struktury rynku par walutowych G10 na sygnały makroekonomiczne z wykorzystaniem minimalnych drzew rozpinających na przykładzie ogłoszeń wskaźnika nonfarm payrolls*, Studia Ekonomiczne, Zeszyty Naukowe Uniwersytet Ekonomicznego w Katowicach, vol. 339, pp. 112–129 [available in Polish only].

Pino, G., Sharma, S.C., (2019). On the Contagion Effect in the US Banking Sector, *Journal of Money, Credit and Banking*, vol. 51, no. 1, pp. 261–280.

Syczewska E., (2014). Przyczynowość w sensie Grangera – wybrane metody, *Metody ilościowe w badaniach ekonomicznych*, vol. XV/4, pp. 169–180 [available in Polish only].

8 Concluding Remarks

Interest rates and their application as a monetary policy tool are well established in both theory and policymaking. However, the post-GFC years brought significant challenges to the long-established consensus on zero-lower bound, which were prolonged by the outbreak of the coronavirus pandemic. Due to the pandemic and, later, the outbreak of the war in Ukraine, monetary authorities in many countries became prisoners of ultra-low, or negative, nominal interest rates in times of increasing inflation. As the period of ultra-low nominal interest rates has been until now sufficiently long, the question of their role in the systemic risk has gained importance. In this monograph, we investigated how negative interest rates impact systemic risk. Based on the multifaceted review of literature and data analysis, we find support for our six research hypotheses.

The goal of this study was to analyse the role of negative nominal interest rates for the systemic risk. We confirmed that monetary policy has a significant impact on systemic risk in the banking sector, regardless of the monetary policy tool applied; however, the NIRP environment favours the amplification of risk. It needs to be emphasized that the monetary policy *per se* is not a source of the systemic risk, but adds to its existing level.

In the economic theory, there is a differentiation between nominal and real interest rates, short and long-term interest rates, paper and non-paper interest rates, as well as the concepts of the natural interest rate originated by K. Wicksell and the zero lower bound. Recent years brought another concept, which accounts for the application of unconventional monetary policy instruments, i.e., shadow interest rates. This economic figure helps achieve comparability. After the outbreak of the GFC, the role of the short-term interest rates has been expanded – they started to be not only the operational goal but also the tool to reduce long-term interest rates. This was aimed to stimulate the economic cycle and was one of the key factors determining the application of the negative nominal interest rates. The concept of ZLB is based on the assumption that the costs of holding cash are negligible. In the real life, however, for large amounts of cash, the holders (especially businesses) are ready to accept negative interest viewed as compensation for access to services offered by banks.

DOI: 10.4324/9781003312116-8

Our first research hypothesis (H1) referred to the transmission of the interest rates to the real economy. We found that during the period covered in this study, the transmission of the negative policy rates follows the same path as in the case of the positive ones, so no new transmission channel has emerged under NIRP. However, the characteristics of negative rates weaken the transmission, as observed in deposit and loan interest rates (see also H4), since banks are unwilling or unable to reduce deposit and loan interest below zero. The transmission channel, which is the most important in our view from the NIRP perspective, is the lending channel, in which the ultra-low interest rates improve the creditworthiness of the entities, constituting, however, the significant risk driver in the case of the future jump in interest rates. NIRP strengthens also the role of the expectations channel as the expectations of market participants are asymmetric towards future interest rate increases. Additionally, under NIRP, investors seek for attractive investment projects to improve their profitability, which may however represent higher risk. The negative rates stimulated the real estate market and gave rise to the (further) relaxation of the fiscal policy, which is overall similar to other periods of expansionary monetary policy.

Our second research hypothesis (H2) is linked to the ways in which NIRP may be implemented by the central banks to mitigate its consequences on the banking sector. We presented experiences of five central banks, pioneering NIRP, i.e., European Central Bank, Swiss National Bank, Sveriges Riksbank, Danmarks Nationalbank and Bank of Japan in the aftermath of quantitative easing. Worth noting, their decisions on NIRP implementation were synchronized around 2014–2015, except for Bank of Japan. The main reason for pushing interest rates below zero was to continue the expansionary monetary policy aimed at reducing the risk of deflation and the global economic downturn or, in some countries (especially Switzerland), reducing the pressure on the exchange rate appreciation. Among the analysed countries, the importance of NIRP was the greatest in the euro area and the lowest in Japan. Under the same label, i.e., NIRP, there are differences in implementation, including so-called tiering, which determines the actual costs borne by banks due to negative interest rates. Tiering helped mitigate the burden on the banking sector, accounting for the necessary buffers. Although NIRP was supposed to be of a temporary nature, it has been used for quite many years together with asset purchases.

The interbank interest rates followed the central bank rate to the same degree as in the case of positive rates (except for Denmark), combined with the central bank's unconventional tools. NIRP *per se* was not a crucial factor for the change in the turnover on the interbank market. Although the role of NIRP for the interbank market was not a game-changer, it was the case for the bond market on which the impact of NIRP was multifaceted. The bond market was affected by NIPR not only because of the valuation in differentiated timeframes but also due to short-lived operational issues (if and how to charge bondholders with a negative interest). In the environment of the positive interest rates, short-term bonds reacted to the largest degree, while under NIRP, also medium- and long-term bonds reacted considerably, showing their role in the expectations of the future interest rates. Regardless of the differences in country risk levels, the transmission of NIRP to treasury bond yields was effective. It is worth noting, that in the euro area, the prices of selected financial assets adjusted relatively to the lowest, while in small open European economies (Switzerland, Denmark) and partly in Japan, to the largest degree to NIRP conditions. Additionally, under NIRP, the average annual yields on the bond market dropped from about 5% to around 1%; however, the share of bonds offering yields below 1% has not changed significantly. In the case of other financial instruments or asset classes, we found NIRP supported companies' valuation (equity market) and was rather neutral in the short run for the exchange rates, except for Denmark and Switzerland. Thus, we provide support for (H3).

The banking sector profitability is under pressure during the times of decreasing interest rates and the net interest margin banks earn is the main transmission belt of central bank monetary policy into banks' profitability, although indirect. As observed on both macro- and microeconomic levels, banks adjusted to a larger extent the interests on loans than on deposits in the NIRP environment, which has led inevitably to the decrease in net interest margins. We found that commercial banks from the euro area were the least willing to transmit the central bank's interest rates to the retail market. This renders support for our (H4). Worth underlying, long-lasting lower profitability reduces banks' capacity to accumulate the capital needed to expand on the market and meet increasing regulatory capital requirements. Therefore, banks had to adjust to NIRP conditions by using alternative tools, e.g., cost-cutting, increasing risk margins (premiums) on loans and their volumes and increasing fees and commissions. Some of these adjustments may lead, however, to entering into more risky areas.

The direct transmission of NIRP is linked to the costs of storing liquid funds with central bank and plays a role when the banking system is over-liquid, which is the case of NIRP economies. Although banks may search for alternatives to invest their liquid resources (e.g., T-bonds), they have to account for negative interest rates in their overall policy. As mentioned above, this may lead to increased risk in the banking sector on the liabilities and assets sides. Under NIRP, depositors face very low interests (or sometimes even negative) on their deposits and may decide to withdraw their funds from the bank in search of a more profitable alternative. This challenges banks' funding structure. Therefore, instead of relying on time deposits, banks rely to the greatest extent on current accounts, which balances are the "stickiest" due to transactional motives. Only in two countries (Switzerland and Denmark) banks decided to "offer" negative interests on new deposits in order to reduce over-liquidity. In the case of firms, such a decision occurred faster than in the case of households. Interestingly, the cash in circulation in times of NIRP has not significantly increased with exception of Switzerland. Moreover, the negative interests on amounts over a certain threshold helped reduce banks' interest expenses, as depositors (especially businesses) are not expected to clear their balances to zero. Thus, we confirmed that banks did not transmit negative rates to household deposits. Our analysis shows that although banks cut largely interest on loans than on deposits, they were also reluctant to transmit negative rates to loans rates. This is aimed at improving (or keeping) their net interest margins at a reasonable level. To achieve this, there are two other measures to reduce the overall consequences of negative central bank rates, namely the reduction of the share of variable interest rate loans in the loan portfolio and the introduction of zero lower bound into loan agreements. Both help reduce the sensitivity of banks' interest income. It is necessary to underline that on both micro- and macroeconomic levels, initial sensitivity depended on the share of fixed-interest rate loans in banks' balance sheets.

In the pre-GFC era, there was a general consensus that price stability is enough to ensure financial stability. This consensus failed and in the post-GFC era the need for studies linking the monetary policy and the financial stability considerably increased. Our last two research hypotheses refer directly to the role of interest rate policy, especially NIRP, for the systemic risk. Based on an in-depth analysis of different systemic risk definitions and measures, we selected a broad set of analytical tools (i.e., systemic risk measures, network connections and monetary policy impulses propagation) for a comprehensive empirical analysis presented in the previous chapter. Our empirical analysis was based on about 430 banks from 12 countries, including NIRP countries and others acting as a benchmark. Altogether we covered about 80% of the world's GDP and about 60% of banking sector assets for the period from 2000 to 2019 and additionally for the sub-period characterized by NIRP. Both direct and indirect impacts of monetary policies were analysed. First, we present conclusions for the full period. We found that the expansionary shock is transmitted to the systemic risk measures in a similar way as the restrictive one. The contagion effect occurs among all groups of entities regardless of their size, and it is similar in the eurozone and in other NIRP economies. Additionally, the contagion effect identified for the euro area is weaker than in the case of the United States and materializes later, but holds longer. Based on CoVaR and SRISK, the aggregate effect of monetary policy on systemic risk was estimated. We found that the higher the interest rates, the lower the systemic risk, both for direct and indirect effects, while the lower interest rates drive up systemic risk. As the strength of the monetary impulse grows, the indirect effect prevails and becomes non-linear due to the contagion effect across the network. Second, for NIRP sub-period, we identified those common characteristics as compared to full period results. This renders support for (H5). Again, NIRP did not occur to be a systemic risk event. However, under NIRP in the eurozone in the case of a relatively minor shock, the response, as well as transmission, is higher than in full period results. In NIRP environment, the network is more condensed and increases the vulnerability of single entities and the financial sector in the short term. In the long term, however, banks operating under NIPR represent higher immunity than the ones from countries with positive interest rates. These conclusions do not hold for non-eurozone NIRP countries. All in all, NIRP added more to the systemic risk than a positive interest rate policy, mostly due to changing structure of interconnections (H6).

As the NIRP has not finished yet (May 2022), the question of when NIRP would end in times when the economies face already high and rising inflation level is important for both policymakers and market participants. Of course, we do not aim at forecasting the date, when NIRP would end, but our goal is to present the challenges the policymakers may face in this respect. Additionally, there is a question of what is next due to many other challenges on the horizon. Among these challenges, we would like to mention new technologies and following digital transformation, demographic changes, especially ageing, and ESG-related issues, especially climate-related.

After the outbreak of the pandemic, the United States and some European countries outside the eurozone decided to cut central banks' interest rates. The goal of central banks was to mitigate the economic consequences of the pandemic and moderate the expected economic downturn. In the eurozone, the ECB's interest rates remained unchanged. In a response to the pandemic, the governments approved fiscal packages to alleviate the economic consequences of the lockdowns. These packages were targeted at enterprises and/or households. As a result of these monetary and fiscal measures, the economies in many countries managed to return to the growth path after the pandemic shock. These loosen monetary and fiscal policies enhanced the "blooming" period for debt increases and the survival time of so-called zombie firms. Not only public sector increased its debt to finance COVID-19 fiscal packages, but also firms and individuals. Zombie firms due to the still low cost of the financing were able to keep on operating. In the second part of 2021, after the revival of many economies, the inflation level started to speed up due to, e.g., higher demand than supply and certain shortages on the global markets. Also, the "green" transformation is mentioned among inflation stimulating factors. In recent months (i.e., from February 2022), the energy prices soared after Russia's attack on Ukraine, thus fuelling the increase in other prices. Increasing inflation plays a role for savings, especially stored in the form of banks' deposits or in the form of fixed-coupon bonds. Depositors and bondholders experience a decrease in their wealth in real terms and therefore the stability of funding may be questioned if interest rates remain low or negative in nominal terms and significantly negative in real terms. In such a case, these may be savers who would pay the highest price for NIRP. This may also disrupt the classical mechanism of transforming savings into investments, which is one of the fundamental tasks of the financial system.

Accounting for all these factors, the policymakers, including bodies responsible for the conduct of monetary policy and for macroprudential supervision, have to find a balance between increasing interest rates in order to cut the inflation level and support savers and increasing the credit risk of counterparties financed by the banking sector and other entities. This is a kind of a trap, because too radical interest rate increases may cause abrupt deterioration in the quality of loan portfolios. The credit risk is somehow mitigated by the restrictive regulations imposed on the banking sector. Nonetheless, such regulations do not apply to, e.g., traditional finance companies, near-bank lenders and lend-tech companies (i.e., a group of fin-tech companies which provide loans, mostly to individuals), which expanded their activities during the period of NIRP, thanks to the increasing role of new technologies in finance. All these entities often finance borrowers with more risky profiles. Although in most cases non-bank lenders are not treated as systemically important, they may be a source of potential widespread difficulties. For example, if the credit risk materializes on their assets side, the non-bank lenders may default to meet their obligations to investors (e.g., bondholders) and therefore the contagion may spread over various financial institutions. The evaluation of the risk of non-banks (excluding insurance and investment firms) is a challenge for policymakers due to the lack of a comprehensive reporting system. Even more challenging may be the decision to embrace these entities by public supervision, keeping in mind they may freely operate on a cross-border basis.

While looking at the interest rate policy from the perspective of new technologies, not only potential threats increasing overall risk should be underlined but also the advantages of using them. Because of NIRP, banks were forced to cut their costs and the application of new technologies appeared to be one of the ways to boost efficiency. For many internal processes, banks started to use machine learning and artificial intelligence (ML/AI) which allowed them to reduce costs and improve profitability. Even if the changing market conditions and expectations of younger generations were not sufficient to start the digital transformation, NIRP and, later, the outbreak of COVID-19 pandemic appeared to be great stimuli for banks in their digital transformation. In the future, this may be, however, also the source of (additional) systemic risk. Algorithms based on the same tools and data sources would indicate the same decisions and cause herding. Further digital transformation seems to be inevitable and therefore more attention should be paid to technological risks (including cyber risks).

The additional factors amplifying systemic risk under NIRP are derived from other spheres, which often are neglected. First, we refer to the role of demography, then to ESG-related issues. The population in Europe has been ageing faster than in the United States, while in emerging markets, the situation is regarded as more comfortable due to the higher rate of birth. Japan represents the highest proportion of the population aged 60+.

In some studies, the ageing of societies is treated as one of the factors important for the interest rate policy. It has been observed that demographic changes explain a large part of the real natural interest rate decrease. Therefore, the question arises, is this possible to exit NIRP in fast-ageing (like the eurozone) or already old-aged (such as Japan) countries? This requires further in-depth research, but it may be regarded as one of the backstops to resigning NIRP. "New Deal" for such economies should be discussed and prepared to avoid excessive shrinking.

ESG has been an important factor on the policy agenda, especially in the EU, over recent years. Much effort has been involved on regulators' and financial institutions' sides to build a framework to achieve sustainable development goals and reduce the speed of climate change. Green transformation, however, has been blamed also for increased inflation ("green inflation") due to the increased burden on conventional or "brown" energy sources. Policymakers are forced to balance the "future" (i.e., climate change) and the "present" (i.e., increasing energy cost and thus dissatisfaction of households being the voters). Searching for such a balance may lead to another wave of the increase in the public debt to finance new "packages" for which the NIRP acts like a respirator.

All in all, the return to positive interest rate policy requires a lot of analysis of potential, various side-effects that may hurt households, businesses, financial institutions and state budgets. It was much easier from the policy perspective to push nominal interest rates below zero lower bound that to push them back to positive values. Therefore, the escape from NIRP in times of rising inflation is challenging.

Index

For Product Safety Concerns and Information please contact our EU representative GPSR@taylorandfrancis.com
Taylor & Francis Verlag GmbH, Kaufingerstraße 24, 80331 München, Germany

www.ingramcontent.com/pod-product-compliance
Lightning Source LLC
LaVergne TN
LVHW021124300926
849160LV00010B/859

* 9 7 8 1 0 3 2 3 1 9 5 0 6 *